Technology to Teach Literacy
A Resource for K–8 Teachers

Second Edition

Rebecca S. Anderson
University of Memphis

Michael M. Grant
University of Memphis

Bruce W. Speck
Austin Peay State University

PEARSON

Merrill
Prentice Hall

Upper Saddle River, New Jersey
Columbus, Ohio

Library of Congress Cataloging-in-Publication Data

Anderson, Rebecca S.
  Technology to teach literacy : A resource for K-8 teachers / Rebecca S. Anderson,
  Michael M. Grant, and Bruce W. Speck. — 2nd ed.
     p. cm.
   Prev. ed. has title: Using technology in K-8 literacy classrooms. c2001.
   Includes index.
   ISBN 0-13-198975-8
     1. Language arts (Elementary)—Computer-assisted instruction.
2. Computers and literacy.   3. Critical thinking—Computer-assisted
instruction.   I. Grant, Michael M.   II. Speck, Bruce W.   III. Title.
   LB1576.7.A43 2008
   372.133'4—dc22   2006036761

Vice President and Executive Publisher: Jeffery W. Johnston
Editor: Linda Ashe Bishop
Editorial Assistant: Laura Weaver
Production Editor: Mary M. Irvin
Production Coordination and Text Design: Carlisle Publishing Services
Design Coordinator: Diane C. Lorenzo
Cover Art: Jupiter Images
Cover Designer: Candace Rowley
Production Manager: Pamela D. Bennett
Director of Marketing: Dave Gesell
Senior Marketing Manager: Darcy Betts Prybella
Marketing Coordinator: Brian Mounts

This book was set in Garamond by Carlisle Publishing Services. It was printed and bound by R.R. Donnelley & Sons Company. The cover was printed by R.R. Donnelley & Sons Company.

Pearson Education Ltd.
Pearson Education Singapore, Pte. Ltd.
Pearson Education Canada, Ltd.
Pearson Education—Japan

Pearson Education Australia Pty, Limited
Pearson Education North Asia Ltd.
Pearson Educación de Mexico, S.A. de C.V.
Pearson Education Malaysia, Pte. Ltd.

10 9 8 7 6 5 4 3 2 1
ISBN-13: 978-0-13-198975-7
ISBN-10: 0-13-198975-8

We dedicate this book to our student-colleagues in Computer Applications in Reading Instruction and the many preservice and inservice teachers with whom we have collaborated, inside and outside of classes, who have helped us understand ways to use technology effectively in the literacy classroom.

Rebecca S. Anderson
Michael M. Grant
Bruce W. Speck

TEACHER PREP

MERRILL
PRENTICE HALL

Teacher Preparation Classroom

Your Class. Their Careers. Our Future. Will your students be prepared?

We invite you to explore our new, innovative and engaging website and all that it has to offer you, your course, and tomorrow's educators! Preview this site today at www.prenhall.com/teacherprep/demo. Just click on "go" on the login page to begin your exploration.

Organized around the major courses pre-service teachers take, the Teacher Preparation site provides media, student/teacher artifacts, strategies, research articles, and other resources to equip your students with the quality tools needed to excel in their courses and prepare them for their first classroom.

This ultimate online education resource will provide you and your students access to:

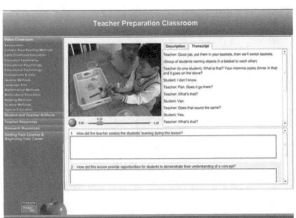

Online Video Library. More than 250 video clips—each tied to a course topic and framed by learning goals and Praxis-type questions—capture real teachers and students working in real classrooms.

Student and Teacher Artifacts. More than 200 student and teacher classroom artifacts—each tied to a course topic and framed by learning goals and application questions—provide a wealth of materials and experiences to help your students observe children's developmental learning.

Lesson Plan Builder. Step-by-step guidelines and lesson plan examples support students as they learn to build high-quality lesson plans.

Articles and Readings. Over 500 articles from ASCD's renowned journal *Educational Leadership* are available. The site also includes Research Navigator, a searchable database of additional educational journals.

Strategies and Lessons. Over 500 research-supported instructional strategies appropriate for a wide range of grade levels and content areas.

Licensure and Career Tools. Resources devoted to helping your students pass their licensure exam; learn standards, law, and public policies; plan a teaching portfolio; and succeed in their first year of teaching.

How to ORDER *Teacher Prep* for you and your students:

- For students to receive a *Teacher Prep* Access Code with this text, please provide your bookstore with ISBN 0-13-615355-0 when you **place** your textbook order. The bookstore **must** order the text with this ISBN to be eligible for this offer.

Upon ordering *Teacher Prep* for their students, instructors will be given a lifetime *Teacher Prep* Access Code. To receive your access code, please email **Merrill.marketing@pearsoned.com** and provide the following information:

- Name and Affiliation
- Author/Title/Edition of Merrill text

○ Intent

Technology to Teach Literacy: A Resource for K–8 Teachers is designed to provide K–8 teachers with an array of computer tools to promote reading, writing, and critical thinking in their classrooms. This text can be used not only in a preservice course, but also by seasoned teachers who recognize the need to continue their education by becoming adept at using computers in their classrooms. Each chapter provides rationales for using computer technology to teach literacy and gives many examples of how teachers can use technology effectively. In addition, chapters cover how teachers can facilitate students' use of technology, how the Internet can enhance students' literacy education, how to develop integrated lesson plans, how technology can be used to help students write and publish their work, how teachers can use technology to work with ESL and special-education students, and how assessment can be facilitated with technology. Each chapter provides information teachers need to feel confident in using technology in the literacy classroom by following sample lessons that can be imported into instructional planning.

This two-fold intent, providing continuing teacher education and pedagogical materials for classroom use, structures the chapters. Beginning with a classroom scenario, each chapter includes a Classroom Snapshot of an actual teaching situation whereby a teacher handles a dramatized topic in his or her classroom and provides discussion of the topic. Additional chapter features include Computer Classroom Lessons, Techno-Teacher Tips, and Frequently Asked Questions. In short, this book covers the major concerns K–8 teachers face as they integrate computer technology into their classrooms and provides numerous suggestions for applying the ideas described in the text in their classrooms. The discussion of literacy topics and pedagogy is grounded in research literature, best practices for teaching, and current successful technology strategies.

○ Features

The following features make this book particularly valuable:

- ○ Provides teachers with theoretical information so that they have the assurance that the information conveyed is based on solid research.
- ○ Focuses on major issues and gets to the point. Teachers can save time by looking at the significant issues without getting bogged down in the details.
- ○ Features Computer Classroom Snapshots, which provide real-life examples of how teachers are integrating technology into the K–8 literacy curriculum.

- ◯ Lists electronic sources to give teachers easy access to Web addresses and thus more materials for their classes.

- ◯ Provides Techno-Teacher Tips with important pointers on using technology in the classroom.

- ◯ Cites numerous print resources throughout, including references at the end of each chapter that identify resources to promote the integration of technology and literacy in the classroom.

- ◯ Includes figures throughout the text with screen captures of well-known and well-respected software applications, Web sites, and technology integration examples.

- ◯ As an ancillary text, *Technology to Teach Literacy: A Resource for K–8 Teachers* does not belabor points but treats each subject in enough detail to get the message across.

◯ Acknowledgments

This book would not have been possible without the support and help of many people. That the book was published was due to the faith that our editor, Linda Bishop, had in us, and we know that we tried that faith during our prolonged period of writing the text. We thank Linda for bearing with us and giving us the opportunity to provide a book that will help K–8 teachers integrate into their classrooms literacy using computer technology. We are also grateful to the reviewers who provided helpful comments on drafts of the book: Laurie Ayre, King's College; S. Kim MacGregor, Louisiana State University; and Mary Tipton, Kent State University. We appreciate the many useful responses they provided to enable us to revise our drafts effectively.

Because the Computer Classroom Snapshots are a significant part of the chapters, we are indebted to the classroom teachers who wrote those snapshots—John Bauer, Kim Buie, Elizabeth Heeren, Ginger Joe, Sonja Bell-Joyner, David Page, and Candace Pauchnick. Our goal was to produce a book that would be useful to classroom teachers, and the snapshots help readers see that their peers, other classroom teachers, are successfully dealing with issues of integrating computer technology into the K–8 literacy classroom. Two professorial colleagues also helped us by writing chapters related to their disciplines. In Chapter 6, Anita Pandey provides expert instruction in using technology to promote ESL students' literacy. In Chapter 7, Janna Siegel Robertson provides expertise and insights into the use of technology to promote literacy among special-needs students and especially among struggling readers.

Others at the University of Memphis—Jim Kelley, Jada Meeks, and Katie Grant—were instrumental in helping us prepare the book for our editor's approval.

We also acknowledge Carmen Speck for her many comments and corrections that provided us reasons for revising the text.

To all our collaborators, we offer our gratitude for the many ways you have worked to make this book a reality.

Contents

Chapter 3   **Using Technology to Teach Reading   55**

Chapter 4   **Teaching Students to Write and Publish with Computers**   88

Chapter 5   **Literacy in the Information Age**   119

Chapter 6   Technology-Enhanced ESL Instruction and Learning in K–8 Classrooms   144

Chapter 7   Using Technology to Teach Literacy to Struggling Readers   166

Chapter 8   **Assessing Students' Work   194**

Literacy and the Technology-Supported Classroom

"I like to read *books*," Alex says, with barely detectable irritation in his voice. "You know, the kind with paper pages. The kind you buy in a bookstore."

Alecia grins as she listens to Alex, but she understands that he is making a valid point. "Oh, you don't like listening to books when you drive long-distance to visit your mother in Seattle?" she says playfully, to engage Alex in debate.

"That's different, Alecia. I thought we were talking about reading *books* via computer screens."

"Well, what we're really talking about is using technology to engage people in reading and writing. If we narrow the conversation to reading books via computer screens, we're merely talking about eye strain, and nobody wants to promote thicker contact lenses."

Alex chuckles. "OK, OK. I see your point. I just don't want all this talk about technology to eclipse the good ol' page-turning experiences I love so much. You know what I mean? Sitting at home late at night in a comfortable stuffed chair, with a good cup of coffee, engrossed in a great novel, feeling the texture of the pages, and . . . "

"The point I started to make before you clutched your beloved books, Alex, is that, as teachers, we have a wealth of electronic opportunities to help our students learn how to read and write. We'd be fools not to use those opportunities. Many of our students are accustomed to using electronic means to become literate."

"Dare I add a bit of evidence to support your argument? My nephew doesn't bother with a paper dictionary. He goes to his laptop and uses some sort of electronic dictionary. That's his first choice. I guess he knows what a *real* dictionary looks like, but . . . " Alex's voice trails off.

"The issue is not what is real," Alecia responds. "The issue is what is available, and how can we use various means to achieve literacy ends. Our students will progress to college and the workplace, where they will find an amazing array of electronic applications that will be essential if they are to function successfully. We need to prepare them for that future—not a future that may exist someday down the road, but a future that exists now and that is only becoming more sophisticated. We're past the point of wondering whether teachers need to be adept at using computer technology in their classrooms. The question now is 'How much technology can we use to help students learn?' "

"Despite my seeming appearance as a Luddite, I share your concerns about marrying technology and literacy." Then, in conspiratorial tones, Alex whispers, "I even bought a laptop last week."

"You're awful," she laughs. "Seriously, though . . . we have to push for the effective use of technology to educate students to become literate in as many ways as possible. They need to learn how to read, but reading is not merely the mechanical process of teaching students how letters and words are strung together to produce phrases, sentences, paragraphs, various documents, and various genres. Reading is a matter of interpreting, and interpretation is not limited to words, but also includes other symbols. We need to teach students how to read a bar graph and how to understand what is being said in it. We need to teach students how to read cultural symbols such as crosses, swastikas, and advertising insignia so that they can learn how to critically analyze a barrage of symbols to make sense of life. Reading is a matter of analyzing symbols so that they make sense, then determining whether what has been understood is worth believing. Need I note that writing is how reading materials are created? So we need to engage students in hard thinking about what they write, teaching them how to think critically about how to construct a document that is worth reading and believing in."

"But since we're deep into confessions," Alecia says, as though she is acknowledging a great error, "I, too, read *real* books. In fact," she pauses, preparing Alex, "I subscribe to a book club and have a stack of unread books at my bedside."

"Alecia! I'm proud of you. I thought you were just a literacy geek. You've restored my faith in teachers who walk around talking in gigabytes."

"Alex, it's a whole lot easier to talk in gigabytes than it is to integrate useful technology into the classroom so that students can learn the tools of literacy and apply those tools with increasing skill and sophistication. I vote for walking the walk."

"You're right, of course," Alex acknowledges, with a twinkle in his eye. "And now the real question is 'Can you help me change the preferences in my word processor so the "track changes" has my name and not "Teacher Computer 12?" ' "

"You're learning—slowly . . . but you're learning. I think you've transformed the old adage into 'Computer literacy begins at home.' Well, welcome home, Alex."

⊙ Attacking Literacy with Computers

In one sense, computer technology is so pervasive at all levels of education that the question is no longer whether a teacher should use technology, but instead it is *how* should it be used to support literacy. Alex is not arguing against the use of technology because, whether he knows it or not, even the production of paper books requires sophisticated computer technology. This book, for instance, was produced using computers—from the desktops of the authors to the computers that were used to typeset and ultimately print everything in the book.

The real issue, as Alecia points out, is how to use technology effectively to help students become more literate. What tools are available to enable teachers to promote literacy effectively in their classrooms? We all need to remember that today's students automatically use a computer dictionary instead of a paper copy of a dictionary. Our students are computer savvy, and we can expect them, in the lingo of "computerland", to consider computers as the default method of learning how to read and write. Newspaper publishers have realized that more and more people are reading the news via the Internet, so newspapers are now online. Streaming video is also replacing or supplementing the nightly news hour. What we as teachers need to know is how to capitalize on students' default method of learning so that students can become increasingly literate as readers and writers. We also want to follow the position statement, published by the International Reading Association (2001), which outlines what teachers need to know about integrating technology into the curriculum (see Figure 1.1). We would also like to follow the National Education Technology Standards for Students (see Figure 1.2).

In this chapter, we will discuss what it means to use computers in the literacy curriculum in order to promote literacy and why we advocate this approach. We believe that before teachers can communicate with students, parents, and administrators about how

**Figure 1.1 Integrating Literacy and Technology in the Curriculum:
A Position Statement of the International Reading Association.**

According to the International Reading Association, students have the right to:

- Teachers who are skilled in the effective use of ICT (Information and Communication Technology) for teaching and learning.
- A literacy curriculum that integrates the new literacies of ICT into instructional programs.
- Instruction that develops the critical literacies essential for effective information use.
- Assessment practices in literacy, including reading and writing with technology tools.
- Opportunities to learn safe and responsible use of information and communication technologies.
- Equal access to ICT.

Figure 1.2   National Education Technology Standards for Students.

1. **Basic operations and concepts:** Students demonstrate a sound understanding of the nature and operation of technology systems. Students are proficient in the use of technology.
2. **Social, ethical, and human issues:** Students understand the ethical, cultural, and societal issues related to technology. Students practice responsible use of technology systems, information, and software. Students develop positive attitudes toward technology uses that support lifelong learning, collaboration, personal pursuits, and productivity.
3. **Technology productivity tools:** Students use technology tools to enhance learning, increase productivity, and promote creativity. Students use productivity tools to collaborate in constructing technology-enhanced models, prepare publications, and produce other creative works.
4. **Technology communications tools:** Students use telecommunications to collaborate, publish, and interact with peers, experts, and other audiences. Students use a variety of media and formats to communicate information and ideas effectively to multiple audiences.
5. **Technology research tools:** Students use technology to locate, evaluate, and collect information from a variety of sources. Students use technology tools to process data and report results. Students evaluate and select new information resources and technological innovations based on the appropriateness for specific tasks.
6. **Technology problem-solving and decision-making tools:** Students use technology resources for solving problems and making informed decisions. Students employ technology in the development of strategies for solving problems in the real world.

they are going to use computers in their classrooms to promote literacy, they must first have a clear vision about what they are trying to do and why they are doing it. To set the stage for discussing the use of computers to promote literacy, the following electronic classroom snapshot about Kim Buie, a first-grade teacher who decided to use technology in her classroom, relates her first adventure in integrating computers in her literacy curriculum.

Computer Classroom Snapshot

Context

My name is Kim Buie and, as a first-grade teacher, I did not always appreciate a computer's potential to impact literacy. But I began to feel as if I was missing out on something that could enhance my teaching, so I enrolled in a class at the University of Memphis in hopes of finding out what all of the excitement was about.

My first attempt at putting all that I was learning into practical use began during a problem-based project involving my first graders. Because my computer experience had been so limited, I started with a simple project with the following goals:

1. Introduce the computer keyboard.
2. Encourage and motivate students to write.

To accomplish these goals, I decided that I needed help to oversee and facilitate my first graders on the computer. I realized that I couldn't give my students the one-on-one attention they needed, so I enlisted the help of a colleague who taught a third-grade class. I suggested to my colleague that her students pair up with my students as one-on-one tutors. The students consisted of 16 first graders and 16 third graders. The ethnic makeup was 29 African Americans and five Hispanic students. My colleague liked the idea of pairing our students, so I had some confirmation that I was on the right track in integrating technology into my literacy program.

What I Did and Why

To meet my goals of introducing my students to the computer keyboard and to encourage and motivate students to write, I decided to have each first-grade student write a story and then compile the stories in a book. To prepare students, I reviewed the steps in the writing process and discussed potential topics.

Then we went to the computer lab to begin writing. The lab contains 25 Macintosh computers, but computer time was difficult to obtain because other classes were scheduled throughout the day. We were allowed 30 minutes, from 1:00 to 1:30 p.m., twice a week. Each first grader, with the help of a third-grade tutor, wrote his or her story at the computer without the use of pencil or paper. First, each student created a file for his or her story. Second, students typed their stories with the help of their tutors, who assisted them in learning the keyboard. In addition, the tutors acted as peer reviewers for the students' stories. Third, the students learned to print their stories so they could combine them into a book. (Alternatively, the students could have learned how to compile their stories into one file and use publishing software to produce a book; however, as I noted, we had limited time in the computer laboratory.) My first goal of introducing the function of the computer keyboard was achieved with the help of the third-grade tutors.

What I Learned

After the project was complete, I read over the notes I had taken, and I found that my second goal of encouraging and motivating students to write was achieved. In fact, my first graders' motivation for writing increased. For instance, many times I overheard my students engage in lively discussions about their stories. Not only were they concerned with their own writing, but they also were curious about each other's writing. My students were full of excitement and pride about what each one in the class was accomplishing. According to my notes, while at the computers, the students' interactions were more spontaneous and extensive than I had ever seen. In addition, I was amazed at some of the storylines my first graders were generating. This was the first time during the year—and it was late in the school year—that I had seen so much interest in and excitement about writing. In fact, every day my students would excitedly ask if that day was a computer day. Overall, I was extremely pleased with the change in my students' attitudes and motivation to write.

(continued)

My project was also a success because I learned ways to improve my writing program for the following year. The first part that I would change would be to start going over the keyboard at the beginning of the year and spend time letting the students become familiar with the keyboard. I would also spend more time with the tutors and find out exactly how much computer experience each student has. I will continue to use the computer as a tool to enhance my students' desire to write, because I now realize how much of a positive impact technology can have on my teaching and in the lives of my students.

○ Why Teach Literacy With Computer Technology?

Technology has revolutionized the way people function in society (Anderson & Lee, 1995; Friedman, 2005; Means, 1994). Computers are common in the workplace and in homes. A strong argument for increasing computer technology in schools is that computers are essential for preparing students for the digital future (Murray, 2003; Reinking, 1997). If teachers accept that "To prepare our students for the challenges of their tomorrows, the Internet and future technologies will be central to our mission" (Leu, 1997, p. 63), they need to provide the tools so that it can happen. Add to this the likelihood that the school will be the only place the urban poor will ever use a computer before going into the job market, and it becomes even more imperative that schools make the most of the time dedicated to computer use. Just as schools have always stressed the lifelong importance of good reading and writing skills, the word *computer* must be mentioned in the same breath.

Many state and national educational initiatives are supporting technology reform efforts in the schools. Educators realize that electronic communication has become a requirement for students' success in the 21st century. Little wonder, then, that government officials at the national level are advocating that every student in the United States have access to the Internet. Federal and state programs, such as the Universal Service Fund, the Technology Literacy Challenge Fund, and Technology Innovation Challenge Grants, have attempted to address these access issues (see **http://www.ed.gov/MailingLists/ EDInfo/Archive/msg00075.html**). The primary goals of these programs have been to reduce the student-to-computer ratio and to increase Internet access for libraries, schools, and instructional classrooms (Puma, Chaplin, & Pape, 2000; Revenaugh, 2000; U.S. Department of Education, 2004). As a result, computer and network technologies have been increasingly available in schools. In 1984, the ratio of students to computers was 125 to one (Smerdon & Cronen, 2000). By 2003, the ratio had dropped significantly to one computer for every 4.4 public school children (National Center for Educational Statistics [NCES], 2003). Access to the Internet and the World Wide Web has continued to increase as well. Approximately 35 percent of elementary and secondary schools in 1994 had access to the Internet; in 1998, the access increased to 89 percent (NCES, 1998). With most recently analyzed data in 2003, nearly 100 percent of schools were connected to the Internet (NCES, 2003).

Teachers have come to appreciate the manifold possibilities that creative software and Web sites offer to enhance traditional teaching methods. In fact, it is much easier to access the Internet than it is to pore over dated texts for fresh ideas. If a paper text such as a book doesn't have a good search engine, such as a useful index, finding a discrete bit of information can be a tedious process and, perhaps, futile. For many students, the computer is the default mode of finding information because search engines can pinpoint information relatively easily. Paper texts are becoming optional resources. As the current gale-force wind of technology becomes a hurricane, paper texts will be replaced more and more by electronic texts. Morrison and Lowther (2005) suggest that the time is ripe for a computer revolution in schools. These authors base their claim on the new knowledge gained throughout the course of the past few years about how to use computers in the classroom. For example, instead of being used as a delivery mechanism, computers are now used as problem-solving tools to augment student thinking (Jonassen, 2000; Jonassen & Reeves, 1996).

Redefining Literacy

Our vision of using computers to teach literacy is connected to our understanding of what it means to be literate. As literacy teachers, we must first ask ourselves, "What are we trying to teach our students?" Historically, we have based our understanding of literacy—and our understanding of what we are trying to teach students—on paper texts. For instance, we have read newspapers, novels, term papers, letters, and a host of other documents printed on paper. We have written directly on paper (even when using a typewriter), not on a computer screen. Discussions inside and outside of classes have been referenced to print documents, whether basal readers or trade books. As educators, we have read paper texts—such as picture books or poems—to students, so they were listening to spoken words read from a paper text. In fact, we have asked students to point to a specific place in a text to provide evidence of the validity of a particular interpretation of the text.

However, many scholars are challenging us to expand our definition of literacy to regard it as a social process that is dependent on cultural and electronic contexts (Bishop, 2003; Flood & Lapp, 1995; Gallego & Hollingsworth, 1992; Hobbs & Frost, 2003; Leu, 1997; Reinking, 1995; Schmar-Dobler, 2003). Their arguments are grounded in the assumption that students are expanding their reading and writing activities beyond traditional print texts to include electronic contexts that incorporate print and nonprint forms of communications. As El-Hindi (1998) notes, we are revising traditional notions of reading and writing because "Literacy now involves being able to make sense of and navigate through several forms of information including images, sounds, animation, and ongoing discussion groups" (p. 694). For example, students now spend time responding to e-mail messages, engaging in online conversations, and navigating through vast amounts of information in a combination of print and nonprint forms (Ryder & Graves, 1996–1997). Although students are interacting with electronic contexts through reading and writing, this electronic communication is described as a "new literacy" (Reinking, 1992, 1994, 1995) that forces us to rethink what we teach as literacy and how we teach it. Adhering to the current standards for the English language arts, we must ensure that "students use a variety of technological and informational resources (e.g., libraries, databases, computer networks, video) to gather and synthesize information and to create and communicate knowledge" (NCTE & IRA, 1996, p. 3). What principles, therefore, should guide our teaching? The shift from a traditional behaviorist paradigm to a constructivist learning perspective provides insights to this question.

Shifting Paradigms

For many years, literacy was taught from a behavioral paradigm. Essentially, this paradigm assumes that all students should learn a finite list of language arts skills, that it is the teacher's responsibility to teach students facts, and that students demonstrate their learning by "regurgitating" facts on a test. When the behavioral paradigm was the ruling paradigm in literacy education, students worked independently in straight rows of desks, and teachers provided lecture or direct instruction, followed by worksheet assignments. Most classrooms did not have even one computer. Instead, computers were located in a computer lab where, once a week, students generally received computer instruction in the form of keyboarding skills. Fortunately, this scenario is changing in many schools. Many literacy educators are moving away from a behaviorist perspective and instead are embracing a social-constructivist learning paradigm that advocates using the computer as a problem-solving tool (e.g., Bickford, Tharp, McFarling, & Beglau, 2002; Bruffee, 1986; Dixon-Krauss, 1996; Gavelek & Raphael, 1996; Gould, 1996; Morrison & Lowther, 2005; Willis, Stephens, & Matthew, 1996).

The social-constructivist learning paradigm is based on a theory of learning that regards learning as a problem-solving activity. Students are actively engaged in their learning, not passively absorbing information via a lecture method so that they can parrot the same information on an exam. The social-constructivist paradigm, by focusing on exploring and solving cognitive conflicts, calls into question a major premise of the behaviorist paradigm, namely, that for every question, there is one correct answer. For some questions, this may indeed be the case. However, for other questions that require higher-order thinking skills where students are asked to analyze, synthesize, and evaluate sources, options, or problems, there could easily be more than one appropriate solution.

If the goal of education is to provide students with the necessary conceptual tools to respond to complex life situations and to apply those tools in the classroom, then the social-constructivist perspective has a great deal to offer teachers. Many life problems do not yield to the easily measured answers that a true-false or multiple choice test provide, two of the premier ways behaviorists promote the assessment of student learning. For example, what is the cause of cancer and how can it be prevented or cured? Why do people of different nationalities and skin color fear each other, and how might people create harmonious multiracial communities? How does a person determine when to stop life support for a loved one? How should an employee—the hoped-for future status of our students—evaluate ethical dilemmas in the workplace? These and many other tough issues can be addressed in practical and informative ways by using a constructivist learning paradigm. A constructivist perspective takes into account the cultures and contexts in which learning occurs (Moll & Greenberg, 1990; Tittle, 1991).

What exactly are the principles associated with a constructivist pedagogy? Brooks and Brooks (1993), building on the work of Piaget (1970), Bruner (1986), and Vygotsky (1978), outline five overarching principles of a constructivist pedagogy:

1. Pose problems that are relevant and meaningful to students.
2. Structure learning around "big ideas" or primary concepts.
3. Seek and value students' points of view.
4. Modify curriculum to address students' suppositions.
5. Assess student learning in the context of teaching.

In constructivist classrooms, students learn through active participation and have opportunities to explore their own ideas through discourse, debate, and inquiry (Anderson & Piazza, 1996; Applefield, Huber, & Maollem, 2000; Bufkin & Bryde, 1996; Davydov, 1995; Duckworth, 1987; Gruender, 1996; Kroll & LaBoskey, 1996). Teachers assume a facilitator's role, and students assume more responsibility for their own learning (Fosnot, 1996). Skills, although necessary components of instruction, are not the goal. Rather, the goal is to promote concept development, deep understanding, and active learning (Brooks & Brooks, 1993). The focus is not on concrete thinking but on abstract synthesis, or higher-level mental development, that occurs through verbal interaction and use. For instance, as Dixon-Krauss (1996) points out, "This Vygotskian idea is in direct opposition to the traditional basic skills view that a child must learn a word before she can use it. From the Vygotskian perspective, the child would learn the word by using it" (p. 14).

In fact, a field of study—problem-based learning—has emerged that can be directly linked to constructivist assumptions. In particular, technology has become prominent in promoting problem-based learning (Knowlton & Sharp, 2003). In a sense, learning is sparked by problems. If no problem needs to be solved, learning appears to be no more than an intellectual activity of flexing one's mind. But the relationship between daily problems and classroom learning is so intimate that to disregard the world's problems in the classroom is to reduce "learning" to memorization of established facts. Education, however pleasurable, is not an end in itself. A major concern of public education is to produce educated citizens who will know how to govern wisely. Problem-based learning helps in the effort to produce such a citizenry.

In all that we have said about constructivism and problem-based learning, we are not negating the use of direct instruction methods, including lectures, note taking, and practice worksheets. In fact, literature on effective teaching takes note of the fact that some exemplary teachers are celebrated for their ability to lecture well (e.g., Baiocco & DeWaters, 1998; Epstein, 1981). Nevertheless, a steady diet of lecture neither effectively feeds active learning nor helps nurture higher-order thinking skills (O'Donnell & Dansereau, 1994; Speck, 2002). Direct instruction methods can be effective if they are used judiciously as a way to support constructivist assumptions.

○ Linking Constructivism, Literacy, and Computers

Even though constructivism is not a theory about using technology, constructivist assumptions are guideposts for developing a vision for integrating technology into the literacy curriculum (Brown, 1997; Wolffe, 1997). In fact, researchers consistently agree that the pedagogy that emphasizes constructivist elements makes best uses of technology (Bickford, Tharp, McFarling, & Beglau, 2002; Morrison & Lowther, 2005). The assumptions associated with constructivist pedagogy are outlined in Figure 1.3 and described above.

Knowledge Has Multiple Interpretations

One assumption of a constructivist approach is that knowledge is complex and can be interpreted in various ways. It is extremely difficult, if not impossible, for everyone to reach a consensus about meaning, because each individual brings his or her background and interpretation to situations that change over time. With this assumption in mind, teachers create classroom environments where students talk, collaborate with, and question others (Applefield, Huber, & Moallem, 2000). In addition to conversations within the classroom, teachers create activities that involve conversations via the Internet. For example, it is not uncommon for students to be engaged in online projects with students in a different state or country and for them to gain new insights about different cultures that lead them to develop different perspectives on current literature they are reading in class.

Learning Is an Active Process

Students actively search for meanings to transform their present understanding instead of parroting standard interpretations (Greene, 1988). Students do not sit passively while teachers pour knowledge into their heads. Teachers assume a new role in a constructivist classroom. Instead of being dispensers of knowledge, teachers are facilitators (e.g., Grant & Hill, 2006; King, 1993). For example, teachers develop tasks that require students to tap into the Internet and other informational sources to find answers to their questions and to explore ideas (e.g., Eisenberg, 2003; Eisenberg & Johnson, 2002).

Figure 1.3 Assumptions of Constructivism.

- Knowledge has multiple interpretations.
- Learning is an active process.
- Process and product are emphasized.
- Problem solving is the focus.
- Power and control are shared among students and teacher.
- Learning is a collaborative process.
- Reflection is promoted.

Process and Product Are Emphasized

Generally, what has been valued and assessed in traditional classrooms are students' final products; the assessment is usually based on some sort of objective test (Bertrand, 1993). The final outcomes of students' efforts are assumed to be representative of their learning, with less consideration given to the "how and why" of their learning. In constructivist classrooms, however, the process is valued as much as the product (e.g., Grant, 2005). What, how, and why students learn are given significant consideration (Hutchings, 1993; Johnston, 1992). For example, when students have access to a word processor, they can use technology to engage in process writing by receiving feedback from others electronically and by making revisions to their drafts.

Problem Solving Is the Focus

In constructivist classroom environments, students develop real-world problem-solving skills that lead them to observe, think, question, and test their ideas. These problem-based learning environments encourage students to make decisions about how to approach a problem. They call into question the traditional approach that focuses on the teacher as the sole authority in the classroom and the *primary* source of knowledge. In the traditional approach, the teacher singularly dispenses information, and the students absorb it in order to demonstrate on a test that they have understood what the teacher has said. Under a constructivist paradigm, teachers are facilitators who scaffold instruction to assist students' growth while the students assume more ownership and responsibility for their learning, using a variety of instructional methods and strategies, including direct instruction (Applefield, Huber, & Moallem, 2000; Grant & Hill, 2006). In this environment, technology tools such as word processors, spreadsheets, and concept maps can be used to collect, analyze, and display information. In addition, primary and secondary source documents on the Internet enable students to explore and gather information on a variety of topics.

Power and Control Are Shared Among Students and Teacher

One assumption of social constructivism is that teachers share the power with students in making decisions about what is to be learned and how it is to be assessed. In this context, students negotiate the curriculum by having a voice in selecting and defining activities that are relevant and meaningful to them as well as in evaluating the outcomes. For example, it is well documented that students are more intrinsically motivated and show greater growth in their writing when they are allowed to write on topics of their choice (Calkins, 1994; Graves, 1983). In today's classroom, the Internet provides numerous sources from which to gather information on topics the students find interesting, not topics the teacher assigns. This does not mean, however, that the teacher has no part in developing assignments. On the contrary: In a constructivist classroom, the teacher is in charge as a manager.

For example, a sixth-grade teacher might determine that the students will read and study Shakespeare's plays and, at the same time, might give students a great deal of freedom in selecting topics for such a study (e.g., Elizabethan costumes, Shakespeare's use of humor in his plays, the politics of Elizabethan England as reflected in the plays). A work of literature exists in a social context, and students can approach that work from a variety of viewpoints, choosing a perspective that is appealing to them.

Learning Is a Collaborative Process

In contexts that embrace a social-constructivist perspective, students and teachers are co-learners, freely expressing and testing their ideas together (Applefield, Humber, & Moallem, 2000). In these social settings, collaborative communication helps students achieve their goals and also builds community. For example, peer writing conferences help "children connect with another human being in order to learn from him or her, to empathize, to hear peers' stories and to understand their own stories more fully, to care about another person's interpretation of the world, and to be able to identify and respond to another person's perspective" (Gould, 1996, p. 98). Thus, students are not always working independently on reading and writing tasks—they are often working in collaborative groups, fulfilling Vygotsky's notions of zone of proximal development and scaffolding, using computers as tools to facilitate the collaborations. Leu (1996) points out that learning "is frequently constructed through social interactions in these contexts, perhaps even more naturally and frequently than in traditional print environments" (p. 163). In addition, these collaborative groups have expanded beyond the traditional brick-and-mortar classroom to groups throughout the world via the Internet. For example, students are able to read, write, and collaborate with others through e-mail, instant messaging, and Web logs (blogs).

Reflection Is Promoted

In constructivist classrooms, students are given opportunities to reflect on their learning. Reflection encourages students to respond to what they are reading and to think about their own learning. Reflection enables them to make informed decisions about what they should learn next (Grant & Hill, 2006). This type of thinking promotes metacognition and self-regulation, where students are able to recognize what they know and what they don't and to make purposeful decisions to address learning deficiencies. One example of how teachers are promoting reflective behavior is electronic journals, or blogs.

Constructivist classrooms that make use of computer technology to teach literacy are busy, interactive environments. Students reflect within themselves and they freely interact with others to enhance their own learning, both online and in the classroom. Teachers do not teach literacy skills in isolation but instead create meaningful and purposeful tasks that are open ended and problem based. Students become researchers, exploring numerous sources to collect and analyze data to make informed decisions about their learning. Serving as mentor and coach, teachers use computers not only as a delivery mechanism for drill and practice of skills, but also as a tool to enhance students' learning in numerous ways.

◯ Enhancing Teachers' Skills to Integrate Technology with Literacy

Regardless of how knowledgeable and skilled we are in using computers to teach literacy, the need for professional development is constant. Advancements are occurring rapidly, and even the technology "gurus" are challenged to stay abreast of the knowledge and skills they need to maintain their status.

Fortunately, today it is easier than ever to collaborate with like-minded teachers. If you have not already done so, you can subscribe to a listserv, such as the Technology and Literacy List (**http://www.nifl.gov/mailman/listinfo/Technology**), the Poverty, Race and Literacy Discussion List (**http://www.nifl.gov/mailman/listinfo/Technology**), the Learning Disabilities List (**http://www.nifl.gov/mailman/listinfo/Learningdisabilities**), or the TESL-LIST and Linguist List for ESL, where you can read about instructional tools, discuss teaching strategies, or pose questions about virtually any topic in the field. You can also pose a question or respond to one at a discussion forum, such as Teach-nology.com (**http://www.teach-nology.com/forum**). One of the main advantages of subscribing to a listserv and participating in discussion forums is that you are connected to thousands of professionals from all over the world in a matter of minutes.

Professional learning communities are another example of a growing movement in the field that brings together preservice and inservice teachers for the purpose of meeting online to discuss and reflect on their teaching. For example, the University of Indiana is currently funded through the National Science Foundation to support student learning and teacher growth through inquiry in a project entitled Inquiry Learning Forum (ILF). At the University of Memphis, Dr. Kathy Cooter directs an initiative funded by Microsoft Corporation to implement and sustain professional learning through online discussions. Their first topic centers on the bigotry of low expectations. They are using the very popular Tapped In (**http://tappedin.org**) online discussion boards to facilitate their conversations.

A traditional, ongoing form of professional development that should not be overlooked is joining professional organizations that offer conferences and publish journals on the topic of using technology to teach literacy, such as the International Reading Association (IRA), the National Council Teachers of English (NCTE), and Teaching English to Speakers of Other Languages (TESOL). Also, organizations that are technology focused, such as the International Society for Technology in Education (ISTE), Society for Information Technology and Teacher Education (SITE), and Association for Educational Communication and Technology (AECT), have divisions and interest groups that emphasize teacher education and literacy. By far the largest technology conference that focuses on K–12 teaching and learning is the National Education Computing Conference (NECC) sponsored by ISTE, which offers various topical strands dealing with integrating technology into classrooms. In addition, there are numerous professional publications that offer case studies, descriptions of classroom research initiatives, and innovative practices: *The Computing Teacher*, *Learning and Leading with Technology*, *Technology and Learning*, and *Teaching Pre-K–8*. You also might find these two publications helpful: Blanchard and Marshall's (2004) *Web-based learning in K–12 classrooms: Opportunities and challenges,* and Greenlaw and Ebenezer's (2005) *English language arts and reading on the Internet: A resource for K–12 teachers.*

Another traditional form of professional development is graduate school. Many school districts provide teachers with incentives to take graduate courses to improve their teaching, which often leads to an add-on endorsement in reading, technology, or ESL. This is particularly timely and imperative given No Child Left Behind's emphasis on teachers' highly qualified status and the mandate for technology literacy for all students by the eighth grade.

Recently, the enrollment in online courses has soared, with not only universities offering online courses, but also with numerous companies offering online workshops. For example, Thirteen Ed Online sponsors the Concept to Classroom site (**http://www.thirteen. org/edonline/concept2class**) that offers a series of free self-paced workshops covering a variety of topics such as "WebQuests," "Constructivism as a Paradigm for Teaching and Learning," and "Why the Net? An Interactive Tool for the Classroom," which are all topics emphasized in this text to support literacy. Additionally, there are numerous summer workshops and institutes being offered, such as the Big6 Academy, which is in such high demand that if you don't enroll early, you won't be able to participate.

When attempting a new lesson, content area, or grade level, it is often helpful to see what other teachers have implemented in their classrooms. The number of online sites housing lesson plans is plentiful, but their quality can be uncertain. In addition to the great number of digital resources we suggest throughout the remainder of this text, two sources for reputable lesson plans include TrackStar and netTrekker. TrackStar (see Figure 1.4) represents online lesson plans and digital resources for lessons created by other teachers. The powerful search engine allows you to search by topics and grade levels. The immense value of this site is that another teacher has already found the digital

Figure 1.4   One of the great tools available to teachers from 4teachers.org, TrackStar is where teachers go to collate and organize Web sites to use in lessons. Teachers create a track, which is a "hot list" of Web addresses for students to visit and use during a lesson. Once the track has been saved, other teachers can search and use the track.

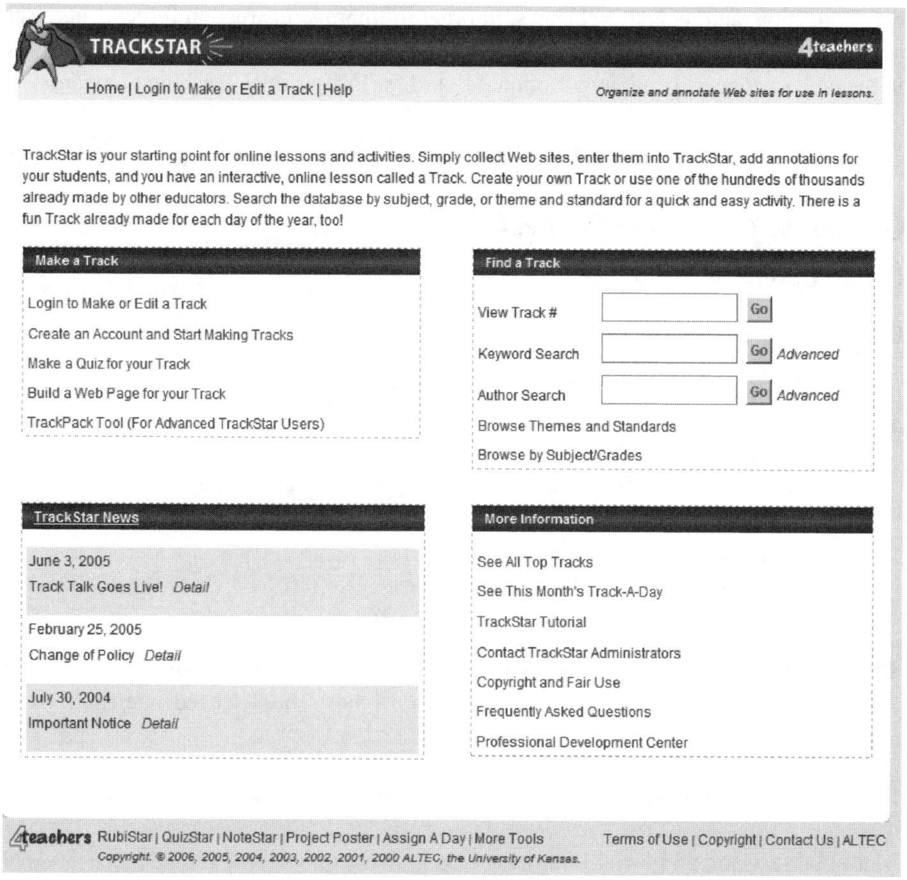

Screenshot copyright 1995–2006 ALTEC, the University of Kansas. Funded by the U.S. Department of Education, Regional Technology in Education Consortium, 1995–2005 to ALTEC (Advanced Learning Technologies in Education Consortia) at the University of Kansas, Center for Research on Learning.

resources to be helpful. So, it's sort of like peeking inside another teacher's bookmark list. netTrekker, similar to TrackStar, also offers lesson plans and digital resources for teachers. Going even further, netTrekker has teachers and content-experts rate and approve the quality of the resources, so teachers can be confident using the materials. net-Trekker's rating process is similar to Amazon.com's rating system. While TrackStar continues to be a free service, netTrekker requires a subscription fee. In addition to TrackStar and netTrekker, many state departments of education maintain lesson plan databases aligned with their respective state's curriculum standards, such as Georgia (**http://georgiastandards.org**), and nationally, the Gateway to Educational Materials (**http://thegateway.org**) maintains.

Although the previous suggestions for professional development have been outside your classroom, one growing trend is inside your classroom with using the approach of studying your practice, known as teacher-as-researcher, or action research. Specifically, action research provides a mechanism to strategically improve your teaching through reflection, data collection, and recursive changes, in order to improve instruction for students. Not only is it required in many masters programs throughout the country, it is also embedded in the process for certification by National Board for Professional Teaching Standards.

COMPUTER CLASSROOM LESSONS

Getting the Genie out of Genealogy

Grade Level: 6–8

Objective: The learner will:

1. Become aware of human migratory habits.
2. Establish a personal relationship with the past.
3. Develop a sense of history.
4. Have fun researching a nonacademic topic using the Internet.
5. Think more about families and family values.
6. Develop a keener self-awareness.
7. Search for and maybe find new relatives.
8. Discover that the Internet can generate personal information.

Time: 50 minutes (Note: This lesson plan is for day one of a longitudinal project intended to last about two weeks, depending on other school-related interruptions to classroom time.)

Problem to Be Solved: How far back can you trace your family?

Materials: Computers with Internet access
Printer
List of Web sites
World map
Handout

Steps:

1. Students are shown pictures of older European, Asian, or other people in traditional or native outfits. The teacher asks if there are any guesses to identify who or what they are.
2. When this is established, the teacher announces probable origins, finds the location on the map, and then asks if any student is aware of his or her ancestry or ancestral country.
3. The teacher (very enthusiastically) announces that the students are going online to search for and discover their family history (which is called genealogy). Students should be told this is a fun assignment and that participation and effort are a main source of their grade.

First-Day Activities:

1. Divide students into groups of three or four. Friends in a group are okay.
2. The teacher demonstrates a Web site devoted to genealogy and also locates a search engine, such as Google or Yahoo!, and types in the word *genealogy* to see what comes up.
3. After being encouraged to help each other and to share in equal time amounts, groups go to the computers and are off and running to look up their ancestral information.
4. The teacher has provided a handout identifying what to look for and how to organize it. Students also should look for clues as to when and how their family migrated to their present location, and they should feel free to speculate about why they did so.
5. Before the bell rings, the teacher asks for a progress report and states that such reports will be a normal routine on subsequent days as more information is researched.

Assessment: Did the students participate and make an effort by self-, peer group, and/or teacher assessments? And/or: Brief oral report by a group member on anything found, including a written summary for inclusion in a portfolio.

Rubric for expanded assessment:

    25 percent participation using peer/group assessment
    25 percent data collection
    25 percent oral report of findings to class
    25 percent written report for portfolio inclusion

Balking in the Balkans

Grade Level: 8

Objective: The learner will:

1. Develop a sense of teamwork to solve problems and complete projects.
2. Gain insight into unfamiliar social and political issues.

3. Be able to converse online with people in other countries.
4. Come to a greater appreciation of his or her own country.
5. Provide an outlet for Balkan residents to share feelings.

Time: 50 minutes (Note: This lesson plan is for day one of a longitudinal project intended to last about two weeks for the field work and several more days for report preparation.)

Problem to Be Solved: What's happening in the part of Europe known as the Balkans?

Materials: 6 or more computers with Internet access
Printer
List of e-mail Web sites
Map
Handout

Steps:

1. Students are shown pictures of refugees from Kosovo Province (overhead, or on large screen), scenes of violence or devastation, and pictures of American soldiers in uniform. The teacher does not say they are Kosovo people but asks the class for a probable identity.
2. Question by question, the teacher finds out how much students know about the Balkan situation, such as place names, map location, U.S. involvement, and so forth. This serves as a preevaluation. Extra credit can be given to anyone making contact within the former Yugoslavia.

First-Day Activities:

1. Formation of groups (called teams) in accordance with model description.
2. Teams are assigned a country: Yugoslavia (Kosovo or Serbia), Bosnia, Albania, or Macedonia. They should be made aware that computers are in short number in Kosovo.
3. Students are given a primer by the teacher on accessing e-mail, Web sites, and chat rooms.
4. Class expectations are explained verbally and with a handout. Students should ask questions about subjects such as changes in school life, sports, after-school and weekend activities, and whether things are improving or worsening since the revolution.
5. The teacher provides general guidelines on writing proper questions. Questions and answers tend to be self-generated, but actual questions are written by the team.
6. Remaining time is to be spent collecting initial questions or getting online.
7. The teacher re-emphasizes the important of going outside the local circle and comfort zone to establish contact with people living in the rest of the world and learn more about important world issues from nontraditional sources.

Assessment: 25 percent list of events happening in Macedonia, Bosnia, Albania, Yugoslavia (Serbia)

25 percent data collection: e-mail contacts, information

25 percent oral report of findings

25 percent written report for inclusion in portfolio

○ Techno-Teacher Tips

Classroom Instruction

Very few teachers have as many computers as they would like, and even those who do have enough are challenged to determine how to structure classroom time so that students can use the computers. In addition, integrating the computer into existing curriculum may be quite challenging. For instance, perhaps you are accustomed to teaching your students process writing, and you intermittently use the school computer lab. Now, however, your grade level has a laptop computer cart for you to use. When you are developing lesson plans, you will need to consider how best to integrate word processing and the new computers. You may wonder what to eliminate from the curriculum to make time for additional computer instruction. Although these types of curriculum and instructional decisions may not be too difficult to think through, they will require additional time on your part.

Balancing Constructivist Approaches with Standardized Testing

Integrating many of the constructivist and computer-based approaches outlined in this chapter does not address the current educational climate's value on standardized testing as the primary assessment mechanism and the broad curriculum these tests address. Later chapters cover content-area reading, publishing, and project-based learning in greater depth. As a guide for now, having students complete two to three extended projects during an academic year will give them the experience of working in a more constructivist, student-driven learning environment without sacrificing the need to attend to a broad curriculum. Also, as these projects are developed, the teacher should link both previously covered material and future curricular goals to situate knowledge, facts, and skills within an authentic use of the constructivist lessons.

○ Frequently Asked Questions

1. **I'm unfamiliar with many of the computer techniques you've briefly mentioned in this chapter. How do I begin using them with my students when I'm not yet comfortable with my own abilities?**

   Expertise in using technology does not necessarily rest on the teacher alone. Technology in the classroom can be regarded as a tool that is everyone's responsibility, including your students. The teacher should not fear not knowing any particular aspect or feature of the technology, but should instead view his or her technological knowledge and skill as blended with the overall knowledge and skill integrated in the classroom. Leveraging your students' knowledge and skills about the technology can motivate the learners and advance the teacher's own knowledge and skills, developing a classroom community of practice (Wenger, 1998). One teacher expressed that technology in the classroom has allowed for students to become experts, redefining the student-teacher relationship (see e.g., Bryan, 2000). Remember, teaching and learning constitute a reciprocal process. You teach the students, and they invariably teach you.

2. **I've read about constructivist approaches before, but they seem to be unfocused and unstructured. I can't teach that way. Is there a way I can compromise?**

Applefield, Huber and Moallem (2000) present five myths about constructivist teaching:

1. There is no focus for learning, no clear goal in constructivist-based instruction;
2. Constructivist-based instruction is not thoughtfully planned; careful preparation is less important than in traditional instruction;
3. There is an absence of structure for learning in a constructivist learning environment;
4. As long as learners are involved in discussion and other forms of social interaction, learning will take place; and
5. Since teachers are not primarily engaged in delivering instruction (lecturing and explaining), their role in the classroom is less important.

As shown above, constructivist lessons are not unstructured. There is a guiding task, question, or topic that provides direction for discusions and investigations. In addition, the teacher provides scaffolding in the form of student-teacher conferences, job aids, and questioning in order to shape the direction of the discussion and lesson. Constructivist lessons involve intricate planning with a variety of different resources, all initially driven by the teachers themselves.

○ References

Anderson, J., & Lee, A. (1995). Literacy teachers learning a new literacy: A study of the use of electronic mail in a reading education class. *Reading Research and Instruction, 34,* 222–238.

Anderson, D. S., & Piazza, J. A. (1996). Changing beliefs: Teaching and learning mathematics in constructivist preservice classrooms. *Action in Teacher Education, 18*(2), 51–62.

Applefield, J. M., Huber, R. L., & Moallem, M. (2000). Constructivism in theory and practice: Toward a better understanding. *High School Journal, 84*(2), 35–53.

Atkinson, R. C., & Hansen, D. N. (1996). Computer-assisted instruction in initial reading: The Stanford project. *Reading Research Quarterly, 21,* 5–25.

Baiocco, S. A., & DeWaters, J. N. (1998). *Successful college teaching: Problem-solving strategies of distinguished professors.* Old Tappan, NJ: Allyn & Bacon.

Becker, H. J. (1994). How computers are used in United States schools: Basic data from the 1989 I.E.A. computers in education survey. *Journal of Educational Computing Research, 7*(4), 385–406.

Bertrand, J. E. (1993). Student assessment and evaluation. In B. Harp (Ed.), *Assessment and evaluation in whole language programs* (pp. 19–35). Norwood, MA: Christopher-Gordon.

Bickford, A., Tharp, S., McFarling, P., & Beglau, M. (2002). Finding the right fuel for new engines of learning. *Multimedia Schools, 9*(5), 18–26.

Bintz, W. P. (1991). "Staying connected:" Exploring new functions for assessment. *Contemporary Education, 62*(4), 307–312.

Bishop, K. (2003). What in the world is happening with information literacy. *Knowledge Quest, 31*(5), 14–16.

Blanchard, J., & Marshall, J. (Eds). (2004). *Web-based learning in K–12 classrooms: Opportunities and challenges.* Binghamton, NY: Haworth Press.

Bork, A. (1987). *Learning with personal computers.* New York: Harper & Row.

Brooks, J. G., & Brooks, M. G. (1993). *In search of understanding: The case for constructivist classrooms.* Alexandria, VA: Association for Supervision and Curriculum Development.

Brown, D. (1997). Kids, computers, and constructivism. *Journal of Instructional Psychology, 23*(3), 189–195.

Bruffee, K. A. (1986). Social construction, language, and the authority of knowledge: A bibliographical essay. *College English, 48,* 773–790.

Bruner, J. (1986). *Actual minds, possible worlds.* Cambridge, MA: Harvard University Press.

Bryan, S. (2000, May 1). SWAT savvy: A model for effect classroom technology using student experts. *Technology and Learning.* Retrieved June 26, 2003, from http://www.techlearning.com/db_area/archives/WCE/archives/bryan.htm

Bufkin, L. J., & Bryde, S. (1996). Implementing a constructivist approach in higher education with early childhood educators. *Journal of Early Childhood Instructor Education, 17*(2), 58–65.

Calkins, L. (1994). *The art of teaching writing.* Portsmouth, NH: Heinemann.

Costanzo, W. (1994). Reading, writing, and thinking in an age of electronic literacy. In C. L. Selfe & S. Hilligoss (Eds.), *Literacy and computers: The complications of teaching and learning with technology* (pp. 11–21). Urbana, IL: National Council of Teachers of English.

Davydov, V. V. (1995). The influence of L. S. Vygotsky on education theory, research, and practice. *Educational Researcher, 24*(3), 12–21.

Dixon-Krauss, L. (1996). *Vygotsky in the classroom: Mediated literacy instruction and assessment.* White Plains, NY: Longman.

Duckworth, E. (1987). *The having of wonderful ideas.* New York: Instructors College Press.

Eisenberg, M. B. (2003). Technology for a purpose: Technology for information problem-solving with the Big 6. *TechTrends, 47*(1), 13–17.

Eisenberg, M. B., & Johnson, D. (2002). Computer skills for information problem-solving: Learning and teaching technology in context. *Emergency Librarian, 21*(2), 8–16.

El-Hindi, A. (1998). Beyond classroom boundaries: Constructivist teaching with the Internet. In D. J. Leu Jr. (Ed.), Exploring literacy on the Internet. *The Reading Teacher, 51*(8), 694–700.

Epstein, J. (Ed.). (1981). *Masters: Portraits of great teachers.* New York: Basic Books.

Flood, J., & Lapp, D. (1995). Broadening the lens: Toward an expanded conceptualization of literacy. In K. A. Hinchman, D. J. Leu, & C. K. Kinzer (Eds.), *Perspectives on literacy research and practice* (pp. 1–16). Chicago: National Reading Conference.

Fosnot, C. W. (1996). Constructivism: A psychological theory of learning. In C. W. Fosnot (Ed.), *Constructivism: Theory, perspectives, and practice* (pp. 8–33). New York: Instructors College Press.

Friedman, T. L. (2005). *The world is flat.* New York: Farrar, Straus, and Giroux.

Gallego, M., & Hollingsworth, S. (1992). Multiple literacies: Teachers' evolving perceptions. *Language Arts, 69,* 206–213.

Gavelek, J. R., & Raphael, T. E. (1996). Changing talk about text: New roles for teachers and students. *Language Arts, 73,* 182–192.

Gould, J. S. (1996). A constructivist perspective on teaching and learning within the language arts. In C. Fosnot (Ed.), *Constructivism: Theory, perspectives, and practice* (pp. 92–102). New York: Teachers College Press.

Grant, M. M., & Branch, R. M. (2005). Project-based learning in a middle school: Tracing abilities through the artifacts of learning. *Journal of Research on Technology in Education, 38*(1), 65–98.

Grant, M. M., & Hill, J. R. (2006). Weighing the risks with the rewards: Implementing student-centered pedagogy within high-stakes testing. In R. Lambert & C. McCarthy (Eds.), *Understanding teacher stress in an age of accountability* (pp. 19–42). Greenwich, CT: Information Age Press.

Graves, D. H. (1983). *Writing: Teachers and children at work.* Portsmouth, NH: Heinemann.

Greene, M. (1988). *The dialectic of freedom.* New York: Teachers College Press.

Greenlaw, J. C. & Ebenezer, J. V. (2005). *English language arts and reading on the Internet: A resource for K-12 teachers.* Upper Saddle River, New Jersey: Pearson.

Gruender, C. D. (1996). Constructivism and learning: A philosophical appraisal. *Educational Technology, 36*(3), 21–29.

Hobbs, R., & Frost, R. (2003). Measuring the acquisition of media-literacy skills. *Reading Research Quarterly, 38*(2), 330–355.

Hutchings, P. (1993). Principles of good practice for assessing student learning. *Assessment Update, 5*(1), 6–7.

Johnston, P. H. (1992). *Constructive evaluation of literate activity.* White Plains, NY: Longman.

Jonassen, D. H. (2000). *Computers as mindtools for schools: Engaging critical thinking* (2nd ed.). Upper Saddle River, NJ: Merrill Prentice Hall.

Jonassen, D. H., & Reeves, T. C. (1996). Learning with technology: Using computers as cognitive tools. In D. H. Jonassen (Ed.), *Handbook of research for educational communications and technology* (pp. 693–719). New York, NY: Simon & Schuster Macmillan.

King, A. (1993). From sage on the stage to guide on the side. *College Teaching, 41*(1), 30–35.

Knowlton, D. S., & Sharp, D. C. (Eds.). (2003). *Problem-based learning in the information age.* New Directions for Teaching and Learning, no. 95. San Francisco, CA: Jossey-Bass.

Kroll, L. R., & LaBoskey, V. K. (1996). Practicing what we preach: Constructivism in a teacher education program. *Action in Teacher Education, 18*(2), 63–72.

Labbo, L. D. (1996). A semiotic analysis of young children's symbol making in a classroom computer center. *Reading Research Quarterly, 31,* 356–385.

Labbo, L. D., Reinking, D., & Mckenna, M. G. (1995). *Incorporating a computer into the classroom: Lessons learned in kindergarten* (Instructional Resource No. 20). Athens, GA: National Reading Research Center, Universities of Georgia and Maryland.

Leu, D. J. (1996). Sarah's secret: Social aspects of literacy and learning in a digital information age. *The Reading Teacher, 50*, 162–165.

Leu, D. (1997). Caity's question: Literacy as deixis on the Internet. *The Reading Teacher, 51*(1), 62–67.

Leu, D. J., Jr., & Leu, D. D. (1997). *Teaching with the Internet: Lessons from the classroom.* Norwood, MA: Christopher-Gordon.

Leu, D. J., Jr., & Reinking, D. (1996). Bringing insights from reading research to research on electronic learning environments. In H. van Oostendorp & S. de Mul (Eds.), *Cognitive aspects of electronic text processing* (pp. 43–76). Norwood, NJ: Ablex.

Means, B. (Ed.). (1994). *Technology and education reform: The reality behind the promise.* San Francisco: Jossey-Bass.

Moll, L. C., & Greenberg, J. B. (1990). Creating zones of possibilities: Combining social contexts for instruction. In L. C. Moll (Ed.), *Vygotsky and education: Instructional implications of sociohistorical psychology* (pp. 319–348). Cambridge: Cambridge University Press.

Morra, L. G. (1995, April). *America's schools not designed or equipped for the 21st century.* Washington, D.C.: Health, Education, and Human Services Division. (ERIC Document Reproduction Service No. ED 381 153)

Morrison, G. R., & Lowther, D. L. (2005). *Integrating computer technology into the classroom* (3rd ed.). Upper Saddle River, NJ: Merrill.

Murray, J. (2003). Contemporary literacy: Essential skills for the 21st century. *Multimedia Schools, 10*(2), 14–18.

National Center for Educational Statistics. (2003). *Internet Access in U.S. Public Schools, Fall 2003.* Washington, D.C.: U.S. Department of Education.

National Council of Teachers of English & International Reading Association. (1996). *Standards for the English language arts.* Newark, DE: Author.

O'Donnell, A., & Dansereau, D. F. (1994). Learning from lectures: Effects of cooperative review. *Journal of Experimental Education, 61*(2), 116–125.

Piaget, J. (1970). *The science of education and the psychology of the child.* New York: Basic Books.

Puma, M. J., Chaplin, D. D., & Pape, A. D. (2000). *E-rate and the digital divide: A preliminary analysis from the integrated studies of educational technology.* Washington, D.C.: The Urban Institute for the U.S. Department of Education. Available from http://www.ed.gov/offices/OUS/PES/erate_fr.pdf

Revenaugh, M. (2000). Beyond the digital divide: Pathways to equity. *Technology & Learning, 20*(10), 38–40, 44–50.

Reinking, D. (1992). Differences between electronic and printed texts: An agenda for research. *Journal of Educational Multimedia and Hypermedia, 1*(1), 11–24.

Reinking, D. (1994). *Electronic literacy* (Perspective in Reading Research No. 4). Athens, GA: National Reading Research Center, Universities of Georgia and Maryland.

Reinking, D. (1995). Reading and writing with computers: Literacy research in a post-typographic world. In K. A. Hinchman, D. J. Leu, & C. K. Kinzer (Eds)., *Perspectives on literacy research and practice, 44th yearbook of the National Reading Conference* (pp. 17–33). Chicago: National Reading Conference.

Reinking, D. (1996). Reclaiming a scholarly ethic: Deconstructing "intellectual property" in a post-typographic world. In *Literacies for the 21st century: Research and practice, 45th yearbook of the National Reading Conference* (pp. 461–470). Chicago: National Reading Conference.

Reinking, D. (1997). Me and my hypertext: A multiple digression analysis of technology and literacy (sic). *The Reading Teacher, 50*(8), 626–643.

Ryder, R., & Graves, M. (December 1996–January 1997). Using the Internet to enhance students' reading, writing, and information-gathering skills. *Journal of Adolescent & Adult Literacy, 40*(4), 244–254.

Schmar-Dobler, E. (2003). Reading on the Internet: The link between literacy and technology. *Journal of Adolescent and Adult Literacy, 47*(1), 80–85.

Speck, B. W. (2002). *Facilitating students' collaborative writing.* ASHE-ERIC Higher Education Report, *28*(6). New York: Wiley.

Smerdon, B., & Cronen, S. (2000). *Teachers' tools for the 21ˢᵗ century: A report on teachers' use of technology* (Publication No. NCES 2000102). Washington, D.C.: National Center for Education Statistics, U.S. Department of Education.

Tittle, C. K. (1991). Changing models of student and instructor assessment. *Educational Psychologist, 26*(2), 157–165.

U.S. Department of Education. (2004). *Technology Innovation Challenge Grant Program.* Retrieved March 23, 2004, from http://www.ed.gov/programs/techinnov/index.html

Vygotsky, L. S. (1978). *Mind in society: The development of higher psychological processes.* Cambridge, MA: Harvard University Press.

Wenger, E. (1998). *Communities of practice: Learning, meaning, and identity.* Cambridge, U.K.: Cambridge University Press.

Willis, J. W., Stephens, E. C., & Matthew, K. I. (1996). *Technology, reading, and language arts.* Needham Heights, MA: Allyn & Bacon.

Wolffe, R. (1997). The constructivist connection: Linking theory, best practice, and technology. *Journal of Computing in Teacher Education, 12*(2), 25–28.

Technology Tools to Support Literacy

Jamila Davis, a second-grade teacher for seven years, sighed to the library media specialist, "Mrs. Bishop, I want to do something with technology in this next unit on similes and figurative language. I feel like there's just so much more that I could be doing, but I just don't know how to." The two colleagues sat beside one another at a large, round table in Green River Elementary School's media center just after the last bell of the day.

"Well, Mrs. Davis, what's the lesson that you usually do?" inquired the calm media specialist, a large woman with salty-blond hair and deep green eyes.

"We usually read a book that uses figurative language like *Quick as a Cricket*. Then we discuss the pattern, and we take a look at some other figurative language patterns. Next, the students usually do a worksheet to identify the figurative language, and maybe they take another worksheet home for homework."

"Well, that gives us a wonderful place to start, Mrs. Davis. I really like how you started with the literature, so the students could see the language in action. It also does a little discovery learning as well. Let's focus on similes first, since that's what you mentioned. It seems like what you want your students to be able to do is to define what similes are and identify them in print. Is that correct?"

"Yes, it is. You sound just like the curriculum standards, Mrs. Bishop," Jamila grinned.

Mrs. Bishop smiled affably. "Have you considered extending the lesson?" Mrs. Bishop suggested. "Maybe instead of having the students do the worksheets, they could create their own sentences with similes. You could even have them pattern it after *Quick as a Cricket*."

25

"I like that idea, but we usually don't focus on creative writing until later, in the second nine weeks. It would probably be okay, though."

"Well, then, here's an idea. You could have students create a story patterned after *Quick as a Cricket* that describes themselves. They could write their sentences on paper first and jot down some ideas of the type of graphics that might go with their sentences. Then they—"

"So, we could use Microsoft Word for them to type their sentences," Jamila interjected, becoming excited with the idea.

"You could do that, or you could use Microsoft PowerPoint and have each sentence be on a new slide with the space already set aside for clip art."

"Oh, that sounds easier," Jamila added. "But would I use the laptop cart or—I only have four computers in my classroom, and I've only used the laptops to do the online testing." Jamila seemed puzzled.

"Well, Mrs. Davis, you could do either. If you wanted to use the laptops, then you could have the students type the sentences they wrote on paper and choose clip art to illustrate them. If you wanted to use the computers in your classroom, then I would suggest having the students illustrate their own sentences."

"And why would we do that instead of clip art?" Jamila inquired.

"One of the classroom management strategies that I like to use with computers is to plan what happens before the kids go to the computers, plan what they do at the computers, and plan what they do after the computers. In this case, before the computers, we would have them write their sentences on paper and write down some ideas for illustrations. That reduces the amount of time they are actually on the computer."

"Wow! That's a good idea," Jamila said.

Mrs. Bishop continued. "Then while they're at the computers, they just have to type what they wrote. Not a lot to think about and take up time. If you choose to use the laptops, then they could choose clip art, which takes up some time. The kids will be picky when looking for the perfect picture," Mrs. Bishop said smiling and rolling her eyes. "If you were going to use your classroom computers, for us to rotate all the kids through the computer stations, you need something for them to do after they are done at the computers. So letting them illustrate their sentences gives them something to do afterward."

The light bulb went on. "Oh, I get it. Before, during, and after the computer. It creates rotation."

"You got it!" Mrs. Bishop added.

"Mrs. Bishop, will you be there to help me make sure it goes OK?" Jamila asked with concern in her voice.

Mrs. Bishop flashed her confident smile again, and her emerald eyes seem to smile, too. "Of course, Mrs. Davis. We'll do it together. I won't let you have all of the fun."

○ Integrating Technology for Literacy

In later chapters, we will examine the processes of literacy and how technology may be integrated to support teaching and learning with these processes. However, it will be helpful for us to explore the wide range of technology tools that are available. These tools offer a wide array of possibilities to augment the ways we teach literacy. In Chapter 1, we discussed moving away from solely didactic instruction and moving toward more constructivist student-centered pedagogy. Researchers (e.g., Applefield, Huber, & Moallem, 2000; Morrison & Lowther, 2005) consistently suggest that student-centered practices make best use of the technology tools we have at our disposal. Before we survey the potential tools, let's take a look at Candace Pauchnick's classroom and notice how she has changed her practice to integrate technology for improved writing and communication skills.

 ## Computer Classroom Snapshot

Context

I'm Candace Pauchnick, and I have been teaching in the San Diego, California, school district secondary education system since 1974—long before computer technology was an everyday presence on school campuses. As technology has advanced and schools have been provided with computers, software, and the Internet, I have seen significant changes in the tools teachers have available to engage students in learning. They enjoy doing research on the Internet, and they demonstrate enthusiasm presenting reports electronically.

I teach at Patrick Henry High School, located in an upper/middle income-bracket area of San Diego. To provide equal educational opportunity, this school district allows parents to choose a school for their child that may be located outside of their neighborhood. Patrick Henry receives many students from other areas. The school ethnicities include approximately 50 percent Caucasians and 50 percent Hispanics, or Latinos, African Americans, Vietnamese, Chinese, Filipinos, American Indians, Cambodians, and several other nationalities, for a total of about 2,400 students. The top nine languages represented in the school consist of, in order of most common to least common, English, Spanish, Vietnamese, Farsi, Somali, Arabic, Cambodian, Chinese, and Lao.

What I Did and Why

I am required to teach about cultural lifestyles in the sociology section of my curriculum. My students used to research a country (using the library), write a

(continued)

report, and then share it with the class. In 2000, I stumbled across an e-mail exchange program as I was surfing the Internet. I did not have any experience in this area, nor did I know anyone who had used e-mail exchanges with their students. During my first year in trying the exchanges with my students, the project was a failure. I collected names and e-mail addresses of many students from all over the world, and I handed them out to my students. I did not do any recordkeeping, and I innocently assumed my students knew how to write proper letters. I fully expected this "e-pal exchange" would be very successful and that my students would learn all about other countries through their connections.

With no monitoring of letters and record keeping, everything fell apart. Students told me they weren't getting replies. Some told me they were sure they sent letters, but when I asked to see them, they couldn't be found. I realized some of my students didn't have enough technology experience to fully understand the e-mail system. I also learned my students didn't really know how to write proper letters. For example, some would just tell about themselves and never ask questions. Others would only list a lot of questions without sharing about themselves Some would write with very poor grammar and spelling errors. I needed to give lessons on proper letter writing.

On my Web page explaining our program (**http://henry.sandi.net/staff/cpauchni/pals0506.html**), I have directions and an example of how to write a letter, plus a rubric for grading. I also have the California English curriculum standards listed. This project targets the following English standards:

> **1.0 Writing Strategies:** Students write coherent and focused letters that convey a well-defined perspective. The writing demonstrates students' awareness of the audience and purpose.
>
> **2.0 Writing Applications:** Student writing demonstrates a command of standard American English and the research, organizational, and drafting strategies outlined in Writing Strategies 1.0.

The students are also required to write a final report on what they learned from this experience.

When I discovered the ePALS.com program, I especially appreciated the built-in e-mail monitoring system. A student's e-mail letter wouldn't be sent until it had my approval. If an e-mail letter needed improvement, I would just send it back to the student for corrections. Students learned to write near-perfect letters.

> **The purpose of the project for students really centered on helping them:**
> - Learn about world cultures and traditions.
> - Become more aware of their own culture.
> - Develop interest in geography and world events.
> - Build understanding and tolerance of others.
> - Practice "Netiquette" skills in writing letters.
> - Inspire positive attitudes within self and others.
> - Create friendships promoting world peace.

- ⅃ Improve proper letter-writing skills.
- ⅃ Become proficient with e-mail computer skills.

The benefits across the curriculum were:

- ⅃ **English:** Students write e-mail letters that demonstrate coherent and focused writing skills with awareness of the audience and purpose.
- ⅃ **Social Studies:** Students learn about cultural diversity (including family life and traditions) from their e-pals. They also do research on geographical, political, and economic topics of their e-pal's country.
- ⅃ **Math:** Students compute the currency exchange rate of the country in which their e-pal lives. They also compute their height and weight in the metric system.
- ⅃ **Technology:** Students become experts in using computers to write e-mails and to communicate with their e-pals through blogs. They also make a PowerPoint presentation of themselves to share with their e-pal.

What I Learned

The greatest joy has been that the students usually didn't mind correcting their e-mail letters because they cared about doing a good job. The focus changed from the desire of earning a good grade to wanting to write letters their e-pals could understand. This practical English education held much more meaning for my students. I kept charts of who wrote to whom and when replies were received. I had to have close, continuous communication with my international colleagues, and we had to work diligently together on keeping records of our exchange. If an e-mail wasn't received for some reason, we would have that student send it again. This was the only way for this type of project to be successful.

The Internet has been a revolution to education. Many of my students are quite enthusiastic about using the Internet. Most of them have personal blog pages, such as MySpace.com, and they spend between 30 minutes to three hours on their pages everyday. When I tie in educational lessons to activities they already are intensely interested in, I have success in the classroom. It was a natural progression from my students exchanging e-mails to posting messages on our school blog page. They are comfortable with blog pages, and they enjoy sharing events with their e-pals from other countries. Having such a broad audience gives students another reason to write as well as they can. They take their writing much more seriously because they see the value of doing a good job. They enjoy the opportunity to interact with their e-pals on blog pages. It's very stimulating to me to see how technology has enhanced learning.

Note: The previous Classroom Snapshot is just beyond the K–8 focus of this book. However, Candace and her class represent one of the most vigorous and meaningful uses of blogs we have seen. So we chose to include her example and to encourage K–8 teachers to use it as a model for adaptation to their own classrooms. For another example of blogs in action inside a fifth-grade classroom, see Linda Well's (2006) award-winning project.

○ Technology Tools for Learning

At first glance, Candace's experiences above and the list of technologies on the next pages may seem overwhelming. But you should set aside those concerns. You have probably already been using these technologies for personal projects or for administrative and classroom management functions. Now, we will take a look at how these same tools can support literacy. First, we will examine productivity tools, followed by visualization and multimedia tools. Second, we will take a look at the Internet and different types of communication tools. Third, the varieties of educational software that can be used will be described, and finally, we will survey some emerging tools that have promise for literacy instruction.

Productivity Tools

Productivity tools are the software applications that are commonly found in an office suite. These may include word processors, databases, and spreadsheets. Typically, electronic presentations are included with this category of software; however, we have reserved electronic presentations to discuss later with visualization and multimedia tools. You are probably familiar with how most of these tools function, so consider how you can translate those functions to support student literacy.

Word Processors. Word processing applications have become extremely robust and rich in the different options available. Applications such as Microsoft Word, Corel WordPerfect and AppleWorks word processor allow students and teachers to perform a variety of functions. Morrison and Lowther (2005) suggest how word processors' different functions can be used to support student learning. Some examples include editing and formatting text, which can be used with summarizing, paraphrasing, and peer reviews. Creating outlines can help students determine key ideas and sequence the ideas. Creating and inserting graphics allow students to match graphics to key ideas and to create original graphics to demonstrate ideas. Finally, creating tables helps students determine and organize categorical information, including column and row headings.

Word processors dominate the literacy landscape. They can be used for process writing, vocabulary development, and outlining. Advanced functions also can support peer review and teacher assessment. These could include functions such as tracking changes and inserting comments. Word processors also can be used to simulate authentic products of real-world writing, such as newsletters, newspapers, brochures, and pamphlets.

Databases. Similar to a table in a word processor, databases allow learners to determine categories for a list of different data. Each category is called a field, and new data are added as separate records. For example, a database of parts of speech may include fields for nouns, verbs, pronouns, adjectives, adverbs, prepositions, conjunctions, and interjections. Each record could have a sentence that separates the words into the specific fields. Common databases include Microsoft Access, AppleWorks database, and File-Maker Pro. Databases allow students to organize data into categories (fields), where they can discover common characteristics among categories (Morrison & Lowther, 2005). They can also match data by categories to isolate specific records with common characteristics. For example, a database could annotate works of literature discussed in class using fields for author, date, themes, and plot summaries. Students could match authors who lived during the same time period or authors who used similar themes.

Spreadsheets. Traditionally, spreadsheets have been relegated to the domain of numbers. Mathematical functions and calculations are embedded within cells. As new data are added, the functions and calculations automatically update sums to reflect the changes. With this description, you might be asking, "How could they be used in a literacy classroom?" In fact, the most recent versions of spreadsheet applications are flexible and robust so that they function like databases. Textual data can be organized into categories, then sorted, and matched to specific criteria. For example, Microsoft Access is an extremely powerful database with a relatively high learning curve, but simple functions that you are likely to be using in your classroom can be accomplished with spreadsheets. Instruction could be given using either Microsoft Excel or Apple-Works spreadsheets. A spreadsheet could be used to keep track of spelling or vocabulary words that include columns for a word's part of speech, definition, and use in a sentence. This would be helpful during descriptive writing when students need better adjectives. They would be able to sort by the part of speech column to find adjectives.

Visualization and Multimedia Tools

Electronic Presentations. As we mentioned previously, electronic presentations are typically included with productivity tools. We've included electronic presentations here because of the functions they offer for learning and literacy. Electronic presentations allow the creation of slides with text, graphics and photos, animations, audio, and even video. Students can present key ideas, sequence information, and create animations and graphics to demonstrate concepts. Young learners also can use electronic presentations as an alternative to a word processor for sentence publishing. The most ubiquitous electronic presentation tool is Microsoft PowerPoint; however, other software packages, like AppleWorks slideshow and Apple Keynote, are available. Electronic presentations could be used to present expository writing, or they could be used to publish young writers' works. See the "Computer Classroom Lessons" later in the chapter for a lesson that includes publishing using Microsoft PowerPoint. Another possible use for electronic presentations is to have K–2 students put back in order the parts of a simple story or picture book, with a focus on chronographic references, such as "first," "next," and "last," using the slide-sorting feature.

Concept Maps. Sometimes called "semantic networks" or "graphic organizers," concept maps are graphical representations of concepts and their relationships to one another

(Jonassen, 2000). Concept maps are concrete representations of a student's thinking on a topic. Students create nodes, or concepts, and then the students link them based on perceived relationships. The links themselves can even be defined to make explicit the relationship among nodes. For example, concept maps can be used for literature analysis, such as story webs, with plot, characters, symbols, and themes. Concept maps can also be used as organizers for prewriting. Whole-class, small-group, and individual brainstorming sessions can take advantage of concept maps to organize ideas and assign tasks. Common concept-mapping applications include Inspiration (see Figure 2.1) as well as Kidspiration, which is specifically for elementary grades and includes text-to-speech recognition for young or struggling readers. Another use of concept maps is to demonstrate progress over time. For example, at the beginning of a unit, you may have students complete a concept map that represents their current thinking on a topic, such as story web, prior to discussion. At the end of the unit, you may have students revise their concept maps to reflect the changes in their thinking and the relationships of their ideas.

Multimedia Authoring. Where electronic presentations proceed linearly from beginning to end, such as VCR tapes, multimedia authoring allows branching and nonlinear navigation, such as DVDs use of chapters to skip around. This type of authoring can be used in teacher-centered instruction to create instructional modules for interaction by students. Teachers may like to create a self-instructional module that a student could work on at his or her own pace, or teachers may create a review for a specific topic to provide more practice. In line with the constructivist philosophy, authoring also can be

Figure 2.1 Students can use concept mapping software such as Inspiration shown here to create an outline for a writing assignment or help analyze literature.

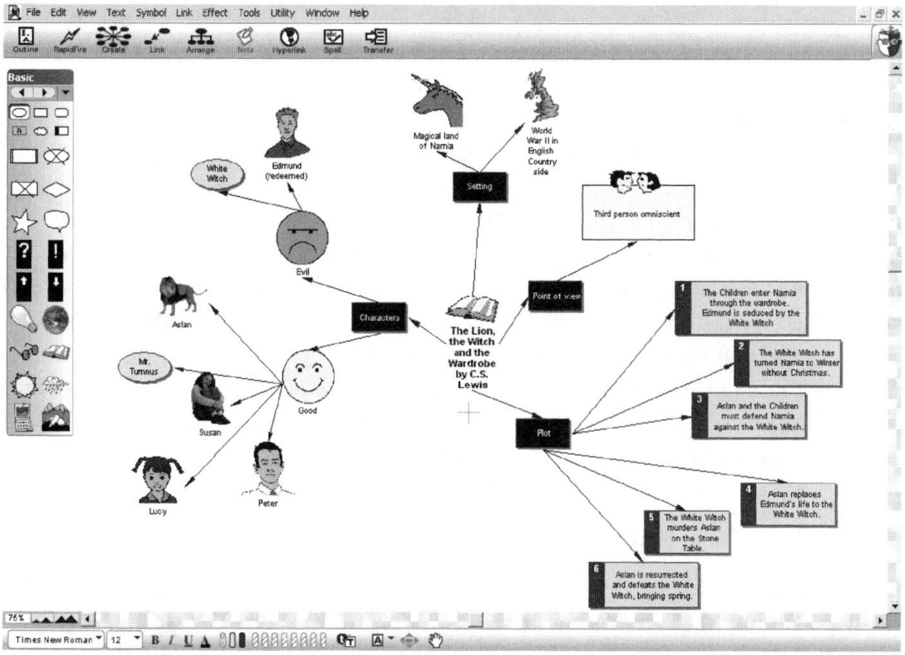

Diagram created in Inspiration® by Inspiration® Software®, Inc.

student centered, where students create nonlinear products to represent their learning. Electronic presentation packages like Microsoft PowerPoint contain advanced functions for hyperlinking that allow them to work as authoring applications. Other dedicated authoring packages that are targeted to children include Hyperstudio, eZedia, and Movie Maker. The most sophisticated authoring tools used by professionals to create CD-ROMs, computer-based training, and many online educational games are Macromedia Authorware, Director, and Flash.

Digital Cameras and Video. Digital cameras and digital video offer two ways for learners to demonstrate their learning with equipment from the real world. Digital cameras capture still photographs that can be used as representations or illustrations to accompany text, such as in word-processed stories, electronic presentations, or "story starters" to inspire students' imaginations. Digital photos must be downloaded from the camera or a camera's memory card to a computer, and they are then inserted into other documents. Digital cameras are widely available with increasing levels of quality, both in terms of the equipment itself and in reproduction of a photograph's detail. The quality we may require at home to print high-quality digital photos is overkill for classrooms.

Instead, lower-cost cameras may be more cost effective, so more cameras can be purchased. Some cameras are specifically designed for small children to use and are in the range of about $20. With more expensive cameras, you may be reluctant to allow students to use them. The quality of the inexpensive cameras is sure to increase with time, and their prices are sure to decrease with time as well.

Digital video is another exciting method for students to showcase their learning and enhance their literacy skills. In the past, digital video equipment has been expensive to purchase and complex to learn. Recently, however, the cost and complexity of these devices have decreased. Digital video requires a digital video camera containing footage wired to a computer with video-editing software. Video footage from the camera is downloaded to the computer, and then the footage may be trimmed, deleted, and sequenced. Video-editing software allows the addition of titles, background music, and sound effects, in addition to transitions between video clips. The edited digital video may be saved to formats appropriate for viewing, including the Internet, CD-ROM, and DVD. Because of the large file sizes associated with digital video, computers need ample hard drive space, as well as internal memory (RAM). Common digital-video-editing software includes Apple iMovie and Pinnacle Studio.

Internet and Communication Tools

The Internet is a vast network of interconnected computers around the world. While many people use the Internet and the World Wide Web or just Web interchangeably, they are different. In fact, the Web is a subset of the tools available on the Internet. We will explore below the tools available through the Internet that can be used for literacy instruction, including the Web.

E-mail. Electronic mail is one function of the Internet. Teachers and students are able to send, receive, and store messages. New messages are available when the teacher or student logs into the e-mail system. The process is asynchronous. Many teachers have tapped the potential of the Internet for literacy; however, in comparison to other types of tools, e-mail is limited in its use. As Ryder and Hughes (1997) emphasize, e-mail is flexible and "can be used as an instructional tool for students, as a communication tool for the teacher, and as a communication tool for the school and the community" (p. 53). Students have success forming electronic "literature partners" (Harris, 1992) along e-mail lines; teachers use e-mail to give and receive assignments and to promote class-wide communication (Parson, 1997). For example, students in one country may exchange messages with students from another country or part of the United States. These "key pals," or "e-pals" as they are called (instead of pen pals), encourage students to write and share with one another (see Rowen, 2005, for a description of writing exchanges about monsters).

Chatting and Instant Messaging. While e-mail may be asynchronous, the synchronous, or real-time, equivalent is text chatting and instant messaging (commonly called "IMing"). Similar to a telephone call, chat and IM enable users at different computers to talk to one another in real time. When one user enters text into the computer, it is immediately viewed on the screen of another person's computer, and that person can in turn respond. When a teacher or student sees that someone they want to talk with is online, they can contact them. Both chatting and IMing can involve two or more participants. Chats occur inside chat rooms hosted on a computer, where all the participants log on through a Web browser. IMs are software programs that reside on each participant's computer, and you can set your status, such as "Busy" or "Away," to prevent unwanted intrusions. The most recent versions of chat and IM software include audio chat (audio conferencing) options or video chat (video conferencing) options. (See the "Emerging Tools" section for more about audio and video conferencing.) Insinnia and Skarecki (2004) offer one description of how chats were integrated into a language arts class to increase enthusiasm, greater reflection, and deeper discussions.

The World Wide Web and Hypertext. The World Wide Web, WWW or Web, is another extremely popular application used with the Internet. In the United States alone, the Web has an estimated 202 million users (Central Intelligence Agency [CIA], 2006). The Web makes use of hyperlinks, which allow users to jump from one Web page to another. In addition, the Web allows the use of multimedia and multimodal learning. Text, graphics, photos, audio, and video can be embedded in Web pages and used with hyperlinks.

Users interact with Web pages using Web browsers, such as Microsoft Internet Explorer, Netscape Navigator, Apple Safari, and Mozilla Firefox. While Web browsers are necessary to view Web pages, Web authoring software, such as Microsoft Frontpage, is required to build Web pages. However, many word processors, including Microsoft Word and AppleWorks word processor, allow the easy creation of Web pages, too.

Broadly, teachers are using the Web to support electronic field trips, electronic publishing, problem-based learning, collaborative product development, and socially responsible projects (Harris, 1998). The multimedia capabilities of the Web also enable visual, aural, and tactile learners to accomplish these activities. More specifically, the Web can be used for researching and information seeking, interacting with online tools and games, and exploring more sophisticated opportunities for distance learning. In addition to being consumers of the Web, students and teachers can be producers, publishing original lessons, journals, reflections, poetry, and essays.

Web logs (Blogs). A recent phenomenon, a Web log, or blog, is a "Web site where entries are made (such as in a journal or diary), displayed in a reverse chronological order" (Wikipedia Foundation Inc., 2006, para. 1). Blog topics may include reflections on current events or personal issues, original prose, or informational text. Like other Web sites, blogs can integrate text, graphics, audio, and video. However, in contrast to other Web sites, blogs are intended to be interactive, whereas many Web sites are merely for passive consumption. Unlike journals and diaries, bloggers are purposefully making their thoughts and opinions public for discussion, comment, and reaction. This true form of interactivity is one of the hallmarks of what is termed Web 2.0. Web logs have several characteristics that make them advantageous to students:

1. Economy – Blogs are concise.
2. Archiving – Blog postings are dated.
3. Feedback – Blogs have comment features that provide opportunities for review or sharing.
4. Multimedia – Blogs can incorporate embedded or hyperlinked graphics, video, and audio.
5. Immediacy – Blogs allow instant publishing.
6. Active Participation – All students can participate in their own time. (Kajder & Bull, 2003, p. 33)

Ray (2006) suggests that blogs can be used with teaching and learning in four primary ways: (a) as a communication tool with students and parents, (b) as an instructional resource Web site, (c) as a collaborative tool to construct group knowledge, and (d) as a showcase for student work (pp. 176–77). Figure 2.2 depicts Blogger, a popular and free blogging tool, and Figure 2.3 highlights ePals SchoolBlog, which is a secure subscription service for students and teachers.

Educational Software

Unlike the other categories presented here, educational software was developed specifically to support teaching and learning. They are often based on specific pedagogy to scaffold learning. We consider four types of educational software appropriate for literacy. See Figure 2.6 later in the chapter for questions to consider when evaluating the quality of educational software, particularly drill and practice.

Writing Aids. Writing aids specifically support the writing process. These tools may provide metacognitive, procedural, conceptual, or strategic types of scaffolding support (Hill & Hannafin, 2001) to help learners perform at a higher level. These types of support help to keep learners in the zone of proximal development (Vygotsky, 1978), which is just above their current performance level, allowing them to be challenged at their appropriate levels without becoming frustrated with learning. Examples of software in this category may include Storybook Weaver Deluxe, which supports the writing process and the creation of illustrations for print or multimedia. NoodleTools (see Figure 2.4) and NoteStar (see Figure 2.5), both available online, aid with student research and citation referencing.

Talking/Electronic Storybooks. Talking storybooks are available on CD-ROM, online, and as hand-held devices. Reinking (1992, 1994) highlights that electronic texts are different from printed texts because (1) readers and electronic texts can interact,

Figure 2.2   One of the most well-known and widely used blogging sites is Blogger.com. Students and teachers can create their own blog, search for blogs on specific topics, and respond to others' blogs for free.

Screenshot © Google, Inc. Reproduced with permission.

(2) electronic reading can be guided, (3) electronic texts have different structures from printed texts, and (4) electronic texts employ new symbolic elements. More recently, LeapFrog LeapPad devices, while common as educational toys, are being considered in some schools as legitimate educational tools and are showing promise (see for example **http://www.leapfrogschoolhouse.com/do/findpage?pageKey=research**). While some research has been conducted with these devices, little has been published in rigorous academic journals.

Figure 2.3 ePals SchoolBlog is one commercial site that securely hosts student blogs for students to reflect and exchange comments. This example is from Candace Pauchnick's class, introduced earlier in the classroom snapshot.

ePALS product screenshot(s) reprinted with permission from ePALS Classroom Exchange, Inc.

Information Processors. As a less expensive alternative to desktop or laptop computers loaded with a word processor, information processors are an all-in-one solution. A small screen with up to 12 lines of text allows students to focus on writing and/or typing. The powerfully small word-processing software on the device includes spell check, a dictionary, and a thesaurus. Alphasmart, from Renaissance Learning, has successfully built these tools for educators for over a decade. Their newest devices are Neo, the most robust information processor yet, and Dana (see Figure 2.6), which rival other wireless personal digital assistants (PDAs). Because of their rugged, all-in-one design, these devices are well suited for young students who are learning to type, create sentences, or

Figure 2.4   NoodleTools includes a number of helpful tools for student research writing. NoodleBib and MyNotes help students organize notes from various reference sources and cite them properly in MLA and APA formats. In this example, a student is adding a new reference from a magazine.

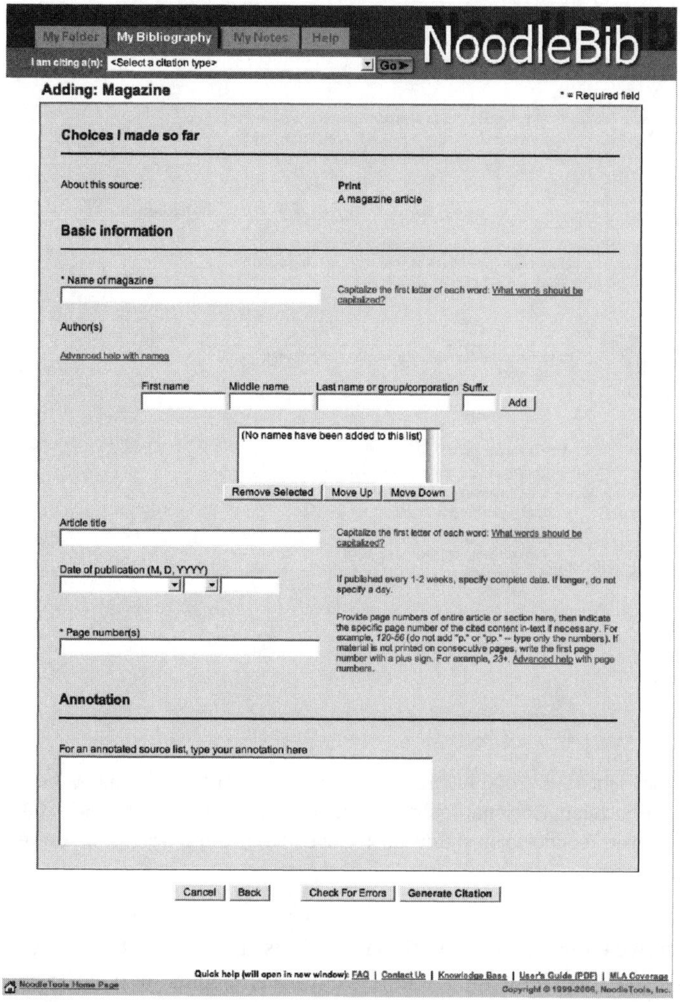

Screenshot used with permission from NoodleTools, Inc.

construct paragraphs. A teacher can quickly pass out the devices, and students can be at work very quickly, with little instruction on how to use the device.

Drill-and-Practice. Drill-and-practice software offers an opportunity for students to memorize and develop fluency with newly acquired knowledge and skills, so its useful-ness is limited (Grabe & Grabe, 2006). These types of applications specifically reinforce

Figure 2.5 NoteStar is similar to the note feature in NoodleTools. NoteStar helps students prepare research papers by collecting and organizing notes from different sources.

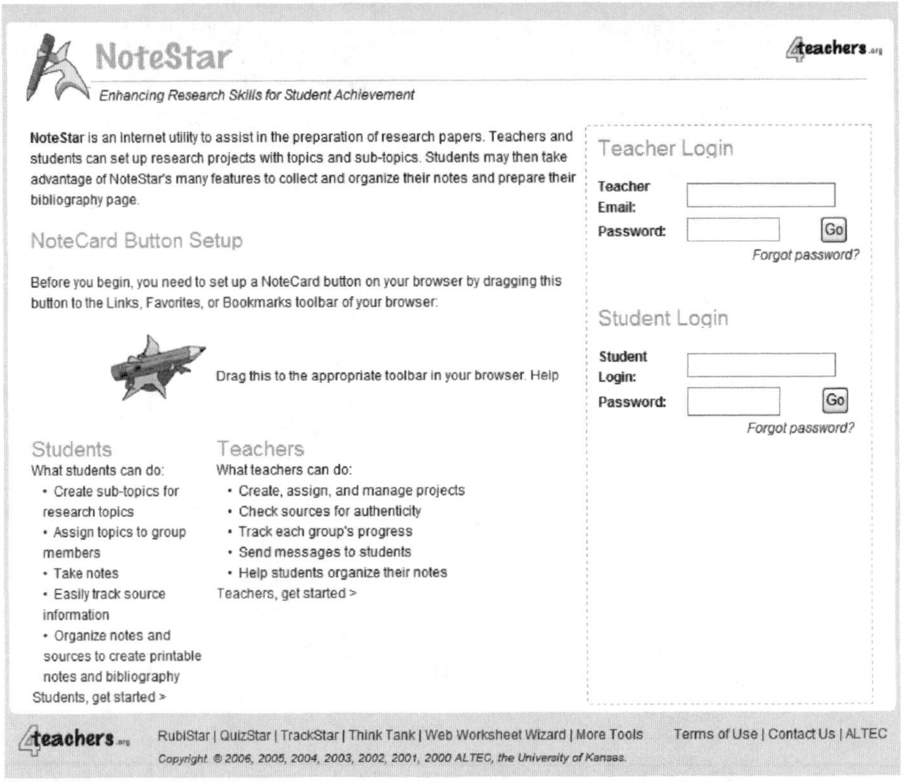

Screenshot Copyright 1995–2006 ALTEC, the University of Kansas. Funded by the U.S. Department of Education, Regional Technology in Education Consortium, 1995–2005 to ALTEC (Advanced Learning Technologies in Education Consortia) at the University of Kansas, Center for Research on Learning.

basic declarative knowledge, or psychomotor skills, and they do little to advance higher-order thinking skills. These applications often are embedded in popular animated characters. Drill-and-practice may do well to rehearse facts and skills plus provide additional self-paced exercises for struggling learners, or below grade-level learners, but they should not be tasked with introducing new content. See Figure 2.7 for questions to consider when evaluating the quality of drill-and-practice software titles.

Individualized Assessment and Instruction. A number of software applications reflect comprehensive curricula. Programs in this category are able, through assessments, to determine the learner's current level of performance on given curricular objectives. The most extensive programs in this category then provide computer-based

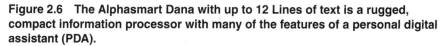

Figure 2.6 The Alphasmart Dana with up to 12 Lines of text is a rugged, compact information processor with many of the features of a personal digital assistant (PDA).

Used with permission from Renaissance Learning.

instruction (CBI) to address deficit skills; this type of application is also called adaptive instruction (Inan & Grant, 2005).

Accelerated Reader (AR) is probably one of the most widely used and widely researched software applications in this category: "The Accelerated Reader program was created to engage students in large amounts of reading practice with authentic material at an individually appropriate reading level, as well as provide rewards for student success in reading achievement" (Melton et al., 2004, p. 19). Books in a school's library have been evaluated using Renaissance Learning's readability formula. A label is placed on the spine of each book, indicating the readability level and point value of the book. After students read a book, they take a computer-based test that focuses on basic facts and comprehension of the story (see Figure 2.8 for an example of the computer-based assessment). Based on the student's performance on the assessment, points are awarded. Students' motivations to read have improved with this incentive program, while current research has questioned the lasting effectiveness of extrinsic motivation (see e.g., Pavonetti, Brimmer, & Cipielewski, 2002). For additional research on Accelerated Reader, see Nunnery, Ross, and McDonald (2006).

Very recently, writing scorers have become viable options to help improve grammar and mechanics for students and reduce some of the drudgery of grading for teachers. These programs have students submit their essays or writing samples, and the automated essay scorer returns a report, noting specific potential problems. Teachers can use these tools in two different ways. First, teachers can allow students to resubmit writing after each draft, or significant revisions (formative assessment). Both the teacher and the learner then can track the changes and monitor the progress and improvements to the work. Second, teachers can have students submit their final drafts

Figure 2.7 Evaluating Educational Software.

The primary purpose for educational software is to enhance the learning goals you have established. These goals are dependent on the age, skill level, and needs of your students. The software may be excellent in terms of the accuracy of subject matter and also technically good if it runs without errors, but if it does not meet the needs of the curriculum, then it is not valuable to you. With this in mind, consider the following general guidelines.

Get to know the software thoroughly. Read the documentation and evaluate it for clarity. Notice if the documentation is laid out in a logical manner and if it is easy to find what you are looking for. Pay attention to the way the information is displayed on the screen. Does the program have a good "Help" function or documentation that replaces the "Help" function? A desirable feature is the ability to leave the program and pick up where you left off without loss of data. It is helpful if software includes suggestions for use in the classroom. When evaluating software, be sure to check if it comes with good lesson plans and resources that support them.

Questions to Evaluate Educational Software Programs

Lesson Content
- Is the topic appropriate for the curriculum?
- Is the information correct?
- Is the content free of bias?
- Are the grammar and punctuation correct?

Interactivity
- How much student interaction is available?
- Is the degree of realism satisfactory?
- Does the learner have control over navigation through the program?
- Does the learner have control over the level of difficulty?
- Does the learner have control over entering and exiting at any place in the program?

Skills Needed to Use
- How much knowledge is needed to use the program?
- Can the learner use the program without help from an adult?

Performance
- Is the program reliable?
- Does it fulfill the promised educational outcome?
- Are the educational strategies sound?
- Is feedback appropriate for correct or incorrect responses?
- Is there effective remediation?
- Are the graphics, animation, and sound used in an appropriate manner, and do they enhance the learning experience?

Student Data
- Does the program collect and evaluate student data?
- Is the student's privacy respected?
- Are collected data secured?

Support
- Does the program include a manual?
- Is there technical support via the Internet or telephone?

Resources
- Does the program have detailed lesson plans and resources?

Figure 2.8   A screenshot of a computer-based reading assessment about
The Borrowers **with Accelerated Reader.**

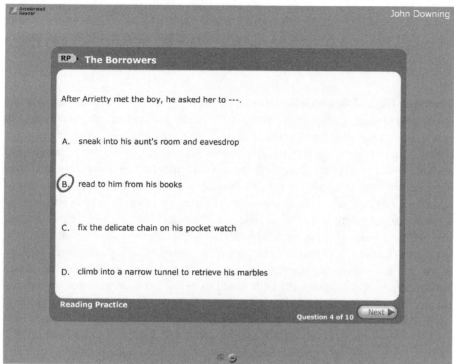

Used with permission from Renaissance Learning.

for scoring, and the teacher can use the report to supplement her own assessment (summative assessment). Two of the most prominent writing scorers are Criterion by Educational Testing Services (ETS) and SAGrader (**http://www.ideaworks.com/ sagrader**). Initial empirical research with these programs is promising (see e.g., Attali, 2004; Scharber, Dexter, & Riebel, 2005). In a recent study, Forbess and Grant (forthcoming) found the essay scorer to be more consistent in assessment of student writing than a trained advanced placement reader.

Finally, as mentioned above, the most robust systems in this category provide both computer-based assessment and computer-based instruction. Often called integrated learning systems (ILS), these applications preassess learners to determine at what level they enter the instruction. Then they trace the learners' progress, providing immediate feedback and specific guidance as necessary (Lockee, Moore, & Burton, 2004). These adaptive instructional systems supplant teacher-led instruction by providing individualized lessons to each learner—a feat the teacher would be unable to do. Examples of ILS systems are PLATO and CompassLearning.

Emerging Tools

Tools in this category are relatively recent innovations or are recently introduced to educational contexts. Specifically, their uses for instruction in general have yet to be determined. However, they represent promise for literacy learning, and the individual teacher will be responsible for determining their utility.

Personal Digital Assistants (PDAs). PDAs are commonplace in businesses for individuals to manage their productivity while on the go. Common applications, such as word processors, databases, spreadsheets, electronic presentation, concept mapping, e-mail, and Web browsing, have been transported, or "ported," to these pocket-sized devices. With access to many of the same software applications as we have described in sections above, their potential seems evident. Baumbach, Christopher, Fasimpaur, and Oliver (2004) describe an extensive unit focused on literacy, creative writing, and science research to create an "autobugography" using PDAs. They argue that the low cost of PDAs makes them approachable for one computer for each student. They also suggest PDAs are less technically complex than desktop or laptop computers, so there is less professional development time necessary to train teachers and less instruction for students on how to use the PDAs. It would seem that PDAs would be an optimal solution. Data suggest PDAs have been implemented in over half of the school districts across the country; however, their effects on student achievement have not been measured (Honey, Culp, & Spielvogel, 1999). According to Molebash and Fisher (2003), PDAs may be more effective as a productivity tool for teachers, conducting running records, updating gradebooks, and managing Individual Education Plans (IEPs). Schools have been reluctant to use these devices in widespread instruction, instead preferring laptop and desktop computers. Possible reasons for this reticence may be the lack of research or experimentation to prove effectiveness across different content areas. PDAs also may be perceived as less powerful than their desktop and laptop counterparts. Lastly, technology specialists may recognize PDAs as a transition technology. Future devices may be more robust, and they may more sleekly combine multiple devices together, such as cell phones, audio recorders and players, digital cameras, and digital video cameras and players.

Wikis. Wikis, at their simplest form, are Web sites that allow all users to collaborate on the creation, editing, and revision of pages (Chawner & Lewis, 2006; Clyde, 2005). Wikiwiki means "quick" in Hawaiian, so Wikiwikiweb is a quick Web site—shortened to Wiki. The most well-known and widely used Wiki is Wikipedia (**http://www.wikipedia.org**), which has been in operation since 2001. Wikipedia is the online equivalent of an encyclopedia; however, since anyone may contribute to the topics, misinformation and inaccuracies are likely. As noted above with blogs, Wikis also represent a category of social software indicative of Web 2.0, pushing toward more authentic interactivity on the Web and less consumption.

Wikis easily support collaborative writing. All contributors are seen as equals in the process, and all previous versions of the text are archived and accessible. In addition, Wikis also take advantage of hypertext and multimedia, so authors are able to link to complementary and supplementary references, as well as embed graphics, sound, and video. Moxley et al. (as cited in Lamb, 2004) at the University of South Florida (**http://writingwiki.org**) are exploring how Wikis can be used to support writing and literacy through collaborative writing, "writing as process" in place of "writing as product," editing and revisions, and preparing students to write for external audiences. Wikis also offer a space to publish student writing.

Because of the open nature of Wikis, teachers should consider some management methods upfront. First, tracking student work can be difficult, since it's collaborative (Lamb, 2004). You may want students to label their contributions in some way, or, more restrictively, require that students only add support materials to any other student's work. This type of restraint opposes the basic premise of Wikis and social software, so you may want to balance your need for classroom management with the purpose of using the tool. In the most open of Wikis, where visitors can contribute, the potential for maliciousness is possible. You may want to restrict the creation and editing to your students or create a common login account and special password that you and the students can share with others to participate in the collaboration.

Electronic Texts and E-books. In an earlier section, we covered talking, or electronic, storybooks. These have been available on CD-ROM and DVD, and they include audio read-alouds, animations, and often interactivity with clickable elements. Electronic texts and e-books are typically only available online. Electronic texts can include both textual and graphical reproductions of copyrighted and non-copyrighted works. For example, all of Shakespeare's works are available online as Web pages with full text (**http://shakespeare-online.com**). Even public libraries, such as the New York Public Library (**http://ebooks.nypl.org**), are beginning to offer current popular fiction and nonfiction e-books online.

In contrast, the International Children's Digital Library (ICDL, **http://childrenslib rary. org**) has digitized scanned images of the original pages from contemporary children's books (Van Horn, 2005). The works in the ICDL are still copyrighted to the original authors, so they should not be downloaded or printed. See Chapter 7 for more resources for electronic texts and e-books.

E-books have been formatted specifically for digital distribution to be "delivered or read online or downloaded to a hand-held reading device," such as a PDA or dedicated e-book reader (Mattison, 2002, p. 15). Some books have been ported to e-books, retaining their printed look and feel such as Adobe's Portable Document Format (PDF), while others have been reformatted and repaginated as text to adapt to the e-booker reading device (Gall, 2005). These options may offer alternatives for schools purchasing class sets of novels or students being assigned summer readings. So far, reports state that schools have been slow to use e-books (c.f., Scott, 2005). Universities and college bookstores have been more likely to explore the use of e-books for course texts (Heyboer, 2005;

Jesdanun, 2006). Recently, the World eBook Library Consortia celebrated 35 years of Project Gutenberg, a free Internet library, by allowing downloads of over 300,000 free e-books and fee-based e-books at no cost for one month (**http://www.worldebookfair.com**) from July 4, 2006, through August 4, 2006, (Young, 2006). Currently, Project Gutenberg continues to be a free electronic library, while the World eBook Library charges a nominal annual subscription fee to download as many titles as you wish.

Podcasts. What blogs are for text and journaling, podcasts are for audio recording and talk radio. In their simplest form, podcasts are simply audio recordings. What makes them special? When you subscribe to a podcast through a program like Apple iTunes, which is freely available for both Macs and PCs, new episodes of your podcast are automatically downloaded the next time you launch iTunes (Godwin-Jones, 2005). Named after Apple's iPod, you do not need an iPod or other audio MP3 players to listen to a podcast. Instead, podcasts can be played right on your computer. One of the bonuses to podcasts is that they can be transferred to an MP3 player and listened to at any time.

Podcasts have two advantages for literacy instruction—for listening and for creation. Currently, over 35,000 different podcasts are registered with Apple iTunes, one of the largest services to register and locate podcasts. Listening to downloaded podcasts of foreign languages (Godwin-Jones, 2005), "period music, historical speeches, radio plays, interviews with experts, and audio books" (Flanagan & Calandra, 2005, p. 21) allows students to align or reinforce discussions and analysis of those topics. Similarly, in Texas, kindergartners are checking out iPods to practice vocabulary while English-as-a-Second-Language learners are practicing oral language skills (Shen, 2005).

Another way podcasts can impact literacy instruction is when students create podcasts. Currently, there are numerous accounts of students from kindergarten through middle grades creating original podcast episodes. For example, a fifth-grade class in Omaha, Nebraska, researched the American Revolution (Shen, 2005). Although students eagerly wrote scripts to be graded, more importantly, they hoped to be chosen for a short eight-and-a-half minute recording. Similarly, at Wells Elementary in Maine, a group of third and fourth graders produces a weekly podcast that begins with brainstorming, interviewing, writing, and recording (Fish, 2005). As is evident from these examples, when students are producing writing and knowledge that is authentic for an external audience, the task is extremely motivating (Anderson, 2005; Shen, 2005). This type of construction also embodies many of the characteristics of project-based learning that we'll discuss later in Chapter 3 (Grant, 2002; Grant & Branch, 2005).

Voice and Video Technologies. This category of technologies is not new, but it is maturing. We will discuss voice recognition, audio conferencing, and video conferencing technologies. Voice-recognition software, such as Dragon Naturally Speaking, and text-to-speech capabilities have been available for some time; however, the quality of both has been mediocre at best. They both were dependent on computer hardware. In recent years, these technologies have advanced. Voice recognition has improved for use with personal digital-audio-recording devices, and the speech training necessary to improve accuracy has become less arduous. In addition, the price of the software is affordable. Text-to-speech capabilities began as digitized voices reminiscent of the movie *War Games* from the 1980s. Currently, speech is much more natural and humanistic, and it has been integrated into a number of software applications, such as Kidspiration, to support language learners, struggling readers, and visually impaired individuals. Molebash and Fisher's (2003) survey of the literature notes examples of voice recognition with dyslexic individuals, visually impaired students, non-native language learners, and mentally and physically challenged students.

In addition, a number of audio conferencing technologies, similar to those described in the "Chat" section above, have become prominent. For example, Skype **(http://www. skype.com)** and the Gizmo Project **(http://www.gizmoproject.com/)** allow your "computer to act like a telephone" (Godwin-Jones, 2005, p. 9). Both run with voice over IP (VoIP), meaning voice over the Internet. Calls can be person-to-person or in small groups. For language learners and culturally aware thematic units, audio conferencing could permit conversations with native speakers in other parts of the world (Godwin-Jones, 2005). However, these conferences could also work locally on a smaller scale if students wanted to interview or question an expert outside their classroom without leaving their classroom for a field trip.

Similarly, desktop video conferencing is quickly becoming a viable option for schools. Previous video-conferencing systems with which you may be familiar were expensive stationary systems set up in dedicated rooms. Often these were used for statewide or districtwide teacher professional development. Newer systems are much less expensive, run on desktop/laptop computers, and use inexpensive Web cameras (Webcams). Apple iChatAV probably represents the easiest video conferencing software. The system resembles instant messaging, so it is a familiar set up. Other online chat hosting services also offer video conferencing, such as America Online and Yahoo! Like audio conferencing, video conferencing could be used to bring external experts into the classroom or to connect with other students around the world, creating vPals (video pals).

There are currently two important challenges to using video conferencing. First, the software is typically not compatible with other software. Both parties engaged in a video conference have to use the same system. Also, the software is generally not cross platform. Mac users and PC users cannot conference together. This is particularly true of Apple iChatAV, which only runs on the Mac OS, and which does not currently connect with any other video conferencing services. Second, video conferencing means sending very large files across the Internet. A fast Internet connection is necessary to be successful. Unfortunately, because of the large file sizes, some Internet Service Providers (ISPs) will block video conferencing to reduce the load on their networks.

COMPUTER CLASSROOM LESSONS ◀

Creating a Story Published Through PowerPoint

by Katie Grant

Grade Level:　1–3

Objective:　The student will write a simple story, publish his story on the computer using PowerPoint as the media, and illustrate the story with or without clip art.

Time:　30-minute blocks over 3 or 4 days

Problem to Be Solved:　How do authors publish their own stories?

Materials:　Pencil
　　　　　　　Lined writing paper
　　　　　　　Computer with Microsoft PowerPoint and printer
　　　　　　　Crayons (optional)

Steps:

1. Day One: The teacher will have the students brainstorm story ideas based on a recently studied topic (ex: science topic for the previous week). This will give students parameters for creating their stories and will give them a comfort level because they already have some background knowledge about that topic.
2. The students will write a story about their topic. The story can be just one or two sentences because the writers are so young.
3. The student will read the story to the teacher, and the student will focus on having strong sentence structure (noun, verb, capital at the beginning of the sentence, period at the end of the sentence).
4. The student can start sketching an illustration for the story if there is time.
5. Day Two: The teacher will read "his or her story" that he or she wrote to the students. He or she will introduce the blank PowerPoint template to the students, showing them how to type in the box provided, where the "caps lock" is for capital letters, and where the period is for the end of their sentences. He or she will type his or her two-sentence story onto the screen thinking aloud the entire time so the students will be able to learn from his or her thoughts. (Ex: "I need a capital letter here at the beginning. I should press this button to make a capital letter. Now I should press it again to make the letters small." or "Oh, I need a space because this is a new word. Here is the space bar. I need to press it.") The teacher will read his or her published story to the class and have the class help him or her check for mistakes (missing spaces, capital letters, missing period).

6. Day Two or Three: Students who are ready to publish their work will be allowed to take their story from the previous day and start "publishing" at a computer. The students will actively be problem solving during the entire publishing activity. If there are not enough computers, students can publish their story anytime during the day that there is a break or when they finish work early.

7. Day Three or Four: The teacher will have printed the "published" works and will have returned them to the students. Students are to draw an illustration to match their story.

8. If there is time, each student can select one piece of clip art to go along with the story. For example, if the story was about a dog, the student chooses a dog from the clip art and places it above the story in the space available for illustrations. That clip art would be printed with the published story. Then the student can add the other details from the story to the clip art and create a unique illustration for his or her first computer published work.

Assessment: The student should have at least a sentence-long story "published" through Microsoft PowerPoint. The student should have a capital letter at the beginning, spaces between words, and a period at the end of the sentence. The student should have an illustration that matches the published story. These criteria can be listed on a simple rubric for self, peer, and teacher assessment.

A Podcast Tour of Washington, D.C.

Grade Level: 2–8

Objective: Learn about Washington, D.C. Students demonstrate their creativity by making a podcast tour of D.C. Students develop their writing skills by generating scripts about the monuments and historical sites.

Time: 1 week

Problem to Be Solved: You have been commissioned by the Visitors Bureau of Washington D.C. to create a podcast tour of the city so visitors may learn about the historical sites prior to their visits.

Materials: Computer
Web browser (e.g., Microsoft Internet Explorer, Netscape Navigator)
Pencil
Journal or notebook paper for learning log
Chart paper
Map of the United States
Microphone
Audio recording software, such as Apple GarageBand or Audacity (free for Mac and PC)

Steps:

1. Locate Washington, D.C. on a map of the United States. Show and discuss the areas where the White House, the Capitol, the Supreme Court, Washington Monument, and other landmarks are located.

2. As a group, complete a KWL (What You Know, What You Want to Know, and What You Learned) chart about Washington, D.C. Write the chart on large paper for future reference.

3. In small-group settings or as an individual assignment, use your Web browser to take a virtual tour of Washington, D.C. Use the following URLs: The White House at **http://www.whitehouse.gov/history/life/** and America's home page at **http://ahp.gatech.edu/dc_map.html.**

4. Instruct students that they are to look for information and pictures of important buildings and monuments in Washington D.C. Require that each student keep a learning log documenting URLs and important monuments sighted. Allow each student sufficient time to search the Internet. To reduce the amount of searching, provide students with a "hot list" of possible links to research specific monuments.

5. Consult the KWL chart completed in Step 2. Using learning logs, ask students to fill in on the chart what they have learned about Washington, D.C. Discuss the chart and student findings. Discuss Web sites and hyperlinks for documenting findings.

6. As a class, brainstorm and determine which monuments to include in the tour.

7. Allow students to choose or divide the monuments among groups or individuals.

8. Each individual or small group should write a script describing the physical features of the monument and the historical details. Have students complete these in their learning logs.

9. If using individuals, have the class vote for best scripts to create about 20- to 30-minute audio recording. If using groups, determine if all groups' scripts can be included.

10. Record each script. Have students listen to recordings and rerecord if necessary.

11. Combine recordings. Add background music or sound effects, if desired. Save as/Export as an MP3 file.

Assessment: Create a rubric that accounts for the depth of the Internet research as well as the quality, mechanics, and creativity of the script.

○ Techno-Teacher Tips

Promoting Your Technology Program

As you gradually integrate a technology design into your classroom procedures, pay particular attention to those most likely to scrutinize your activities—parents and principals. The principal already knows you have the hardware and software, but he or she needs to be brought up to date on lesson planning, particularly under the heading of goal setting and meeting curriculum standards.

Parents are sometimes skeptical of new approaches to learning old behaviors. Technology won't sell itself at parent-teacher conference night. You will have to do it. After a general discussion of why you are using the new technologies, provide parents with a handout giving more detailed explanations of the software you are using in class and how the technology is helping their children learn language arts, math, science, social studies, and the arts. It's always a good idea to show examples of student work generated by the software.

Keep Your Focus

With so many tools to choose from and many new ones to learn, it would be very easy to lose your focus—or for your students to lose their focus. While the technology tools are considered "cool" and novel, we are still in the business of teaching content. A middle school in Wisconsin explained allure of one "hip" technology—podcasting: "The technology is a tool to implement the curriculum.... Podcasting is all about learning the content. If you don't have educational content, you have no podcast. No amount of sound effects, visuals, or music can hide a lack of content in an educational podcast" (Anderson, 2005, Three C's in a Pod section, para. 4).

○ Frequently Asked Questions

1. **With so many technologies to choose from, how do I know which one to use when?**

   Morrison and Lowther (2005) offer a feasible method for designing lessons that take advantage of the functions and features of the technology tools discussed earlier in this chapter. They recommend first *specifying the content objectives* you would like to address in the lesson. Second, *identifying the functions of the different computer tools*, such as summarizing in word processors, or presenting key ideas with electronic presentations. Finally, *matching the content objectives to the computer functions*. Some matches are easy and obvious. "Brainstorm writing topics" would easily align with concept-mapping software or lists in a word processor. However, other higher-order thinking skills, such as evaluating, judging, and analyzing, may require spreadsheets, databases, or word processors. In some cases, multiple technologies may be appropriate, such as using a database to collect and analyze specific pieces of information, and then reporting the findings in a word-processed document.

2. **With so many Web sites on the Internet—some good, some bad—how do I know which ones to use with my students?**

There is no censorship of the Internet. Essentially, the material on the Internet is unrestricted, making the accuracy and reliability of the information questionable (Hittig, 1995). In Chapter 5, we discuss more about evaluating Web sites for accuracy and bias. A particularly good strategy for basic Internet research is for teachers to hand out a list of acceptable sites applicable to a given project. This strategy takes some teacher planning, but in addition to keeping students on safe sites, it will speed up their information gathering. WebQuests (Dodge, 1995, 1998; **http://webquest.org**) take advantage of this strategy of providing students with a number of previewed Web sites to accomplish specific curricular tasks. Also, netTrekker (**http://school.nettrekker.com/**), a fee-based service, offers a search engine that uses only educator-selected online sites. Similarly, TrackStar (**http://trackstar.4teachers.org**) is a free service where teachers have created lists of online links, often called hot lists, that deal with specific topics, such as *Number the Stars* by Lois Lowry, parts of speech, and writing letters.

⊙ References

Anderson, L. S. (2005). Podcasting: Transforming middle schoolers into 'middle scholars.' *THE Journal (Technological Horizons in Education), 33*(5), 42–43.

Applefield, J. M., Huber, R. L., & Moallem, M. (2000). Constructivism in theory and practice: Toward a better understanding. *High School Journal, 84*(2), 35–53.

Attali, Y. (2004, April). *Exploring the feedback and revision features of the Criterion service.* Paper presented at the National Council on Measurement in Education Annual Meeting, San Diego, CA.

Baumbach, D., Christopher, T., Fasimpaur, K., & Oliver, K. (2004). Personal literacy assistants: Using handhelds for literacy instruction. *Learning & Leading with Technology, 32*(2), 16–21.

Central Intelligence Agency [CIA]. (2006, July 11). The world factbook. Retrieved July 15, 2006, from http://www.odci.gov/cia/publications/factbook/fields/2153.html

Chawner, B., & Lewis, P. H. (2006). Wikiwikiwebs: New ways to communicate in a Web environment. *Information Technology and Libraries, 25*(1), 33–43.

Clyde, L. A. (2005). Wikis. *Teacher Librarian, 32*(4), 54–56.

Dodge, B. (1995, May 5, 1997). Some thoughts about WebQuests. Retrieved August 7, 2001, from http://edweb.sdsu.edu/courses/edtect596/about_webquests.html

Dodge, B. (1998, June 22–24). *WebQuests: A strategy for scaffolding higher level learning.* Paper presented at the National Educational Computing Conference, San Diego, CA.

Fish, J. (2005, May 31). Airtime for young podcasters: Wells students write and produce weekly audio Web program. *Portland Press Herald,* p. B1.

Flanagan, B., & Calandra, B. (2005). Podcasting in the classroom. *Learning & Leading with Technology, 33*(3), 20–22, 25.

Forbess, J., & Grant, M. M. (forthcoming). *The effects of online essay scoring on the improvement of writing of high school sophmores.* Unpublished manuscript, the University of Memphis, Memphis, TN.

Gall, J. E. (2005). Dispelling five myths about e-books. *Information Technology and Libraries, 24*(1), 25–31.

Godwin-Jones, R. (2005). Skype and podcasting: Disruptive technologies for language learning. *Language Learning & Technology, 9*(3), 9–12.

Grabe, M., & Grabe, C. (2006). *Integrating technology for meaningful learning.* New York: Houghton Mifflin.

Grant, M. M. (2002). Getting a grip on project-based learning: Theory, cases, and recommendations. *Meridian: A Middle School Computer Technologies Journal, 5* (Winter). Retrieved November 13, 2006, from http://www.nesu.edu/meridian/win2002/514/index.html

Grant, M. M., & Branch, R. M. (2005). Project-based learning in a middle school: Tracing abilities through the artifacts of learning. *Journal of Research on Technology in Education, 38*(1), 65–98.

Harris, J. (1992, August–September). Electronic treasures by electronic mail. *The Computing Teacher,* 36–38.

Harris, J. (1998). *Virtual architecture: Designing and directing curriculum-based architecture.* Eugene, OR: International Society for Technology in Education.

Heyboer, K. (2005, September 8). Campus bookstores begin large-scale offerings of e-books. *The Star-Ledger.* Retrieved November 13, 2006, from Lexis Nexis Academic database.

Hill, J. R., & Hannafin, M. J. (2001). Teaching and learning in digital environments: The resurgence of resource-based learning. *Educational Technology, Research & Development, 49*(3), 37–52.

Hittig, J. (1995, July). Free speech or online slime? *PC Novice,* 74–79.

Honey, M., Culp, K. M., & Spielvogel, R. (1999, 2005). *Critical issue: Using technology to improve student achievement.* Retrieved August 29, 2006, from http://www.ncrel.org/sdrs/areas/issues/methods/technlgy/te800.htm

Inan, F.A., & Grant, M. M. (2005, October 18–22). *Design and development of strategies for adaptive Web-based learning environments.* Paper presented at the annual meeting of the Association for Educational Communications and Technology, Orlando, FL.

Insinnia, E., & Skarecki, E. C. (2004). Power chatting: Lessons for success. *Voices from the Middle, 11*(3), 10–16.

Jesdanun, A. (2006, February 14). Despite youths' comfort with technology, e-textbook demand is slow. *Associated Press Financial Wire.* Retrieved November 13, 2006, from Lexis Nexis Academic database.

Jonassen, D. H. (2000). *Computers as mindtools for schools.* Upper Saddle River, NJ: Merrill Prentice Hall.

Kajder, S., & Bull, G. (2003). Scaffolding for struggling students: Reading and writing with blogs. *Learning & Leading with Technology, 31*(2), 32–35.

Lamb, B. (2004). Wide open spaces: Wikis, ready or not. *EDUCAUSE Review, 36*(5), 36–48.

Lockee, B., Moore, M., & Burton, J. (2004). Foundations of programmed instruction. In D. H. Jonassen (Ed.), *Handbook of research for educational communications and technology* (pp. 545–569). Mahwah, NJ: Erlbaum.

Mattison, D. (2002). Alice in e-book land: A primer for librarians. *Computers in Libraries, 22*(9), 14–21.

Melton, C. M., Smothers, B. C., Anderson, E., Fulton, R., Replogle, W. H., & Thompson, L. (2004). A study of the effects of the Accelerated Reader program on fifth-grade students' reading achievement growth. *Reading Improvement, 41*(1), 18–23.

Molebash, P., & Fisher, D. (2003). Teaching and learning literacy with technology. *Reading Improvement, 40*(2), 63–70.

Morrison, G. M., & Lowther, D. L. (2005). *Integrating computer technology into the classroom* (3rd ed.). Upper Saddle River, NJ: Pearson Merrill Prentice Hall.

Nunnery, J. A., Ross, S. M., & McDonald, A. (2006). A randomized experimental evaluation of the impact of Accelerated Reader/Reading Renaissance implementation on reading achievement in grades 3–6. *Journal of Education for Students Placed at Risk, 11*(1), 1–18.

Parson, T. (1997). Electronic mail: Creating a community of learners. *Journal of Adolescent and Adult Literacy, 40*(7), 560–565.

Pavonetti, L. M., Brimmer, K. M., & Cipielewski, J. F. (2002). What are the lasting effects on the reading habits of middle school students exposed to Accelerated Reader in elementary grades? *Journal of Adolescent and Adult Literacy, 46*(4), 300–312.

Ray, J. (2006). Blogosphere: The educational use of blogs (aka edublogs). *Kappa Delta Pi Record, Summer*, 175–177.

Reinking, D. (1992). Differences between electronic and printed texts: An agenda for research. *Journal of Educational Multimedia and Hypermedia, 1*(1), 11–24.

Reinking, D. (1994). *Electronic literacy* (No. 4). Athens, GA: National Reading Research Center, Universities of Georgia and Maryland.

Rowen, D. (2005). The write motivation: Using the Internet to engage student in writing across the curriculum. *Learning & Leading with Technology, 32*(5), 22–23, 43.

Ryder, R. J., & Hughes, T. (1997). *Internet for educators*. Upper Saddle River, NJ: Prentice Hall.

Scharber, C., Dexter, S., & Riebel, E. (2005, April 11–15). *Formative feedback via an automated essay scorer: Its impact on learners*. Paper presented at the 86th annual meeting of the American Educational Research Association, Montreal, Canada.

Scott, A. (2005, December 23). LBHS to launch e-book program; Students will be able to download text to read, or MP3 audio books for listening. *Sarasota Herald-Tribune*, p. BC1.

Shen, F. (2005, October 24). Podcasts as learning tools; Teachers use trendy technology to turn on students. *The Record*, p. C2.

Van Horn, R. (2005). Online children's books. *Phi Delta Kappan, 87*(2), 103.

Vygotsky, L. S. (1978). *Mind in society: The development of higher psychological processes*. Cambridge, MA: Harvard University Press.

Wells, L. (2006). Blog it: An innovative way to improve literacy. *Reading Today, 24*(1), 40.

Wikipedia Foundation Inc. (2006). *Blog*. Retrieved July 16, 2006, from http://en.wikipedia.org/wiki/Blog

Young, J. R. (2006, June 30). World e-book fair to encourage summer e-reading. *The Chronicle of Higher Education*, pp. NA. Retrieved September 5, 2006, from Expanded Academic ASAP database.

Using Technology to Teach Reading

Chapter 3

"You know, Jody, I never thought that as a math teacher I would be required to teach reading." Jose looks perplexed and just a tad bit angry as he speaks. "I was good at math, but I didn't particularly like to read. Numbers made sense. Words were always slippery."

Jody smiles broadly as she thinks about the implications of what Jose has said. "It's common to hear people say, 'I'm not very good at math,' but you may be the first person who has said, 'I'm not very good at reading.' " Then Jody pauses, thinking about her own situation. "I'm not very good at math," she confesses, "but I love to read, and I can't imagine a world without reading."

"I can't imagine a world without math. Take calculus, for example," Jose begins, warming to his topic.

But Jody interrupts, "Whoa, Jose. Let me repeat, 'I'm not very good at math.' Please put heavy stress on 'not.' But," she stops, allowing for a dramatic pause that lasts until Jose looks at her squarely and seems intent on hearing her. "But," she repeats, "I dare say most people can get by in life without understanding a great deal about math." Jose is about to protest. "Hold on and let me finish. I'm not saying math is not important. Both you and I know that mathematics has all kinds of practical applications that our students can use, and many students must use math if they pursue studies in science, technology, or engineering, not to mention statistics and economics. But for the common person, math works unseen at so many levels." Jody pauses, hoping that Jose will see her point. He is thoughtfully quiet, so she continues. "Reading, however, is central to virtually every transaction people make. Look at all the signs, advertisements, contracts, newspapers, magazines, books—and," Jody starts getting excited, "even computers. The average Joe or Jolene can't begin to operate a computer without reading the instructions to press control and delete simultaneously."

"This is very odd," Jose responds, beginning to grin. "You wouldn't even have computers if Boolean algebra didn't exist. So math allows computers to operate."

"Ironically, yes," Jody agrees, "and we could get into a 'chicken or egg' argument, but the fact is most people who use a computer don't know how to spell 'Boolean' much less understand how ones and zeros could make a computer work. I don't really understand that much about the computer language of ones and zeros, but I read about computers, so I have some idea about the need for ones and zeros. And frankly, I don't need to know. All I need to know is what I have to do to make a computer work for me. All I *really* need to know is how to read instructions."

"I hate to grant your point about the relationship between math and reading. I love math. I feel an obligation to defend math." Jose moves his head side to side slightly as if disagreeing with himself, weighing the sides of Jody's argument, first one side and then the other. "But I see your point, and it's hard to argue that reading isn't foundational to being successful in everyday life. But," Jose pauses, his face tightening, "why do I have to teach reading? I'm a math teacher."

"Jose," Jody begins cautiously, realizing that Jose is perturbed, "in one sense, teaching math is teaching reading."

Jose looks startled.

"Don't you teach students a particular vocabulary? Don't you teach students how to read story problems? You know, 'Train A leaves Boston at 9:00 a.m. going 65 miles per hour, and Train B leaves Chicago at noon going 80 miles per hour.' I never did understand why trains went at different speeds, but maybe that's because my math teacher didn't explain to me *how* to read the story problems."

"OK," Jose admits, "we math teachers do teach reading—of sorts."

"Au contraire, my numero uno, math teachers, like all teachers, have to teach all kinds of reading. You give out instructions for homework, type questions on the computer screen in your classroom, explain the comments you write on your students' tests, compose . . ."

"OK, OK," Jose says, laughing. "Don't be so exponential in your argument."

"You mean, in other words, don't pile it on?"

"You got it. In fact, I'll be exponential and add one more to your list. I have students use word processing to write explanations of how they worked a problem. And if I'm not mistaken, writing produces reading materials, so I'm actually both a reading and a writing teacher!"

"Don't forget math," Jody adds, laughing too. "So you're using math to teach reading fluency, vocabulary, and text comprehension. You get three gold stars."

"I'm honored," Jose says, bowing his head slightly.

"Even though you display mock seriousness," Jody observes with a twinkle in her eye, "you seem to have overcome your dismay at being asked to teach reading. And may I add," Jody says as she gets up from her chair to return to her office, "you've also incorporated computers into your literacy classroom. Come by my office sometime, and I'll show you some software that can make math and reading work together in ways you may not have anticipated."

"Yes, sir, Mrs. Curriculum Leader," Jose says crisply while giving a smart salute.

"That's 'Yes, ma'am,' or else what you said doesn't add up," Jody remarks with a mischievous grin as she walks down the hall toward her office.

○ Importance of Teaching Reading

Why does the teaching of reading today hold a more prestigious position than ever before? For one reason, as a result of No Child Left Behind legislation, reading became the number one focus of many districts, teachers, parents, and students. The message is clear that if students are not performing well in the area of reading, there are punitive consequences for districts and teachers. For instance, schools are taken over by school boards with teachers and principals either being relocated or let go. In some districts, the amount of time spent on reading instruction has expanded until other subjects, such as science and social studies, are totally neglected.

Associated with this increased emphasis on the teaching of reading is a new attitude about being a reading teacher. Most of us would agree that it is the most exciting time in history to be a reading teacher. Fortunately, award-winning teachers are sharing stories of what they are doing in their classrooms, and their excitement is contagious (Leu, Karchmer, & Leu, 1999). It is important to note that by "reading teacher," we agree with Jody in the opening chapter scenario that all teachers are teachers of reading. As she demonstrated, students do not learn content area material for subjects such as science, social studies, and math without engaging in the literacy skills of reading, writing, thinking, listening, and reviewing. When embracing this perspective, all teachers are indeed reading teachers.

Adding to this increased excitement about being a reading teacher is the fact that a great deal has been learned in the past few years about how students learn, and specifically, about how students learn to read. Several important groups have contributed to these new understandings, providing guidance to our work. One seminal document produced by the National Council of Teachers of English (NCTE) and the International Reading Association (IRA) is the "Standards for the English Language Arts" (see Figure 3.1). Although the standards do not prescribe curriculum or instruction, they do emphasize the importance of preschool through adult literacy performance outcomes that are expected for students to become productive members of society. Another seminal publication produced by the National Reading Panel in 2000 identifies five areas of reading grounded in scientific principles: phonemic awareness, phonetics, vocabulary, fluency,

Figure 3.1   NCTE/IRA Standards for English/Language Arts.

1. Students read a wide range of print and non-print texts to build an understanding of texts, of themselves, and of the cultures of the United States and the world, to acquire new information, to respond to the needs and demands of society and the workplace, and for personal fulfillment. Among these texts are fiction and nonfiction, classic and contemporary works.

2. Students read a wide range of literature from many periods in many genres to build an understanding of the many dimensions of human experience (e.g., philosophical, ethical, aesthetic).

3. Students apply a wide range of strategies to comprehend, interpret, evaluate, and appreciate texts. They draw on their prior experience, their interactions with other readers and writers, their knowledge of word meaning and of other texts, their word identification strategies, and their understanding of textual features (e.g., sound-letter correspondence, sentence structure, context, graphics).

4. Students adjust their use of spoken, written, and visual language (e.g., conventions, style, vocabulary) to communicate effectively with a variety of audiences and for different purposes.

5. Students employ a wide range of strategies as they write and use different writing process elements appropriately to communicate with different audiences for a variety of purposes.

6. Students apply knowledge of language structure, language conventions (e.g., spelling and punctuation), media techniques, figurative language, and genre to create, critique, and discuss print and nonprint texts.

7. Students conduct research on issues and interests by generating ideas and questions and by posing problems. They gather, evaluate, and synthesize data from a variety of sources (e.g., print and nonprint texts, artifacts, people) to communicate their discoveries in ways that suit their purpose and audience.

8. Students use a variety of technological and information resources (e.g., libraries, databases, computer networks, video) to gather and synthesize information and to create and communicate knowledge.

9. Students develop an understanding of and respect for diversity in language use, patterns, and dialects across cultures, ethnic groups, geographic regions, and social roles.

10. Students whose first language is not English make use of their first language to develop competency in the English language arts and to develop understanding of content across the curriculum.

11. Students participate as knowledgeable, reflective, creative, and critical members of a variety of literacy communities.

12. Students use spoken, written, and visual language to accomplish their own purposes (e.g., for learning, enjoyment, persuasion, and the exchange of information).

and comprehension. Known as the "Big 5 Components" in the reading world, in this chapter we discuss how to use technology to teach these areas of reading instruction, followed by a discussion on using technology to teach reading in the content area, and using technology in integrated literacy units. But first, Elizabeth Heeren shares in a Computer Classroom Snapshot how experienced classroom teachers are using technology to teach reading.

◣ Computer Classroom Snapshot

Context

My name is Elizabeth Heeren, and I am a doctoral student at the University of Memphis. I also have 20 years of middle-school teaching experience, and I have worked the last four years as a Literacy Specialist with Memphis City Schools. Within that context, I have spent the last four years observing, supporting, and coaching middle-school teachers in literacy strategies. During my career and studies, I have become increasingly interested in how definitions of literacy have changed in the face of new technologies. As literacy definitions and conceptualizations have changed with technological advances, I have observed changes in classroom practices as well. Research supports these universal changes in literacy practice, and experts have coined the term "New Literacy" to define current constructs of literacy. Based on these findings and my observations, I decided to explore specific new literacy classroom practices in a research study, and my dissertation topic emerged.

What I Did and Why

I began my study by finding a sample of teachers who used technology extensively in their classrooms for literacy instruction. Luckily, Memphis City Schools had a recent push toward having teachers include technological instruction in their classrooms. For the last five years, the district has recognized leading teachers of technology by awarding Academy Awards for Technology Instruction. The list of teachers who were nominated during a five-year period or who won these awards formed the sample for my study. I considered these teachers to be master teachers of technology based on their selection. The specific technological application of using the Internet for literacy instruction was chosen for study. To narrow the study even more, I chose to focus on middle-school teachers.

To examine how the designated master teachers used the Internet for literacy instruction, I designed a survey and gathered basic information about teacher approaches toward and practices with literacy and administered it by mail to the 42 middle-school teachers in my sample. From the survey data, I selected a smaller sample of seven teachers to study in a more in-depth manner. For these teachers, I conducted a classroom observation of them teaching an Internet literacy lesson. I also conducted a postlesson debriefing interview and a general interview about their instruction and assessment practices with Internet literacy. With this data I was able to "draw a picture" of what New Literacy classrooms look like as teachers engage in teaching literacy with the Internet.

What I Learned

Several themes emerged from the data, and these themes can be organized into three main components: 1) teacher approaches with Internet literacy, 2) student

(continued)

practices with Internet literacy, and 3) challenges with Internet literacy use in the classroom.

Teacher Approaches with Internet Literacy

The middle-school teachers embrace the Internet as an important tool for literacy instruction. This was evidenced in the considerable time spent planning and preparing for Internet literacy lessons. Several teachers were in the habit of completing Internet lessons themselves before conducting the lessons with their students. Most teachers reported and demonstrated that they used national and state standards to help them determine important Internet literacy skills. To help them design their lessons, the teachers also used their own perceptions about skills that students were going to need in high school, college, and the workplace.

Another common approach with these middle-school teachers was letting students interact collaboratively during Internet lessons. In all classrooms there was some level of student interaction and peer teaching. In some lessons, teachers gave directions for students to discuss and interact, while in others, students just began collaborating naturally. The interesting point is that with Internet literary lessons, students seemed to gravitate naturally toward social interaction, and teachers appeared comfortable with their students' interaction. This observation supports the conceptual framework in which I conducted my study, Vygotsky's (1962) sociocognitive perspective. Vygotsky theorized that social interaction profoundly shapes intellectual development, and he stressed the importance of language in the development of thought. In this study, observations of this phenomenon at work revealed several examples of specific practices that students engaged in during Internet literacy lessons.

Student Practices with Internet Literacy

Student behaviors during Internet literacy lessons were fascinating to watch. First, the level of motivation and student engagement in learning appeared to be high. Students were observed engaging in the following literacy practices:

- Rereading texts for clarification.
- Making predictions.
- Reading aloud to their partners.
- Using online resources for information (dictionary.com, Web links).
- Making inferences about graphics.

The most interesting concept about these observed behaviors was that many of the actions occurred without teacher prompting. As a former middle-school teacher, I knew how difficult it was to get students to reread texts, for example, without hearing, "But I already read it" or having students merely pretend to reread. The students in this study seemed to engage in these practices simply because the activities helped them to understand the material read and the activity assigned, not to merely follow teacher directions. These observations point out the power of the

Internet as a tool to get students actively engaged in learning. Unfortunately, I also observed how students do not have equal access to the Internet, and, therefore, all students do not have exposure and opportunity to engage in the online strategies that undoubtedly could lessen the achievement gaps among students.

Challenges with Internet Literacy Use in the Classroom

The lack of equitable access to Internet-wired computers was the overwhelming challenge reported and observed in this study. Classrooms had every possible configuration of computer access. For example, to illustrate opposite ends of the spectrum in access, one classroom had a laptop cart, with a laptop computer for every child. Another teacher had to take his students on an "in-school field trip" to the computer lab, which was equipped with 20 outdated computers, some broken, for his 28 students. Teachers indicated that providing students with access to the Internet was an ongoing problem, especially in low-income areas. This is a notable challenge, all the more important because in lower-income schools, families are less likely to have Internet access at home as well. Challenges such as this must be addressed by the educational community or gaps between socioeconomic groups are likely to increase rather than decrease.

○ Phonemic Awareness and Phonics Instruction

From the previous classroom snapshot, we learned from Elizabeth Heeren how middle-school teachers are approaching Internet literacy. In this section, we discuss how early childhood teachers approach phonemic awareness and phonics instruction.

Phonemic awareness and phonics is not the same thing. Historically, teachers and teacher educators focused on phonics but not on phonemic awareness. As a result, it is understandable that some confusion may currently surround their differences. Much of the new emphasis on teaching phonemic awareness grew from the National Reading Panel's (2000) work, resulting in today's reading curriculum and instruction clearly addressing both phonemic awareness and phonics. It is important to note, however, that neither phonemic awareness nor phonics is a complete reading program. Both are best combined with the other components of teaching reading, and both are important stepping stones and a major focus of reading instruction in grades pre-K–2. Neither component should encompass a great deal of class time; actually, the National Reading Panel (2000) suggests that phonemic awareness instruction not exceed 20 hours during the school year, and phonics instruction is noted as being most effective when it begins in kindergarten or first grade and lasts approximately two years.

Why Teach Phonemic Awareness and Phonics?

To discuss phonemic awareness and phonics, it is important to review the definitions of several literacy terms. A **phoneme** is the smallest unit of speech that makes a difference in spoken language. For example, *bed* and *red* sound the same except for the /b/ and /r/ sounds, which are different phonemes. We have approximately 44 speech sounds or phonemes in the English language, and most words have more than one phoneme. **Phonemic awareness** is the ability to hear, identify, and work with the phonemes in spoken language. As an example, students who are phonemically aware recognize that a word such as *check* has three phonemes (ch/e/k/), although it has four letters that represent these sounds. When writing words, a **grapheme** represents a phoneme in written language, and **phonics** instruction brings phonemes and graphemes together by helping students learn the relationship between the letters of written language and the sounds of spoken language.

Phonemic awareness and phonics are skills that can and should be taught for several reasons. Once students learn there is a predictable relationship between written letters and spoken words, they can then apply this knowledge to decoding words. This is known as the alphabetic principle, and it is a precursor to learning to read. Phonemic awareness and phonics instruction also aid students' abilities to comprehend because they are less bogged down with word recognition and freer to focus on making meaning of text. Additionally, phonemic awareness and phonics instruction are associated with students' spelling development because, as noted already, they understand that letters and sounds are related in a predictable way (Moxlely, Warash, Coffman, Brinton & Concannon, 1997).

Using Technology with Phonemic Awareness and Phonics Instruction

Early childhood teachers keep several features in mind when they use technology to teach phonemic awareness and phonics (Dahlquist, 2002; Labbo, 2000; Lalley 2001; Partnership for Reading, 2001). First, teachers know that it is important to engage students in a playful, stimulating, and social manner. Making instruction fun for this age is actually quite easy because young children will not only delight in rhythm, rhyme, and alliteration activities, but also they are eager to use computer technology. Be sure to select games and software with attractive visual representation and motivating speech to hold young students' attention. For example, you can use a cloze procedure that consists of text with missing words with an electronically recorded familiar story or poem that allows students to fill in the appropriate word at the appropriate time (Dahlquist, 2002). Note also in this example that the activity reinforces the importance of teaching phonemic awareness and phonics within the context of real reading. Like other reading skills, phonemic awareness and phonics should not be taught in isolation. Teachers find that when activities are purposeful, meaningful, and connected to real reading, students are motivated to learn because they understand the relevance of the task. An important idea here is these skills are not something students will later transfer to reading; instead, students are already using the skills during reading, a guiding principle of teaching children to read. In another example described by Labbo (2000), young children use talking books in learning centers to search for rhyming words or phonic elements, such as using the "Find" feature to locate all *bl* blends or all words of the *ad* word family. This example scaffolds students' learning by enabling them to click on any word and hear the individual sounds or the whole word spoken. It is also important to provide phonemic awareness and phonics instruction on a regular and consistent basis throughout the curriculum. Students need to be provided with individual problem sets and stories to focus on the letter-sound correspondence and on words they have not mastered. This engagement alone can go a long way toward providing students with ample opportunities to practice what they are learning.

As previously mentioned, teaching phonemic awareness involves students in learning how to hear, identify, and manipulate sounds in spoken language. We know that digitized speech helps students with decoding skills (Reitsman, 1988), and we know that all voice-chip technology is not created equally (Lalley, 2001); therefore, it is important to note that while you do not need the latest computer programs or the most sophisticated technology or equipment, you do need a clear digitized natural voice that can be easily reprogrammed (Dahlquist, 2002). Currently, a growing number of electronic devices and online systems are available (Rankin-Erickson, Wood, & Beukelman, 2003), including voice chips that read words and sounds. For instance, the LeapFrog company provides an interactive tool for a child to "touch" words and letters using a specific stylus pen (Lalley, 2001).

Research confirms the importance of teaching sounds along with the letters of the alphabet, and technology must allow students to match sounds and letters and spoken and written words, and alter the speed of speech to meet individual needs. It is also important to select electronic programs that focus on one or two types of phoneme manipulation at a time. Young children can be confused if they are exposed to more than two of the following types of manipulation at the same time: (1) blending individual phonemes to form words, (2) segmenting words into their individual phonemes, (3) deleting or recognizing a word that remains when a phoneme is removed from another word, (4) adding a phoneme to an existing word to create a new word, and (5) substituting one phoneme for another to make a new word (National Reading Panel, 2000). When using computer technology to teach the various types of manipulation, also limit the number of student answer choices to no more than four or five. Remember that students need to receive immediate feedback and to be provided with as many repetitions as necessary.

Effective electronic phonics instruction programs are also systematic and explicit, meaning the instruction is provided on the major oral and written relationship of consonants and vowels in a predetermined sequence. Drill exercises that make use of a number of computer capabilities, such as visual highlighting and synthesized speech, can have a very positive impact on student learning. These tools are resources for teachers that support and enhance their traditional methods of teaching phonemic awareness and phonics (Reitsman, 1988; Barker & Torgesen, 1995; Wise, Olson & Treiman, 1990). Using technology tools to teach reading is evidenced widely in Labbo's work (2004a; 2004b), which has been instrumental in conducting research in early childhood classrooms. She finds that teachers are very successful integrating technology into reading strategies they already know and use. For instance, Labbo provides details of teachers who took the widely accepted strategies of morning message, language experience approach, and author's chair and transformed them by integrating technology resulting in daily digital morning messages, online language experience stories, and author's computer chair. She explains how teachers use a large monitor connected to a computer running KidPix so that all children can watch her model how to write a story. Next, a voice synthesizer on the computer reads the text, called text-to-speech, and sometimes teachers change the computer synthesized voice to read the message in a sing-song way, which, of course, young children find amusing. This is followed with opportunities for students to practice choral reading, when all

Figure 3.2   Web sites for Phonemic Awareness and Phonics Instruction.

Between the Lions—Videos, books, and interactive games by PBS's award-winning program. Includes phonics skills, word activities, and visual and auditory assistance.
(http://pbskids.org/lions/)

Chateau Meddybemps: Fun with Letters—According to the International Reading Association, this is the third best site on the Web for phonics instruction that includes phonics and writers' workshop activities.
(http://www.meddybemps.com/letterary/index.html)

GameGOO: Learning That Sticks—Interactive site based on state standards. Activities use phonic elements and links to the Earobics Literacy site, which provides voice input.
(http://www.cogcon.com/gamegoo/gooeylo.html)

Sounds of the Day—Two letters of the alphabet with accompanying sounds are produced and spoken in context of words.
(http://readmeabook.com/sounds/sotd.htm)

Welcome to the Phonics Link—This San Diego County Office of Education's Web site provides online materials about phonics instruction.
(http://www.sdcoe.k12.ca.us/score/Phonics_Link/phonics.html)

Words and Pictures—Aligns the United Kingdom's standards and teaching words.
(http://www.bbc.co.uk/education/wordsandpictures/phonics)

students read the text together, or students use the highlighting feature to practice specific phonic skills, such as identifying words that begin with the letter "b." Another advantage of using the computer in this example is that teachers can print copies of the stories for students to reread or to use as practice phonics sheets. Students are encouraged to take their stories home and read them aloud to their parents. In these ways, teachers feel more comfortable and willing to experiment with using technology if they are teaching activities that already hold an established pattern and routine in their classrooms.

As previously noted, teachers make sure that students understand why they are learning phonemic awareness and phonics skills to aid in comprehending text. Thus, students need to have ample opportunities to practice these skills in real reading and writing examples. Not only is there a growing number of electronic materials in the form of short books, stories, and activity sheets that allow students to practice their skills, but there are also a number of effective Web sites that provide phonemic awareness and phonics instruction (Bertelsen, Kauffman, Howard, & Cochran, 2003). See Figure 3.2 for a list of publications.

Challenges of Phonemic Awareness and Phonics Instruction

Although phonemic awareness and phonics instruction are critical for students' reading development, Dahlquist (2002) cautions that students may have difficulty with phonemic awareness and phonics instruction for several reasons. First, phonemic awareness entails understanding that words are composed of a series of sounds and understanding the relationship of sounds within a word. This can be challenging because we do not naturally process language this way; instead of attending to specific phonemes, we automatically focus on the meaning of the total utterance. Second, numerous phonemes sound similar and can create confusion for children. Take for example the words *van* and *ban*, although the /v/ and /b/ sound very similar, the word meanings have nothing in common. Many experts additionally warn that a major barrier to learning phonics is the great number of irregularly spelled words in English that do not follow the standard English letter-sound correspondence. Chapters 6 and 7 also offer suggestions for working with ESL and struggling readers, student populations who frequently experience special challenges with phonemic awareness and phonics instruction. In spite of these challenges, as observed already, phonemic awareness and phonics instruction greatly improve students' word recognition, spelling, and reading comprehension and will continue to be a major component of the early-reading program.

◯ Fluency Instruction

Fluency is the ability to read a text quickly, accurately, and automatically with a natural, proper expression. Fluency is a vital component of the reading process and should be taught to children (Osborn, Lehr, & Hiebert, 2003). Similar to phonemic awareness and phonics, fluency is not a stand-alone program, but rather it is one component of successful reading. Again, the work accomplished by the National Reading Panel (2000) and *Put Reading First* (Armbruster, Lehr, & Osbor, 2001) has been instrumental in moving fluency to the forefront of educators' minds. Both organizations report a close relationship between fluency and reading comprehension, even though historically that relationship was a neglected reading skill in classrooms (Allington, 1983; Shanahan, 2002).

Fluency galvanizes the two important cognitive tasks of word recognition and comprehension to produce a successful and competent reader. Teachers know students have a limited amount of attention for any given cognitive task, and obviously attention devoted to one task is attention not given to another (Osborn, Lehr & Hiebert, 2003; Samuels, 2002). In the case here, word recognition and comprehension are competing for the reader's attention, and the more attention given to identifying the printed word, the less attention given to comprehension. An important idea to keep in mind is that non-fluent readers who are focusing hard on word recognition skills have very little attention to devote to developing comprehension skills.

Most children, thankfully, are on their way to becoming fluent readers by second grade, having accomplished the skills of rapid word recognition and familiarity with common text features. Beginning readers and older struggling readers, on the other hand, must stop and use decoding strategies to decipher unfamiliar words. Thus, the one-time appearance of many key words in a selection may disrupt fluency. For these children, even with several readings, selections that contain a large number of one-use multisyllabic content words can interfere with the development of fluency. Additionally, the level of fluency is associated with the familiarity of text (Hiebert & Fisher, 2002; Torgesen, et al., 2002). For instance, a child whose hobby is horseback riding is able to read a story including horse terms such as "saddle" and "stirrup" more easily than a child who has never been on a horse. Overall, most children benefit from fluency instruction, especially struggling readers who need to move beyond word-for-word reading into smooth, fluent reading.

Using Technology with Fluency Instruction

Repeated oral reading and independent silent reading are two instructional approaches recommended by the National Reading Panel (2000) for building reading fluency.

Repeated Oral Reading. In repeated oral reading, students read a passage several times orally with explicit guidance and feedback from a fluent reader (Samuels, 1979). A variety of electronic assisted reading techniques can be implemented to increase students' fluency abilities. Most popular is using software with speech recognition that can provide students immediate feedback and help as they read aloud. Many software programs (e.g., Kidspiration and Kidpix Deluxe) and electronic books allow students to ask the computer to pronounce an unknown word. If the child asks for the meaning of a word, the computer provides on-demand or automated help in decoding individual words so that a problem with a word does not interfere with reading. Depending on the situation, the computer pronounces an unknown word, displays the word's meaning in the context of a sentence, or provides a graphic to illustrate how the word is used. Phrases in the text also can be highlighted to guide students in learning how to read with expression. These features allow students to tackle more challenging texts because they receive additional support and scaffolding with pronunciation and meaning.

When students are successful with reading, they are more excited and more willing to reread and gain additional experience with text. It is also important to remember that students are highly motivated to read when they have an audience for their reading. Two ways to accomplish this scenario are to have students record themselves using either electronic presentations such as Microsoft PowerPoint or audio recording software such as Apple GarageBand and Audacity. This suggestion provides an authentic reason for students to practice reading a passage multiple times and lets them receive positive feedback about their reading. In addition, many of these software programs provide recording and analysis tools of students' fluency and accuracy, enabling teachers to monitor student performance over time and to help inform instructional decisions.

Providing children with many opportunities to practice reading online, showing them electronic examples of how fluent readers read, and giving them effective feedback on their personal reading abilities enables children to self-correct and to make progress with repeated reading. Actually, one of the most significant ways that electronic books and software programs enhance students' fluency is by providing them a model of fluent oral reading. According to experts, when students listen to fluent reading, they learn how a reader's voice can influence the meaning of text (Kuhn & Stahl, 2003).

Repeated oral reading helps improve the reading ability of developing readers and aids struggling readers. In sum, "it is important to note that all effective repeated reading procedures have two features in common: (1) they provide students with many opportunities to practice reading, and (2) they provide students with guidance in how fluent readers read and with feedback to help them become aware of and correct their mistakes" (Osborn, Lehr, & Hiebert, 2003, p. 14). Thus, technology can be used as a very successful support for children's reading fluency.

Independent Silent Reading. In independent silent reading, unlike repeated oral reading, students are encouraged to read extensively on their own, both in and out of the classroom, with minimal guidance and feedback from others. Several studies support independent silent reading by showing a direct correlation between students who read widely and reading success (Juel, 1988). No doubt the most widely used electronic resource for promoting independent silent reading is electronic texts (see Figure 3.3). Several series, such as *The Living Books*, offer many children's books on CD-ROM, DVD, or Internet sites. These electronic books have unique features: for example, the story is read in another language, specific words are pronounced, sound effects are heard, and animated pictures are viewed. According to Lewin (1997), students who use electronic talking books were able to read more independently, develop effective decoding skills,

Figure 3.3   Electronic Book Resources.

"Ask the Author"
(http://ipl.sils.umich.edu/youth/AskAuthor/)

Carol Hurst's Children's Literature Site
(http://www.carolhurst.com/index.html)

Classics for Young People
(http://www.ucalgary.ca/~dkbrown/storclas.html)

The Children's Literature Web Guide
(http://www.ucalgary.ca/~dKbrown/)

Children's Story Books Online
(http://www.magickeys.com/books/)

Childrenstory
(http://childrenstory.com/)

Laura Ingalls Wilder Home Page
(http://webpages.marshall.edu/~irby1/laura.htmlx)

Newberry Award Home Page
(http://www.ala.org/alsc/newbery.html)

Poems, Poetry, Poets
(http://www.spondee.net/)

Project Gutenberg
(http://www.gutenberg.org/)

Reading Rainbow
(http://gpn.unl.edu/rainbow/)

Recommended Youth Reading
(http://www.st-charles.lib.il.us/youth_services/yrl/ythread.htm)

Tales of Wonder: Folk and Fairy Tales from Around the World
(http://www.darsie.net/talesofwonder/)

Winnie the Pooh and Friends
(http://www.worldkids.net/pooh/)

The Electronic Text Center at the University of Virginia
(http://etext.lib.virginia.edu/uvaonline.html)

The Online Books Page
(http://onlinebooks.library.upenn.edu/lists.html)

and read more on their own. Indeed, these interactive books can be effective and motivational for students, including students with reading difficulties (Johnson, 2003).

One example of an activity that entails using electronic books to promote repeated reading involves a comparison/contrast assignment—the CD versus the book. Find several comparable stories, both on CD and in hard copy. Have students list strengths and weaknesses (call the lists "What I liked" and "What I didn't like") and engage them in discussion. After doing this on several occasions, you'll have your own program analysis.

Another valuable tool for improving fluency skills is Readers' Theater, which encompasses both repeated oral reading and silent independent reading. In this situation, students have an authentic reason for practicing repeated reading of texts because they know they will be performing a play by reading it aloud with expression to an audience, even if the audience is a small group of students in their own classroom (Worthy & Prater, 2002). Numerous Web sites are available to choose poems, songs, and scripts for Readers' Theater (Worthy & Broaddus, 2001–02). Other ways to modify the Readers' Theater strategy include having students rehearse a poem, joke, or story that is changed daily or weekly and displayed on the large TV monitor. Another version may ask students to practice a short story to record as an audio recording or podcast for students in a lower grade. Students are also generally eager to participate in choral reading with students reading in unison, another form of oral reading that promotes fluency.

During designated times, teachers often plan for independent silent reading such as Drop Everything and Read (DEAR), Sustained Silent Reading, Uninterrupted Sustained Silent Reading, or free time. One challenge associated with students reading independently is that they often select books on their instructional, frustrational, or listening level, rather than their independent reading level (see Figure 3.4). When this happens, students do not easily read or comprehend the books; instead, they become bored, lose interest in the book, and eventually put it down. Again, to be successful with independent reading, students need to select books on their independent level to ensure they can read the text easily with fluency and comprehend the meaning (Allington, 2002). As noted previously, one advantage of the popular Accelerated Reader program is it identifies the reading level of each student and thus helps students choose appropriate books.

Increasingly computers have been used for fluency instruction, especially with advances in computerized speech recognition and products that assess and provide

Figure 3.4 Student Reading Levels.

READING LEVELS	DESCRIPTION	% FOR WORD RECOGNITION (WR) AND COMPREHENSION (COMP)
Independent Level	Students can pronounce words and comprehend easily on their own.	WR = 99%–100% Comp = 90%–100%
Instructional Level	Students can be successful with teacher's instruction.	WR = 95%–99% Comp = 75%–90%
Frustration Level	Student cannot be successful—too difficult.	WR = Below 95% Comp = Below 75%
Listening Level	Students listen electronically or read aloud.	WR = N/A Comp = Above 75%

feedback to students and teachers. Clearly, the increased use of computers, along with the ease and convenience of using them, are promising and motivating factors in getting children to practice their reading, which is at the heart of producing fluent readers (Osborn, Lehr, & Hiebert, 2003).

⊙ Vocabulary Instruction

An old adage warns, "When buying a house, you need to focus on three things: location, location, location." A related idea is if you want students to become better readers, then you also focus on three things: vocabulary, vocabulary, vocabulary. Obviously, the intended message is that words carry a significant weight in the reading process. What is also important is for teachers to understand this and to develop a passion for integrating vocabulary development throughout all oral and written communication (Johnson, 2001).

What are some of the main reasons that words from both oral (speaking and listening) vocabulary and written (reading and writing) vocabulary are so critical for students to become proficient readers? First, young readers build on their oral language, meaning they use their oral vocabulary to make sense of the words they see in print (Johnson, 2001). Second, there is a direct connection between vocabulary and comprehension. Naturally, if you do not understand the meaning of the words then you will not understand the meaning of the text.

Generally, two types of vocabulary are essential for promoting reading development. First, sight-word vocabulary are those words that you have seen so much in text that you recognize them instantly without attacking them phonetically. Amazingly, only approximately 107 words make up half of the words in written text (Zeno, Ivens, Millard, & Duvvuri, 1995). The other half of the words that we encounter when reading are known as content vocabulary. Words specific to content area reading give meaning to text and require students to use decoding strategies to pronounce.

Using Technology to Teach Vocabulary

The National Reading Panel (2000) recognizes two predominant ways that vocabulary is learned. First, most words are learned indirectly by children hearing and seeing words in various contexts. This is why children need to be widely exposed to and immersed in reading. Some of the best recommendations from experts include reading aloud to children, engaging children in conversations with adults, and supporting children to read extensively on their own.

In the second case, words are learned through direct instruction (National Reading Panel, 2000). Generally these words are not a part of students' daily language, but rather they are associated with new and complex concepts. In this situation, students need specific instruction. For example, (a) having the vocabulary words introduced before reading the text, (b) having students actively engaged with the vocabulary in some manner, such as typing the words in an online vocabulary notebook or spreadsheet, (c) creating

Web pages with tool tips, or (d) providing students with multiple and repeated exposure to words. Perhaps even more importantly, students need to know how to learn new words on their own. As you might expect, individual word-learning strategies are critical for students to become lifelong independent readers.

In numerous ways, computer technology supports both indirect and direct approaches to vocabulary development. First, a variety of interactive and individualized online vocabulary lessons provide feedback to students as well as help teachers keep records of students' progress. Second, a growing number of online texts with hyperlinks give students the definitions of words and explanations of key concepts in the texts. Third, online dictionaries, glossaries, encyclopedias, thesaures, and other traditional reference tools are transformed into hypertext with many interactive features that allow students to cross-reference information, look up words, hear material read back, and access related supplementary material instantly. Many of these reference tools are integrated into word processing software; however, more elaborate individual software packages are available for purchase, and Wikipedia has become a very popular free reference. Fourth, as observed already, extensive reading is a necessary practice for vocabulary development. The growing number of online materials and exchanges available provide infinite opportunities for students to broaden and deepen their word knowledge and to extend their reading. For instance, it is not uncommon for students to engage in online discussions, blogging, Web sites, and other technology-enabled uses of text. In the following cases, studies support the use of computer technology to teach vocabulary. McKenna and Watkins (1996) found primary students who used hypermedia and hypertext features increased their vocabulary and read books above their reading levels. As discussed in Chapter 7, struggling readers experience increased vocabulary scores after using electronic textual aids (Anderson-Inman & Horney, 1988). Numerous studies also confirm that electronic talking books and electronic texts support vocabulary development at different grade levels (e.g., Reinking & Richman, 1990).

○ Comprehension Instruction

Comprehension instruction includes purposeful and active strategies that help students understand what they read (National Reading Panel, 2000). If someone asked you which one of the "Big 5 Components" of reading is the most significant, no doubt you would say comprehension. It is no wonder that comprehension instruction holds this lofty position. It deals with the real reason we read. Indeed, we use our decoding, fluency, and vocabulary skills to aid us in understanding what we read.

Naturally, we read different materials for different purposes, and we adjust our reading accordingly. For instance, we read recipes, newspapers, and biographies for different reasons, and to know how to deal with these differences, we use our background knowledge, vocabulary skills, reading strategies, and language structure knowledge to help make sense of the text. Although comprehension instruction begins in the primary grades, generally students at this time are focusing more on "learning how to read," meaning they are spending more time practicing word recognition and fluency skills than on comprehension. Once students move into the "reading to learn" developmental phase, a heavier focus is placed on teaching comprehension strategies. As previously noted, regardless of the grade level, teachers need to help students understand that the reason "we learn how to read" is to help comprehend texts. Students need to be encouraged to monitor their comprehension by constantly asking themselves if what they are reading makes sense.

Using Technology to Teach Comprehension

Research from the last 30 years clearly demonstrates that students improve their reading skills through learning comprehension strategies. What, then, are some strategies when using technology to teach comprehension? According to the National Reading Panel (2000), six strategies received the strongest scientific support for teaching comprehension. In this section we discuss these strategies and the ways in which technology can provide direct instruction in comprehension strategies.

Monitoring Comprehension Strategies. Teachers use monitoring comprehension strategies to teach students how to know when they know something, how to know when they do not understand, and how to use appropriate strategies to address lack of understanding (National Reading Panel, 2000). Consequently, thinking about your own thinking, better known as metacognition, enables students to learn how to think about and have control over their reading. Frequently teachers demonstrate this strategy by using electronic books and modeling "think alouds," the process of saying out loud what is going through your head as you encounter and solve different reading situations. By employing hypertext features (Harste, 1994; Rowe, 1994) in electronic books, you can model for students how to interlink animations, sounds, movies, and pictures and demonstrate how to use these aids to confirm your thinking about reading issues, such as the uncertainty of how to pronounce a word or how to confirm the main idea of a passage. Note also in this example a fundamental difference in the nature of electronic books and hard copy books. Students who see teachers select different links to create a nonlinear story path can lead to students having greater control and more options for monitoring their own learning (Karchmer, 2001). According to Doty, Popplewell, and Byers (2001), students have greater comprehension gains when using these interactive qualities of electronic books than when using a traditional, static format.

Graphic and Semantic Organizers. When teachers use graphic and semantic organizers, they teach students how to focus on text structure as they read, use visual representation to illustrate concepts and relationships among concepts in the text, and write in an organized way (National Reading Panel, 2000). As previously noted, one of the most popular concept-mapping software programs available is Kidspiration for grades K–3 and Inspiration for grades 4 and above. These programs are especially effective as a prewriting activity tool because students use electronic tools for both outlining and diagramming. They also work well as analysis tools when students identify characteristics of stories, such as plot, setting, and characters.

Question-Answer Strategy. When teachers use the question-answer strategy, they teach students how to establish a purpose for reading, focus on what they are to learn, think actively as they read, monitor their reading, and relate what they learn to what they already know (National Reading Panel, 2000). Questioning-answering instruction is one of the oldest and most widely used strategies by teachers. As mentioned previously, one example of a popular tracking system that uses a question-answer strategy is Accelerated Reader, a system from Renaissance Learning. Extensive research shows that Accelerated Reader enhances students' motivation to read and increases their comprehension skills (Lopez, 2000; Poock, 1998). The program contains a database of quizzes for thousands of books that are listed by grade level, and after a student reads a book, he or she immediately takes an electronic comprehension test. Advantages of the program include students reading books on their individual levels, students working independently, teachers working with small groups or the whole class while individual students use the program, students taking computer-generated tests so there is less work for teachers, and teachers being kept informed through a tracking device about students' progress (Lopez, 2000; Poock, 1998).

Generating Questions Strategy. When teachers use the generating questions strategy, they teach students how to ask their own questions, which improves the active processing of text and comprehension (National Reading Panel, 2000). One creative example of using this strategy is to have students identify the main idea in their reading, generate questions about the main idea, and submit the questions to a school blog, an online discussion group, or a community of experts through e-mail. Similarly, Helt (2003) describes the use of online literature circles between middle-school students and mentors that could easily employ the use of the generating questions strategy. Teachers can also have students respond online to their peers' questions, working either alone or in a small group.

Recognizing Story Structure Strategy. When teachers use the strategy of recognizing story structure, they teach students how to increase their comprehension skills and to develop a greater appreciation of stories (National Reading Panel, 2000). Developing a story schema enables students to understand story elements and to look for these elements in future reading. For instance, teachers frequently use online story maps to quickly and easily allow students to show the sequence of events in a story. Another electronic example is using digital images for storytelling. In this process, the reading is made more visual and is easier to understand because the narrated storytelling video involves children's oral language, linking reading to a lived experience, and sequencing the events (Kajder & Swenson, 2004; Labbo, 2005). Another example, Tom Snyder's Timeliner, also helps students visually organize information on a time line or number line. Additionally, Scott and Harding (2004) point out that script writing for video projects and podcasts is motivating and reinforces the process approach to writing as covered in Chapter 5. Also, because current production tools, such as Apple iMovie for video and Audacity freeware for audio, are simple and easy to use, students are free to focus on the content of the recording instead of worrying about how to operate the technology.

Summarizing Strategy. When teachers use the summarizing strategy, they teach students how to identify main ideas, eliminate unnecessary information, synthesize information, and remember what they read (National Reading Panel, 2002). One current and popular electronic tool used for summarizing is a blog (Web log). It is no wonder students like blogging. It is an informal, journal-like approach for responding to reading, writing, or life, and it also serves as a public discussion forum for exchanging personal opinions (Oravec, 2002). Teachers can structure blogging, however, to achieve specific standards or skills, such as students knowing how to summarize information. With regard to literacy, students can be instructed to first summarize their reading, to next include their personal reaction to the reading, and then to end with an invitation for other students to respond. As you might expect, blogging is also an effective strategy to use with struggling readers, as covered in Chapter 7 (Kajder & Bull, 2003). An idea related to blogs is using threaded online discussions, another supportive, nonjudgmental forum for students to share their thinking. For example, Viani (2004) explains how his school uses the Southern Oregon Write Site for students to discuss their writing; similarly, it can also be used for students to summarize their reading, or any other reading skill that needs to be reinforced.

Using Technology to Teach Reading in the Content Area

As previously discussed, during students' early years, students are heavily engaged with decoding words and learning how to read. Generally, around third grade, this shifts to focusing on reading to learn. Then the goal is for students to understand what they read and to become equipped with using a wide array of self-regulating strategies for reading all types of texts (Snow, 2002). Traditionally, expository texts were used to teach conceptual information. Today, technology expands teaching options in the content areas through: (1) publishing, (2) accessing information, and (3) communicating and collaborating.

Publishing

The Internet is a powerful and innovative tool for publishing students' works (Iannone, 1998). Through word-processing software, students can publish their written texts on their content areas of study in forms such as newspapers, posters, newsletters, and brochures. In addition, the Internet provides an innovative forum for students to publish their written text for audiences in other locations, such as class Web sites, student poetry sites, blogs, and podcasts. Thus, students have authentic purposes for their writing, a proven link to enhance students' motivation. Further examples of how to integrate publishing across the curriculum are provided in Chapter 4.

Accessing Information

The Internet opens doors for teachers and students on all content area topics to easily access a wealth of information. Multimedia information in the form of text, graphics, and sound can be obtained from libraries, businesses, and governmental departments around the world. Many users claim such broad access is the greatest educational strength of the Internet because such access provides extensive sources of information for students, and it assists teachers in developing instructional materials (Descy, 1993, 1994; Tomaiuolo, 1996; Zorn, 1996). One problem is finding the information. You can use several tools to search the Web, such as subject directories like Yahoo!, search engines such as Google, and metasearches such as Vivisimo. In addition, you need to plan how to organize your search and evaluate the quality of search results. These are discussed in Chapter 5.

Of particular interest to teachers is the growing use of WebQuests as a means of accessing information. WebQuests are an inquiry-oriented task or project created in almost any discipline that uses a predefined list of resoures from primarily the World Wide Web, but which also may include textbooks, CD-ROMs, videos, and experts in the field (Dodge, 1995, 1998; Grant, 2002b). Generally, these are interdisiciplinary projects, and because they use a predefined list of resources, students' time is maximized by not having to search for references, and teachers feel secure that students do not visit inappropriate sites. WebQuests focus on using information instead of looking for it (Starr, 2000) and can incorporate collaborative learning. You can find examples on the WebQuest homepage (**http://webquest.org/**). See Figure 3.5.

Communicating and Collaborating

One reason the Internet is such a powerful and exciting tool for teaching content area literacy is that it enables teachers and students to communicate and collaborate in new ways. Expanding beyond individual classrooms, students connect with other schools, experts, and the global community. In particular, the Internet is an exceptional tool for supporting communication and collaboration through project-based learning experiences, publishing students' work, communicating with keypals, fostering discussion groups, and interacting with authors and experts.

○ **Project-Based Learning Experiences.** Essentially, project-based learning experiences are integrated Internet units of study with classrooms around the world (Grant, 2002a, 2000b; Leu & Leu, 1997). This integration of classrooms provides an authentic audience for students' reading and writing.

Figure 3.5 WebQuests, developed by Bernie Dodge and Tom March at San Diego State University, are one instructional strategy to implement integrated learning units and project-based learning.

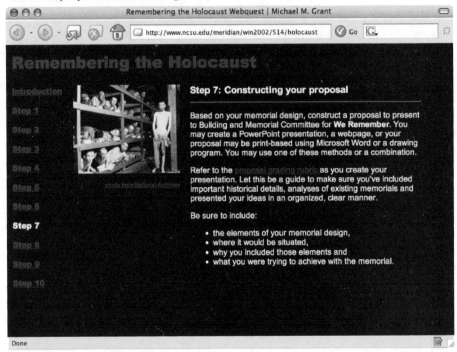

Used with permission from author.

○ **Publishing Students' Works.** Students also use the Internet as a tool for online conferences about their writing, using asynchronous bulletin boards, chat rooms, blogs, and e-mail. By giving and receiving feedback from one another and others on the Web, students engage in process writing and gain responsibility for and ownership of their writing. In addition, many online writing competitions and contests are available. Thus, not only do students publish their work on a classroom home page, but a variety of sites are available on which students can publish. (See Chapter 4 for a list of Web sites.)

○ **Keypals.** Currently, there are numerous classrooms around the world that are engaging in keypal exchanges. Many benefits are associated with keypal projects. Students are engaged in a meaningful and purposeful literacy experience, and they are highly motivated to read their keypals' writing and write to their keypals. A keypal exchange is a natural entrée into studying a different country and gaining insights into a new culture. The following is a sample of popular sites for establishing your keypal relationships: ePals Global Network (**http://www.epals.com/**), (see Figure 3.6); Global SchoolNet Foundation (**http://www.globalschoolnet.org**); Intercultural E-mail Classroom

Figure 3.6   ePals.com is one source for electronic pen pals from across the country and around the world.

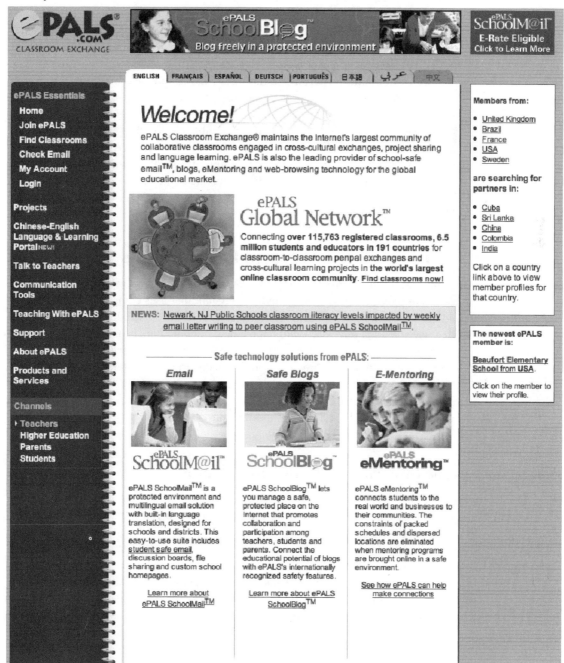

Connections (**http://www.iecc.org/**); and Pitsco KEYPALS (http://www.keypals.com/).

- ◯ **Discussion Groups.** Many teachers and students find great value in having online discussions with people around the world. Students' discussions often focus on books they are reading. Teachers often discuss project ideas and current educational issues.
- ◯ **Authors and Experts.** The Internet affords a unique opportunity for students to seek advice from authors and experts about what they are learning. These discussions can be built around any topic of study. They can be one-time questions or an ongoing collaboration. For examples, visit the Global School House Projects Registry, Kidproject, or Ask an Expert. Wikipedia also may offer an opportunity for students writing on specific topics to have their writing reviewed and augmented by others around the globe.

◯ Facilitating Integrated Literacy Units

Many teachers are currently using integrated literacy units, so the purpose of this section is to provide a model integrated literacy unit that uses computer technology. For additional examples visit **ReadWriteThink.org.** At the outset, this is no way suggests that whatever you have done without the help of computers is obsolete. Rather this is to suggest that computer technology can help you provide integrated literacy units that will give your students more opportunities to integrate their literacy skills, as well as foster critical thinking about content and concepts (Wepner, 1992). The model integrated literacy unit being recommended has several components that need to be planned before the literacy unit is used in your classroom.

The Integrated Literacy Unit Model

Topic: What will be the focus of the unit?

Major Concepts/Goals: What new information do you want students to learn while doing this unit?

Content Areas: Which content areas will be integrated into the unit: reading, writing, social studies, science, math, health?

Audience: With whom will students share their final products: parents, other classes, keypals, senior citizens, siblings, or community citizens?

Purpose/Problem Statement Given to Students: Because the unit focuses on a problem that needs to be solved, when introducing the unit to students on the first day, what will you tell them they are trying to accomplish?

Rationale Given to Students: Why investigate this purpose or problem? When introducing a unit, teachers must explain to students why the unit is important.

Time: How long will the unit last?

Technology Tools: Which technology tools will you use in this unit: database, spreadsheet, word processing, e-mail, Internet, electronic presentations, CD-ROM, Web pages, multimedia, and so forth?

Procedure: What problem-solving activities will students engage in, and how will they complete the activities? Will there be whole-group, small-group, and independent activities?

Assessment/Outcomes: How will you include teacher, self-, and peer evaluation in the unit?

Example of an Integrated Literacy Unit

Following is an example of an integrated literacy unit using the components previously listed.

Topic: Touring the United States.

Major Concepts/Goals: Appreciate geographical and cultural diversity in the United States; learn to manage money; learn to research; examine the relationship of geography to daily life; identify major tourist attractions in the United States; learn how to plan a vacation.

Content Areas: Reading, writing, social studies, science, math in third through eighth grade levels.

Audience: Keypals in schools in other states.

Purpose/Problem Statement Given to Students: What can you learn from your keypals in other schools across the United States that isn't widely known? What are the major attractions in the vicinity of these schools? If you were to visit your keypals, what would you need to consider before going there?

Rationale Given to Students: (Teachers can use the following rationales.) Visiting friends and relatives in faraway places can be fun, but as parents know, a great deal of planning is involved. How much time is to be spent away from home? What are the expenses, such as gas, food, and lodging? What is the distance in miles traveled? What will the weather be like? What do we pack for the trip? These questions, when answered through proper planning, help ensure that a new travel adventure really is exciting—and not frustrating—because, for instance, the traveler packed summer clothes for a December trip to Vermont.

Time: Approximately 3 weeks.

Modified Version of Unit: This unit could be modified by establishing keypals in other countries and making plans to visit those countries.

Technology Tools: Database, spreadsheet, word processing, e-mail, Internet, electronic presentations, printer, CD-ROM.

Procedure: All units have problem-solving activities. Students have to collect data, manipulate the data, analyze the data, and report the data using technology tools. In this unit, students working in small groups will research a specific region of the United States. They will find two or three keypals in schools in states within the region they are researching and make simulated plans to visit them and see local attractions. Students will conduct travel research on the Internet, record expenses, and create a list of places using databases and spreadsheets. The student groups will report their study to the class using an electronic presentation. A word-processed report should be included in a group portfolio.

Assessment/Outcomes: Both teacher and students will develop and use a rubric to assess each group's presentation on its specific region of the United States. In addition, the teacher and students will develop a self-/peer assessment rubric to evaluate individual student contributions during the group project. As a starting point, the following broad rubric for this kind of group project is suggested:

- ◯ 25 percent effort/participation
- ◯ 25 percent data collection
- ◯ 25 percent presentation
- ◯ 25 percent written report

In addition, students can become involved in a peripheral, but important, assessment tactic: Three Stars and a Wish (3SW). After each group makes a presentation, class members write down three things they liked (positive) about the presentation and one thing they wish had happened differently (negative) during the presentation. Each group receives the 3SWs the class writes. The 3SWs are not shared with the class.

Facilitating the Unit Model

The project we have just outlined needs the teacher's facilitation to run smoothly, and teacher facilitation involves proper planning. For instance, students will need to know how to make e-mail contact with schools within the region. The teacher can show students how to use the Internet to make e-mail contact. In addition, students will need guidance in developing questions to ask keypals, so the teacher should lead a brainstorming session at the beginning of the project in which students create a list of generic questions. The teacher also might list projected items for the database and spreadsheet, such as travel time, distances, various expenses, and places to visit. In fact, conducting a class discussion about expenses is a good way to help students calculate the myriad costs of traveling.

As facilitator, the teacher has the responsibility to keep students on track and engaged in activities related to the overriding themes (Wepner, 1993). He or she should ensure that each member of a group has an assignment and makes a contribution to each group session. The teacher also needs to have planned, productive activities for groups that complete their project ahead of other groups. See Candace in Chapter 2's Computer Classroom Snapshot for an example of teacher facilitation.

COMPUTER CLASSROOM LESSONS

Learning About the World Through Keypals

Grade Level: Adaptable for K-8

Objective: The students learn how to write letters and use effective communication. The students learn effective inquiry skills. The students also learn about another country.

Time: 2 hours

Problem to Be Solved: You are planning a trip to a country you do not live in now. Before you go there, you want to know about the people, holidays, etiquette, and customs. Travel brochures tell you some of this information, but you want the information from someone who lives there and is close to your age. What are you to do?

Materials: Computer with Internet access
World map

Steps:

1. Ask students to describe a penpal.
2. Discuss penpals and writing letters in a whole group environment.
3. Use a map of the world, and discuss areas of interest to the students.
4. Ask the students to imagine having penpals or communicating with children in an area of the world that is interesting to them. Discuss these areas.
5. Lead discussion of the similarities and differences in their environment and the environment of the interesting areas. Discuss the people, holidays, and customs of these areas.
6. Introduce the concept of keypals to the students. Keypals are penpals that communicate through e-mail. Discuss how keypals and pen pals are alike and different.
7. Tell the students they will be traveling to a Web site full of students interested in becoming keypals. Ask the students to think about what type of keypals they would like to communicate with.
8. Travel to Pitsco's keypals using this URL: **www.keypals.com**
9. Browse through the information categorized according to age, topics of interest, and collaborative project interests. Choose a group of students to communicate with.
10. Contact the students with an initial class e-mail expressing interest.
11. Decide if the class will compose one e-mail or communicate individually with the students.
12. E-mail the students and wait for responses.
13. Read the responses and enjoy.

Assessment: Students will write a report about the country they have researched.

Bring a Book to Life

Grade Level: Adaptable for K–8

Objective: Students will practice their reading skills by reading *Arthur's Birthday* by Marc Brown. The students will explore the *Arthur's Birthday* CD-ROM to search for hidden objects. Students will enhance their writing skills by writing the directions to a hidden object on a specific page.

Time: 2 hours

Problem to Be Solved: Someone has hidden objects at Arthur's birthday. Can you find them?

Materials: *Arthur's Birthday* by Marc Brown
    Arthur's Birthday CD-ROM (*Living Books*)
    Paper
    Pencils
    Computer

Steps:

1. Read *Arthur's Birthday* by Marc Brown to the class.
2. Discuss setting, characters, problem, and resolution with the students.
3. Introduce the class to the *Arthur's Birthday* CD-ROM. Play the "Read to me" version first.
4. Discuss how the book and CD-ROM are alike and different.
5. Engage the class in the "Let me play" version of the CD-ROM.
6. After reading the text, click on different characters and items on the page. Tell the students that they will be choosing a favorite hidden item to write about.
7. Group the students in pairs.
8. Give the students time to explore the CD-ROM on their own. Assign them a specific page in the CD-ROM.
9. Ask them to find their favorite hidden object. (On each screen of this CD-ROM, there is a hidden party blower with confetti. Students do not have to choose this item. They may select from any of the hidden objects or actions.)
10. Ask the student pairs to plot a course to find their hidden object. You may wish to develop a rubric with the students for this. If not, ask that the students include four or five specific written directions to the object.
11. Have each pair of students exchange directions with another pair of students.
12. Use the CD-ROM to travel to the specific page. Follow the directions to find the hidden object.

Assessment: Develop a rubric with the students for writing the directions to the hidden objects. After exchanging directions and completing the activity, have students share their experiences with writing and following directions. Suggest ways of improving writing and listening skills.

◯ Techno-Teacher Tips

Determining Reading Levels

Traditionally, when educators determined students' independent, instructional, and frustrational reading levels, students were required to read independently and did not receive assistance when they came to unknown words. However, electronic books provide audio assistance in decoding unknown words. This makes it somewhat confusing in determining students' reading levels because the machine, not the teacher, is helping the student. Individualized assessment and instruction software like Accelerated Reader and PLATO track student reading levels. In addition, with Microsoft Word's readability statistics you can check a student's writing level.

◯ Frequently Asked Questions

1. **How do I choose the best software to support print skills?**

   Ernest Balajthy (1998) emphasizes the importance of making sure that the software you select is based on educationally sound practices congruent with how reading is taught today. Although he focuses on struggling readers, his criteria are appropriate for all students:

   1. Reinforces decoding by breaking words into sounds.
   2. Reinforces decoding using meaning cues.
   3. Reinforces decoding using knowledge of sentence structure.
   4. Provides reinforcement of letter/sound relationships.
   5. Strengthens structural analysis skills (i.e., use of affixes, word parts, word families).
   6. Strengthens automatic sight vocabulary.
   7. Provides a variety of supported practice for skills presented.

2. **I have been using integrated units in my classroom for the last five years. I'm not sure how to start using the computer in my units. Do you have any suggestions?**

   Ask yourself about the potential ways to begin:

   ◯ "Are my students producing a piece of writing?" If so, have them word process their stories.
   ◯ "Will my students share their writing or other information they have learned during the unit?" The Internet provides many ways for students to share their work with the outside world. For instance, they can create a chat room or in-house presentations using tools such as electronic presentations or multimedia authoring.
   ◯ "Are my students engaged in collecting information on the specific type of study?" The Internet is an excellent resource. In addition to having students read textbooks, tradebooks, magazines, and the like, introduce

them to Web sites related to your type of study. You will be amazed by the students' motivation and excitement.

3. I'm afraid that when I teach literacy using computer, I will not cover all the literacy skills my students need. How do I make sure I'm covering everything?

It is important to be aware of your local and state grade-level scope and sequence guidelines, as well as the National Language Arts Standards. The computer is a tool that will help you teach the students, and it in no way changes what you expect them to learn. How your students go about learning and how they demonstrate their learning will be what changes.

◯ References

Allington, R. L. (1983). Fluency: The neglected reading goal in reading instruction. *The Reading Teacher*, *36*, 556–561.

Allington, R. L. (2002). What I've learned about effective reading instruction from a decade of studying exemplary elementary classroom teachers. *Phi Delta Kappan*, *83*, 740–747.

Anderson-Inman, L., & Horney, M. A. (Ed.). (1998). *Transforming text for at-risk readers*. Mahwah, NJ: Lawrence Erlbaum Associates.

Armbruster, B. B., Lehr, F., & Osborn, J. (2001). *Put reading first: The research building block for teaching children to read*. Kindergarten through grade 3. Washington, D. C.: National Institute for Literacy.

Baker, A. B., & Torgeson, J. K. (1995). An evaluation of computer-assisted instruction in phonological awareness with below average readers. *Journal of Education Computing Research, 13,* 89–103.

Bertelsen, C. D., Kauffman, S., Howard, K., & Cochran, L. L. (2003, July/August). Web watch: Phonics web sites. *Reading Online, 7*(1). Available: http://www.readingonline.org/electronic/elec-index.asp? HREF-webwatch/phonics/index.htm

Dahlquist, Lori. (2002). Technology and phonemic awareness: A step toward literacy. *Closing the Gap.*

Descy, D. E. (1993). Reviewer. Teleclass teaching (Book Review). *International Journal of Instructional Media, 20*(1), 84–85

Descy, D. E., (1994, November/December). Online Internet resources. *TechTrends, 39,* 13–14.

Dodge, B. (1995, May 5, 1997). Some thoughts about WebQuests. Retrieved August 7, 2001, from http://edweb.sdsu.edu/courses/edtect596/about webquests.html

Dodge, B. (1998, June 22–24). WebQuests: A strategy for scaffolding higher level learning. Paper presented at the National Educational Computing Conference, San Diego, CA.

Doty, D. E., Popwell, S. R., & Byers, G. O. (2001) Interactive CD-ROM Storybooks and young readers' reading comprehension. *Journal of Research on Computing in Education, 33*(4), 374–84.

Grant, M. M. (2002a) *Individual differences in constructionist learning environments: Qualitative inquiry into computer mediated learning artifacts*. Unpublished doctoral dissertation. The University of Georgia, Athens, GA.

Grant, M. M. (2002b). Getting a grip on project-based learning: Theory, cases and recommendations. *Meridian: A Middle School Computer Technologies Journal, 5*(Winter). Available: http://www.ncsu.edu/meridian/win 2002/514/index.html

Harste, J. C. (1994). *Curriculum for the Millenium. Proceedings of the First International Conference on Language and Literacy*. Melbourne, Australia: Australian Reading Association.

Helt, M. (2003). Writing the book on online literature circles. *Learning and Leading with Technology, 30*(7), 28–31.

Hiebert, E. H., & Fisher, C. W. (2002, May). *Text matters in developing fluent reading*. Paper presented at the annual meeting of the International Reading Association, San Francisco, CA.

Iannone, P. V. (1998). Just beyond the horizon: Writing-centered literacy activities for traditional and electronic contexts. *The Reading Teacher, 51,* 438–43.

International Reading Association. (2001). *Integrating literacy and technology in the curriculum: A position statement of the international reading association.* Newark, DE.

Johnson, D. (2003). Choosing the right books for struggling readers. *Learning and Leading with Technology, 31*(1), 22–27.

Johnson, D. (2001). *Vocabulary in the elementary and middle school.* Boston, Allyn & Bacon.

Johnson, D., & Zufall, L. (2004). Web watch—Not just for kids anymore: WebQuests for professional development. *Reading Online, 7*(5). Available: http://www.readingonline.org/electronic/elec-index.asp? HREF=webwatch/webquests/index.html

Juel, C. (1988). Learning to read and write: A longitudinal study of fifty-four children from first through fourth grades. *Journal of Educational Psychology, 80,* 437–447.

Kajder, S., & Bull, G. (2003). Scaffolding for struggling students: Reading and writing with blogs. *Learning and Leading with Technology, 31*(2), 31–35.

Kadjer, S. & Swenson, J. (2004). Digital images in the language arts classroom. *Learning and Leading with Technology, 31*(2), 31–35.

Karchmer, R. A. (2001). The journey ahead: Thirteen teachers report how the Internet influences literacy and literacy instruction in their K–12 classrooms. *Reading Research Quarterly, 36,* 442–466.

Kuhn, M. R., & Stahl, S. A. (2003). Fluency: A review of developmental and remedial practices. *Journal of Educational Psychology, 95,* 3–21.

Labbo, L. D. (2005). Books and computer response activities that support literacy development. *The Reading Teacher, 59*(3), 288–92.

Labbo, L. D. (2004). From morning message to digital morning message: Moving from the tried and true to the new. *The Reading Teacher, 58*(8), 782–785.

Labbo, L. D. (2004). Author's computer chair [Technology in Literacy department]. *The Reading Teacher, 57*(7), 688–691.

Labbo, L. D., Sprague, L., Montero, M. K., & Font, G. (2000). Connecting a computer center to themes, literature, and kindergartners' literacy needs. *Reading Online, 4*(1). Available: http://www.readingonline.org/electronic/labbo/

Lalley, Bob. (2001). Teaching children to read using technology. *Technology Horizons In Education Journal Online.*

Leu, D. J., Jr., Karchmer, R., & Leu, D. D. (1999). The Miss Rumphius effect: Envisionments for literacy and learning that transform the Internet. *The Reading Teacher, 52,* 636–642.

Leu, D. J., Jr., & Leu, D. D. (1997). Teaching with the Internet: Lessons from the classroom. Norwood, MA: Christopher.

Lewin, C. (1997). Evaluating talking books: Ascertaining the effectiveness of multiple feedback modes and tutoring techniques. In L. Kinzer, K. A. Hinchman, & D. J. Leu (Eds.), *Inquiries in literacy theory and practice: Forty-sixth yearbook of the National Reading Conference.* Chicago: National Reading Conference.

Lopez, S. (2000). Cat in the hat and all that. *Time Magazine, 156*(17), 6.

Moxley, R., Warash, B., Coffman, G., Brinton, K. & Concannon, K. (1997). Writing development using computers in a class of three-year-olds. *Journal of Computing in Childhood Education, 8*(2/3), 133–164.

National Council of Teachers of English & International Reading Association. (1996). *Standards for the English language arts.* Urbana, IL: Author.

National Institute of Child Health and Human Development, (2000). *Report of the National Reading Panel. Teaching children to read: An evidence-based assessment of the scientific research literature on reading and its implications for reading instruction* (NIH Publication No. 00-4769). Washington, D.C.: U.S. Department of Education.

Osborn, J., Lehr, F., Hiebert, E. (2003). *A focus on fluency.* Regional Educational Laboratory at Pacific Resources for Education and Learning, Michigan, U.S. Department of Education.

Oravec, J. A. (2002). Bookmarking the world: Weblog applications in education. *Journal of Adolescent & Adult Literacy, 45*(7), 616–621.

Partnership for Reading (2001). *Put reading first: Helping your child learn to read.* Washington, D.C.: The Partnership for Reading.

Pinnell, G. S., Pikulski, J. J., Wixson, K. K., Campbell, J. R., Gough, P. B., & Beatty, A. S. (1995). *Listening to children read aloud: Oral fluency.* Washington, D.C.: National Center for Education Statistics, U.S. Department of Education. Retrieved July 10, 2006, from nces.ed.gov/pubs95/web/95762.asp

Poock, M. M. (1998). The Accelerated Reader: An analysis of the software's strenghts and weaknesses and how it can be used to its best potential [review]. *School Library Media Activities Monthly, 14*(9), 32–3.

Rankin-Erickson, J., Wood, L, & Beukelman, D. (2003). Early computer literacy: First graders use the "talking" computer. *Reading Improvement, 40*(3), 132–144.

Reinking, D. (1992). Differences between electronic and printed texts: An agenda for research. *Journal of Educational Multimedia and Hypermedia, 1*(1), 11–24.

Reinking, D. (1994). Electronic literacy (Perspective in Reading Research No. 4). Athens, GA: National Reading Research Center, Universities of Georgia and Maryland.

Reinking, D., & Rickman, S. S. (1990). The effects of computer-mediated texts on the vocabulary learning and comprehension of intermediate grade readers. *Journal of Reading Behavior, 22,* 395–411.

Reitsman, P. (1998). Reading practice for beginners: Effects of guided reading, reading while-listening, and independent reading with computer-based speech feedback. *Reading Research Quarterly, 23,* 219–235.

Samuels, S. J. (1979). The method of repeated readings. *The Reading Teacher, 32,* 403–408.

Samuels, S. J. (2002). Reading fluency: Its development and assessment. In A. E. Farstrup & S. J. Samuels (Eds.), *Comprehending oral and written language* (pp. 243–270). New York: Academic Press.

Scott, T., & Harding, D. (2004). Splicing video into the writing process. *Learning and Leading with Technology, 32*(1), 26–31.

Shanahan, T. (2002, November). *A sin of the second kind: The neglect of fluency instruction and what we can do about it.* PowerPoint presentation at A Focus on Fluency Forum, San Francisco, CA. Available at www.prel.org/programs/rel/fluency/stahl.ppt

Snow, C. (2002). *Reading for understanding: Toward an R & D program in reading comprehension.* Santa Monica, CA: RAND.

Starr, L. (2000) Creating a WebQuest: It's easier than you think! Retrieved August 7, 2001, from http://edweb.sdsu.edu/courses/edtect596/aboutwebquests.html

Tomaiuolo, N. G., & Packer, J. G. (1996).An analysis of Internet search engines: Assessment of over 200 search queries. *Computers in Libraries, 16*(6), 58–62.

Torgesen, J. K., Rashotte, C. A., Alexander, A. W., Alexander, J., & McFee, K. (2002, November). *The challenge of fluent reading for older children with reading difficulties.* PowerPoint presentation at A Focus on Fluency Forum, San Francisco, CA. Available at www.prel.org/programs/rel/fluency/torgesen.ppt

Viani, N. (2003-2004). The right write site. *Learning and Leading with Technology, 31*(4), 24–27.

Vygotsky, L. S. (1962). *Thought and language.* Cambridge, MA: MIT Press. Adams, M. J. (2002, November). *The promise of speech recognition.* PowerPoint presentation at A Focus on Fluency Forum Available at www.prel.org/programs/rel/fluency/adams/ppt

Wepner, S. (1992). Using technology with content area units. *The Reading Teacher, 45*(8), 644–646.

Wepner, S. (1993). Technology and thematic units: An elementary example on Japan. *The Reading Teacher, 46*(5), 442–445.

Wise, B., Olson, R., & Treiman, R. (1990). Subsyllabic units in computerized reading instruction: Onset-rime vs. postvowel segmentation. Journal of Experimental Child Psychology, *49,* 1–19.

Worthy, J. & Broaddus, K. (2002). Fluency beyond the primary grades:From group performance to silent, independent reading. *The Reading Teacher, 55*(4), 334–343.

Worthy, J. & Prater, K. (2002). I thought about it all night: Readers' theatre for reading fluency and motivation. *The Reading Teacher, 56*(3), 294–297.

Zeno, S. M., Ivens, S. H., Millard, R. T., & Duvvuri, R. (1995). *The educator's word frequency guide.* New York: Touchstone Applied Science Associates, Inc.

Zorn, P., et. al., Advanced Web searching: tricks of the trade [cover story]. *Online (Weston, Conn.) 20*(May/June 1996), 14–16ff.

Chapter 4

Teaching Students to Write and Publish with Computers

*B*ill, a student in Miss Harmon's fifth-grade class, has just talked with Group 1, the Harmonizers, about their contributions to the class book of poetry. Just before he leaves, Jamal asks, "So what you're saying is that we—our group—have to get all our poems on one of our flash drives to you by this Friday?"

"That's right," Bill responds, adding, "I just want one flash drive, rather than trying to fiddle with 17 different ones. One flash drive per group. That makes it easier for my group, because we have to make a draft copy of the entire book for peer review."

"But what if the word processing program I'm using at home doesn't fit the one the rest of the group is using?" Sarah asks with some concern in her voice.

"Sarah," Bill responds, "remember how we discussed in class that we'll save our work as Rich Text Format—that's RTF—to take care of all the different programs you have at home. Remember, you can do that under " 'Save as' . . ."

"We've got everything taken care of," Barbara notes, adding, "I'll help Sarah."

"Any other questions?" Bill waits a moment, and seeing that Barbara has things under control, says, "OK, I'll look for your flash drive this Friday."

Bill then moves to Group 2, the Poe Poets, to confirm the delivery of their drive in the proper format on Friday.

◯ Getting Started with Process Writing and Publishing

In the scenario you've just read, the time Bill spent with Group 1 was devoted to one step in planning a class publication. No writing was produced. No instruction on how to write was given. Yet the time students spend in planning classroom publications is critical to the success of those publications. Indeed, the amount of planning that is needed to produce a group publication—especially if the students take responsibility for the publication—is an added dimension to the writing process.

Any group or classroom publication begins with students' creating written products. How to help students create those products can take two very different approaches. Maybe you're attempting to help your students learn to write by applying the old behavioral model—assigning five-paragraph themes, requiring students to produce a detailed outline of the theme before any text is created, and forbidding any useful help from peers (that would be cheating, after all). That's one approach, and unfortunately, the behavioral model still persists in many classrooms today.

Many college professors are stuck with the legacy of students who have been taught to write according to the behavioral model. Our experience as classroom teachers, college professors, and authors of this book leads us to make the following observations:

◯ The behavioral model makes a poor fit with the way people really write (Forman, 1992; Galegher, Kraut, & Egido, 1990; Odell & Goswami, 1985; Spilka, 1993) and does very little to help students create written products typical of academic or work settings. When was the last time you read a five-paragraph theme in a newspaper, magazine, pamphlet, or journal article? In college, we only read them when our new students replicated those artificial middle-school and high-school norms (often unsuccessfully) to fulfill writing assignments.

◯ If students learn to write according to the behavioral model, they do so despite the model. For instance, some students confide in us that they outline their paper after writing it, even though they produced a feeble outline at the beginning of the writing assignment because they were required to.

◯ Chapter 5 covers the subject of students' nonlinear methods of organizing the information they access from texts (Shen, 1996). The organization of writing works in a similar fashion: The straight-line behavioral method does not take into account the experiential complexities of the individual writer. Each person works from a unique perspective and is perfectly capable of organizing a composition from a nonbehaviorist set of parameters.

In this chapter, we provide an overview of the writing process leading to classroom publications. We begin by providing a snapshot of a classroom publishing activity. Then we explain the writing process, discuss why you should incorporate classroom publishing activities into your literacy curriculum, give instructions on how to use a variety of classroom publishing activities, and discuss issues associated with those activities.

◥ Computer Classroom Snapshot

Context

My name is John Bauer, and I was part of a team-teaching research project involving a sixth-grade class at Campus Elementary School, which is operated under the auspices of the University of Memphis's College of Education and a senior-level college class. The sixth-grade class was taught by Judith Thomson, who had agreed to allow her class to become the "students" of UM seniors about to graduate into the teaching profession. The college class was taught by Professor Becky Anderson, who also wrote the syllabus, and me. A requirement for the college seniors was that they spend 10 hours in an elementary-school setting. The college class, numbering some 28 students, divided itself into seven groups of four, and the 22 sixth graders were assigned as equally as possible to these groups. Each college group, then, became the collective "teachers" of their younger counterparts.

In the abstract, the goal for both sets of students was to learn how computer technology can be an indispensable tool for teaching and learning content literacy: the college students on how to apply such techniques in future classes; the sixth graders on how to use the technology to do research, how to read data, and how to write results.

What I Did and Why

The project was run this way: Each group was to research a topic and to write a chapter for inclusion in a book entitled *A Young Person's Guide to the City of Memphis*. The book features chapters on history, geography, famous personalities, sports, tourism, and entertainment. For a one-hour time slot each week, the sixth graders met with their new sets of teachers, who were armed with lesson plans designed to guide activities in the most productive manner. After initial brainstorming and planning sessions, the groups did their field research, which for the most part consisted of accessing Internet sites using the university's computer labs. Further computer use entailed group members corresponding with each other via e-mail during the week.

The end product notwithstanding, the weekly hour each class spent with each other was the critical period for the project. Could the seniors get the kids to work? Would they all get along? Would there be an even division of responsibilities? Would lesson plans be conscientiously prepared so that members knew where they were headed? Could sixth graders maintain a focus serious enough to be important contributing members? We observed the group dynamic closely and arrived at a resounding "yes" for an answer. The college seniors enjoyed working with the kids immensely, it being the one hour they felt they were gaining good hands-on field experience working with classroom kids. The sixth graders saw the hour as a break from the norm, a chance to enter the new and lofty realm of the university setting, something they could be proud of in front of peers and family. In addition, they

(continued)

used their youthful enthusiasm to attack computer problems and were excited that their work might be part of a published book. Observing this group dynamic at work was for me an unparalleled educational experience. The entire exercise was stretching the outer limits of content literacy in terms of a constructivist design in a real-world setting. What the sixth graders learned was clear: how to work as a team to set goals, perform tasks, and produce a viable end product in a given period of time. They learned the value of Internet technology as a resource tool and that e-mail communication can be used as a valuable link to team members.

What I Learned

The college learning coefficient was relative to the effort and enthusiasm the college seniors put into the project. It was, of course, a class assignment, and some were typically not flexible enough to succeed in a nontraditional setting such as this. Thus, they allowed stronger team members to take charge. It was clear they all learned that there are options when integrating technology into literacy instruction, particularly if they initiated similar techniques as new elementary school teachers.

As I look back on the class, I see certain important restrictions on this particular model but also endless possibilities as well. To begin with, requisite to the design is the location of a college conveniently close to an upper elementary or middle school, since busing over long distances poses logistical difficulties. Second, upfront cooperation between the college and school administrators, teachers, and most likely the school board may be hard to establish, but it is nonetheless an absolute necessity. Third, the grade-school teacher must be thoroughly involved with and in favor of the project. It is possible to have a school nearby whose teachers are reluctant to participate. Fourth, effective motivational talks to both sets of students are needed at the onset so that they can "buy into" the program and make it work. Other factors that may affect outcomes are availability of labs, work areas for groups, and student and/or teacher (college student) absenteeism.

On the other hand, an important advantage of the model is that it can be put to use in a grade school class without the guidance of a college class. Nothing prevents, for example, a fifth- or sixth-grade teacher from accomplishing the same goals in his or her own school setting. Most schools today are equipped with adequate lab facilities to make it happen. In this case, however, the workload in terms of planning and execution falls entirely upon the classroom teacher—not an undaunting task, but one that can be a completely rewarding experience. Even the "publishing" of a book using a school copier can involve students at divergent learning levels, and topics can be tailored to a more localized level than the model's use of a citywide design.

The whole experience of working with the class for this project broadened my outlook on educational possibilities. The flexible nature of the concept allows for success within different parameters. One can pick and choose different elements of the design to fit a number of disparate circumstances. In any case, the use of Internet research and team collaboration on a written product remain the important constants, and these are what drive the design and makes it particularly relevant as schools function in a technological millennium.

○ Understanding the Process Approach to Writing

Imagine yourself taking a graduate class at a local university. The professor enters and announces, "This evening you are going to complete an in-class writing assignment: Explain in lay terms what $e = mc^2$ means. You have 15 minutes to brainstorm, half an hour to write a draft, 15 minutes to discuss your draft with a peer, half an hour to revise your draft, 15 minutes for a formal peer critique, and half an hour to complete a final draft of your paper for a grade." The professor smiles and asks, "Any questions?" What would you feel at that point?

We'd feel trapped, and our first question would be "What does $e = mc^2$ mean?" As educated adults—teachers even!—we should know how to explain that famous formula to a lay audience, but we don't; we don't really know what the formula means. And that's a real problem if the professor expects us to be successful in completing the writing assignment.

Although we may be part of the problem because we didn't study our science well enough, the real problem is the professor's approach to the writing process. Even though she did follow part of a process approach, she failed to understand that a teacher can't use part of the process approach and expect the entire process to work. She has to use the entire process approach (Speck, 2000), which includes letting students write on things that they know about and are interested in (Calkins, 1990, 1986; Graves, 1994). This does not mean, by the way, that students cannot be challenged to learn things they don't know much about and perhaps don't find very interesting. Rather, it means students go through all stages of the writing process as outlined in Figure 4.1: (1) prewriting activities such as brainstorming, (2) writing a rough draft, (3) revising the draft, (4) peer reviewing the draft, (5) revising the draft based on peer reviewers' comment, (6) editing the draft, (7) proofreading the draft, and (8) publishing the completed work. It is important to note that although the stages of the writing process are presented in a linear fashion, in reality writing is a recursive process. For instance, a student may be at the editing stage of a draft and determine that the conclusion needs to be changed and thus will return to the prewriting stage.

Returning to the physics assignment, we've already stated that we don't know much about the formula $e = mc^2$ (and, to be honest, our interest level in that formula is not very high), but if we are aware of a reason why we should know it, we're willing to learn. We're willing to have someone explain the formula to us, answer our questions, work through our uninformed ideas about physics, and get us to a point where we can write sensibly about $e = mc^2$. Then we'd be on the road to fulfilling the professor's assignment. But until we have knowledge about something—not assumed knowledge, that is, the knowledge the professor assumes we have—we're not prepared to write the kind of paper she wants. In fact, even gaining knowledge about something includes forms of writing—lists of questions, notes from readings, thumbnail outlines—that make visible the issues we need to investigate and provide a record of the bits and pieces of knowledge we are gaining as we work toward fulfilling a writing assignment that can be useful to readers both inside and outside the classroom.

Figure 4.1   Stages of the Writing Process.

How to Integrate Process Writing into the Curriculum

- **Brainstorming:** Helping students come up with ideas and narrowing those ideas so that students can write a focused paper.
- **Drafting:** Scheduling time for students to prepare multiple drafts of a project.
- **Revising:** Showing students how to shape their writing to meet the needs of particular audiences.
- **Peer reviewing:** Providing writers with real audiences (their peers) and teaching peers how to respond to writers' writing, while not correcting grammar, mechanics, and spelling.
- **Revising again:** Showing students how to sort through peer response and use what's left to prepare a "final" draft.
- **Editing:** Teaching students how to help each other correct mistakes in grammar, mechanics, and spelling.
- **Proofreading:** Comparing the next to last draft with the "last" draft to catch errors that were supposed to be fixed but were not.
- **Preparing presentation copy for readers:** Printing the final copy so that it can be read, shared (or published), and evaluated.

The writing process extends to the entire curriculum—from using writing to explore topics, to completing writing assignments for a variety of audiences (Fulwiler & Young, 1982). As teachers, then, we need to use writing throughout the literacy curriculum and with other literacy projects, such as keeping journals for reading assignments and constructing writing projects that fit with course content. But we need to allow time for students to use the writing process to complete those assignments that are published for an outside audience. It is important to remember that process writing is not something that is simply added to the literacy curriculum; it must be integrated, infused, or stirred into the curriculum.

Infusion means more than just putting A into B. We could drop a cube of sugar into a hot bowl of chili, but the sugar wouldn't be infused until we stir it in. Similarly, writing must be stirred into the curriculum so that the curriculum cannot be separated from it. Indeed, the literacy curriculum is composed of writing and reading and speaking and listening. Take them all away and there is no curriculum. Take even one away and the curriculum is incomplete.

Teacher's Role as Facilitator in the Writing Process

Chapter 1 covers the constructivist classroom, in which students take an active, not passive, role in their education. We emphasize again the need for such a classroom when we consider integrating writing into the curriculum. The focus of the constructivist classroom is student-centered learning, not teacher-dispensed knowledge. This does not mean that teachers should never present students with background material for a topic, suggest ideas for writing assignments, or respond to students' concerns about their success in meeting requirements for a writing assignment. Teachers should do all those and more, but they should perform their teaching role in the spirit of being a facilitator rather than an authority figure who provides answers to questions (Speck, 1998).

In the facilitator role, teachers have a great deal of control in shaping the classroom so that students feel comfortable exploring ideas. The teacher, as a facilitator, provides a flexible structure within which students learn about limits but are not merely passive receptors of knowledge.

Part of the answer to the question about how to integrate writing into the classroom has nothing to do with technology directly. Teachers can be facilitators without computers. As DeGroff (1990) notes, "It is teachers' beliefs about writing and writing with computers, rather than the technology itself, that makes a difference in how instruction proceeds" (p. 570). Labbo, Reinking, and McKenna (1995) also confirmed this finding in a case study on incorporating the computer into kindergarten—teachers used computers according to their philosophy about how children become literate. Integrating writing into the literacy curriculum has nothing to do with skill-and-drill exercises, whether used with or without a computer.

Abandoning Skill-and-Drill

Writing is not a matter of identifying parts of speech, filling in the proper verb forms in isolated sentences or paragraphs, or identifying the subject and verb in a sentence by putting two lines under the subject and one line under the verb. Such an approach is counterproductive because the focus is on grammar, a technical aspect of language analysis. Indeed, a student may accurately identify subjects and verbs and still not be able to write something that makes sense to an audience. Likewise, a student may not be able to identify parts of speech and still be a good communicator in writing. Skill-and-drill exercises promote one sort of ability, and writing promotes another.

When language-arts teachers truly understand the difference between those two types of abilities, they change the way they teach. They realize that using skill-and-drill exercises as a way to promote writing may be counterproductive to students' ability to write. Why? Because the time a teacher spends on skill-and-drill takes away from the time a teacher can spend helping students learn how to write. Of course, certain standardized tests, including state-mandated instruments, use multiple-choice questions about writing as a way to test students' writing ability, so teachers might wonder why they shouldn't teach skill-and-drill to help students prepare for those tests. There are several reasons.

Teachers should not confuse helping students prepare for such a standardized writing test with actually helping students learn how to write. A multiple-choice test on writing requires students to provide knowledge *about* writing; it does not ask students to demonstrate their writing ability. The scores from such a test reveal nothing about a student's ability to write. This type of test measures the ability to identify language features, and it is not at all clear that a student's ability to identify language features has much relationship to his or her ability to write serviceable prose (Speck, 2002). Skill-and-drill is not a productive way to integrate writing into the literacy curriculum, whether the skill-and-drill takes the form of a pencil-and-paper test or a computer test.

Reasons for Integrating Computers into the Writing Curriculum

If skill-and-drill should be discarded, how can teachers incorporate computers into the mentoring process regarding writing? We will answer that question after we address teachers' possible objections to joining computers and writing. After all, if teachers don't understand why computers should be integrated into the writing curriculum, then they probably won't see any sense in committing themselves to such integration. For instance, a teacher might ask, "Why must I use technology to infuse writing into my classroom? I really don't have time enough to do what I'm supposed to do without getting involved in technology."

The standard answer to that question is this: "Everything is moving toward computers. Computers already have made a great impact on our lives, and that impact will only increase in the years ahead." This answer, which reflects common wisdom, is insufficient because it assumes that simply because something is, people should accept it. Computers are only a tool. They are not a panacea, even if they have become well entrenched in today's world. Instead, we suggest four practical reasons why computers are useful in integrating writing into the language-arts classroom.

1. **Computers allow flexibility.** The teacher can encourage students to take chances with their writing because the computer allows so much flexibility in deleting, moving, and correcting text (Macarthur, 1988).
2. **Computers make revising easier.** Notice we didn't say *easy*. Revising is hard work, but with the computer it is easier than with a typewriter or a pencil and paper. Students don't have to take the intermediate step of writing something out before going to the keyboard. And once they have a document in a file, they can revise it—correcting misspellings, fixing a sentence that doesn't sound right, changing margins, cutting, and pasting—without having to retype the entire document (Baumbach, Christopher, Fasimpaur, & Oliver, 2004). Common tools in word processors, such as tracking changes by different authors or versions and commenting, make editing easier (see Figure 4.2).
3. **Computers widen the concept of audience.** Traditionally, students have written for teachers. Of course teachers are good audiences, but we are only one type of audience; students will have to write for various types of audiences throughout their lives, so we need to provide them with opportunities to write for authentic purposes (Butcheri & Hammond, 1994; Maring, Wiseman, & Myers, 1997; Smede, 1995; Smith, 1995). This means that students need to learn how to write for the audiences they will encounter after their schooling is complete: parents, colleagues, subordinates, bosses, friends, clients, the general public. According to many researchers (Atwell, 1998; Calkins, 1986; Cohen & Riel, 1989; Graves, 1994), when real audiences are involved, students' writing has greater depth because students pay closer attention to content, detail, and clarity. Thus, writing assignments

Figure 4.2   Both the Track Changes and Comments features in Microsoft Word can support peer and teacher editing.

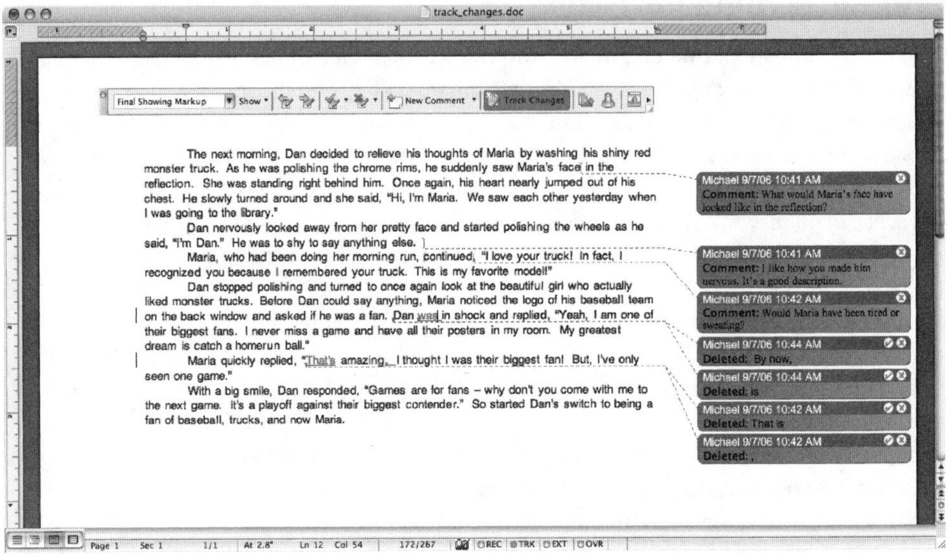

Microsoft product screenshot reprinted with permission from Microsoft Corporation.

should target a variety of audiences. Also, if computers are linked to the Internet, students have lots of opportunities to write for all kinds of audiences, especially using e-mail (e.g., Sullivan, 1998).

4. **Computers raise the stakes on what it means to produce professional-looking documents.** Computers help you show students what a professional document looks like. When kindergarten students construct books using the computer, they develop models of professional documents that can be reinforced throughout their schooling. Part of our job as teachers is to prepare students to be successful employees and citizens, and one aspect of that preparation is to learn that how a document looks has an impact—negative or positive—on the way others read it. Perception is important. After all, even in the elementary grades, a scrawled assignment generally gets a lower grade than a cleanly typed copy of the same assignment (Fuller, 1988; Soloff, 1973).

⊙ Extending the Writing Process to Classroom Publishing

Now we transition to a discussion of classroom publishing by analyzing two types of classroom publishing, traditional and electronic, although both types use electronic media. By "traditional publishing," we mean the production of paper products of students'

work, emulating traditional book and journal publishing. By "electronic publishing," we mean that students make their work available in electronic form, perhaps even creating a Web site so that their work is published on the Internet. Before discussing each type of publishing, we provide reasons why classroom publishing is a useful pedagogical tool.

The major purposes for publishing students' writing are to help students go through the entire writing process and to provide audiences for student writing. When we discussed the writing process, we noted that the process culminates in a written product. Too often, however, students prepare an individual "final" draft for grading, a draft that has yet to undergo the publishing process. That is, either students do not have the opportunity for their individual works to go through the publishing process or students do not have the experience of compiling their works into a cohesive unit, such as a book or magazine. Working with others to publish an individual text and creating a book or magazine made up of peers' texts can give students insights into the entire process of text production that they do not receive when they prepare an individual paper.

In particular, literature on collaborative writing promotes both coauthored works (Comstock, 1993; Long & Bulgarella, 1985; McEachern, 1986; Tsujimoto, 1988; Yanushefski, 1988) and writing projects that include collaborative production of a text composed of students' individual texts (Angeletti, 1993; Doolittle, 1991; Marzano, 1990; Music, 1988; Paeth, 1996; Vincent, 1993). Participation in the development of a composite text mirrors the types of writing activities students will do when they leave school and become employed. In fact, collaborative writing, including the production of books or magazines of students' writing, is not limited to the workplace. Increasingly in higher education, students are asked to participate in collaborative groups to prepare written products, such as reports for engineering classes and research papers for classes in the social sciences. So when K–8 teachers introduce their students to collaborative writing projects, including collaborative construction of books and magazines, they are preparing their students for greater success not only in business and industry, but also in future educational endeavors (Speck, 2002).

Another reason for publishing student writing is because a published book or magazine provides a tangible product that can attract a wider audience beyond the students' classmates and teacher, emphasizing the authenticity of writing we discussed earlier. For instance, parents, grandparents, siblings, friends outside of school, keypals, and a host of other people can have access to the final draft of any given project. A major purpose of writing is to communicate with others; for writing aimed at a general audience, the more readers the better.

In addition, the possibility of more feedback (including praise) is increased when more readers have the opportunity to experience the students' writing. As writers receive more reader responses, such feedback has the potential to teach the value of writing to various audiences. In fact, authentic reader responses may have much greater value than classroom lectures.

Of course, the assumption is that readers will respond in helpful ways. Readers, especially those with a filial relationship to the writer, may give more praise to the writer than the finished text merits. Although the literature on praising writers strongly promotes such cheerleading (Dragga, 1988; Zak, 1990) and although affirmative responses to writers can be a powerful motivator for writing again, it is important to note that helpful response includes more than praise. As a teacher, therefore, you not only have to model a range of responses to students' writing, but you also have to teach students how to respond to peers' writing so that the writer wants to write again, but even better next time. See Figure 4.3 for a process for teaching successful response to writing.

Teaching readers how to help writers improve their work is particularly important when teachers use the publishing process in their classes because the publication of student work raises the bar on quality. When a book or magazine is available for those outside the classroom to read, the quality of learning and teaching becomes public in ways that writing limited to the classroom is not. Thus, teachers have an obligation to prepare students for the higher stakes involved in giving wider audiences access to their written products.

◯ Traditional Classroom Publishing

The traditional publishing forms include books, newspapers, newsletters, and brochures. You can use these traditional publishing forms for a variety of projects. For instance, let's talk about using books in the classroom. Your students may be composing an "All About Me" book, and you decide to have them interview a family member who grew up at least 30 years ago. You lead the class in brainstorming interview questions (e.g., "Where did you live?" "What was your school like?" "How much did a loaf of bread or a gallon of milk cost?" "What did you do for recreation?"). Depending on the age of the students, you or one of the students can use the word processor to type the final questions and make a copy for each student to use for the interviews. Each student can conduct the

Figure 4.3   Process for Teaching Successful Response to Writing.

1. Create effective assignments so that students know what audiences they are expected to address. Effective response depends on identifying the audience for a given piece of writing.
2. Ask students to analyze audiences for their writing. For instance, you can prompt students to analyze their audiences by asking, "Who would want to read what you are writing?" "What kind of people might be interested in your topic?" "How old would a person need to be to understand what you are writing about?" "What would a person need to know to understand what you are describing?"
3. Model response by asking questions and making statements. When responding to students' writing in writing groups or in student-teacher conferences, you can say, "I'm confused. Why did the toy bear lose his ear?" "I'm interested in knowing more about why Simon decided to leave home." "Would your audience understand what you're writing about when you use computer terms?"
4. Train students in ways of responding effectively. Modeling effective response is important, but students also need guidelines such as "The purpose of responding to your peer's writing is to help the peer revise that writing. This means that you *do not* want to argue with your peer. For instance, you do not want to say, 'I don't understand this, and you're a bad writer.' Rather, you want to say, 'I don't understand this and here is why I don't understand it.' Whether the peer takes your suggestions or not is a decision the peer has to make. You also *do not* want to say, 'Wonderful' or 'Terrible!' Neither one of those helps a person revise. What exactly was wonderful? What exactly in the writing caused you to think it was terrible? Tell the writer what the problem is without telling the writer that his or her writing is terrible. You *do* want to say what you like about the writing and why you like it and what could help the writing become stronger (what needs to be added or deleted). In short, *do* say positive things (including what could help the writer improve the piece of writing) in a positive way, and *do not* say negative things in a negative way. Focus on the writing, not the writer."
5. Construct critique sheets that reinforce the instructions you give students. A critique sheet could ask students to identify the main point of a piece of writing (the thesis); to point out a particularly strong image or metaphor; to suggest two ways to make the piece of writing stronger; to cite one or two errors in grammar, mechanics, or spelling; to identify the audience(s) for the piece of writing; and so on.
6. Determine which group of students in the class does a good job of critiquing, and ask them to model their critiquing in front of the class. Alternatively, you could ask a student to volunteer to have you critique his or her writing in front of the entire class.
7. Conduct student-teacher conferences—even mini-conferences during class—and model effective response.
8. Ask students to critique a piece of your writing.
9. Critique a piece of writing by putting it on a transparency and using an overhead projector or computer monitor; ask the entire class to determine (1) the main point of the writing, (2) gaps the writer has left for the audience to fill, (3) other information readers might want to know, (4) errors that might distract readers, and (5) particularly pleasing aspects of the writing. If you can, use a computer instead of an overhead projector—it gives you more options to demonstrate editing techniques.
10. When you make responses on students' writing, ask questions and make statements. Do not use code words (e.g., "awk," "frag") to cite problems in students' writing. Rather, indicate why you think something in the writing is awkward ("Do you mean to say that all the animals jumped over one another at one time?") or why something is an error ("Where is the verb in this sentence?").

Figure 4.4   Quiz for Identifying Possible Members of the Publication Committee.

1. I would rather read than eat.
2. I like to roll words around in my head.
3. Give me a book and leave me alone.
4. My favorite store is a bookstore.
5. I like to spend lots of time watching T.V.
6. Words are wonderful.
7. I am good at finding misspellings in writing.
8. If I could, I wouldn't read anything but labels on soup cans.
9. So far this year, I have read lots of newspapers, magazines, and/or books.
10. I enjoy writing.

interview (and send a thank-you note to the interviewee); write a draft of the results (the class would need to determine the format for the results); and go through the writing process of revising, peer reviewing, revising, and editing to produce a "final" copy. A group of students can compile the final copy into a book.

Style and Format

Putting the book together requires upfront planning. At the outset, students should resolve a variety of issues regarding style and format. For instance, which fonts should be used? You might explain to students that using more than one or two fonts is not a good idea because too much variety in type is distracting to readers. If students want to produce documents with variety, they can use the bold, italics, and roman styles of a particular font. In addition, students can use rules (thin lines used either as ornaments, such as the rules at the top of a magazine page, or as dividers, such as the rule that separates text), centering, bullets, and a variety of tables and figures to enliven a document and enhance its readability. (Tables have columns and rows; figures don't. Charts, pictures, and graphs are figures.)

However, you should caution students not to use various word-processing functions simply for the sake of using them. The purpose of publishing a document is to attract a wider audience than the unpublished document would, so issues of readability are extremely important. Jazzing up a book just because you can is one sure way to produce a gawdy and ostentatious publication, one that may unintentionally amuse and confuse audiences. An easy suggestion is to limit the font choices to two: one font for the titles and headlines and another for the body of the text. You might be interested in learning more about document design so that you can provide students with principles for creating effective documents (Baird, McDonald, Pittman, & Turnbull, 1993; Williams, 2003).

Figure 4.5   Example of Instructions the Publication Committee Might Produce.

1. Please save a copy of your interview into our class public folder and provide a hard copy of your interview on [date].
2. The written product should conform to the following requirements:

   - Length should be between 1,000 and 1,200 words. [Younger students would have a much reduced word requirement.]
   - Use Times New Roman typeface.
   - Single-space all text unless otherwise noted.
   - Center title in 14-point bold on the first line of the page.
   - Center your name in 12-point bold on the next line.
   - Double-space to the first paragraph of text and introduce the person you interviewed. This introduction should be no longer than three lines.
   - Double-space to the first line of the interview. Type "**Interviewer:**" and leave two spaces before you type the first interview question.
   - Double-space between each interview question and each response from the interviewee to the question. For example, double-space after the first question and type "**Eugene Smith:**" (or whatever the interviewee's name is) and leave two spaces before typing the interviewee's response to the question.
   - After you have completed typing the interview, double-space and provide a two-line biographical sketch of yourself.

The Publication Committee

When using classroom publications, it is a good idea to create a publication committee to plan much of the publishing process. We often use the quiz in Figure 4.4 as a lighthearted way to single out those who might have some propensity for publishing. The three or four people with the highest number of true answers to the quiz become members of the publication committee. The purpose of the committee is to work with the class to create instructions on how to plan and put together the publication. Figure 4.5 is an example of the type of instructions the publication committee might produce.

One major purpose of the instructions the publication committee produces is to make more efficient the job of those who will actually produce the book. For example, those who put all the student contributions together do not need to change all the headings in each interview to a particular font style. Each contributor can do that. Imagine, for instance, the work involved in making sure that all the interviews—say, 20 in a class of 20 students—use **Interviewer:** instead of *I:* or *Interviewer:* or some other designation to introduce the questions in the interview. Certainly, technology can make searching and replacing easier than it would be without computer ingenuity, but correcting is something that contributing authors can do before handing in their papers.

So far, we've talked about some of the mechanics of publishing a class book. What needs to be reiterated, however, is that the publishing process includes a heavy dose of the writing process. That is, when students write their interviews (or whatever the assignment might be) for the book, they should be engaged in peer critiques before the individual papers are submitted to the publications committee. Then the committee compiles the papers and goes through the review process again, beginning with the committee members' review of the book in draft form. Once the committee reviews the draft of the book and makes needed adjustments, including editing the text of individual papers, a copy of the book as well as a copy of each author's contribution should be printed for the entire class to review. After authors have had the opportunity to review their contributions, making corrections or questioning changes, they return the contributions to the committee so that it can create a final draft. In terms of the cover for the book and possible art for the cover, the committee can enlist a person in the class to create a cover and ask the class for comments. Alternatively, the committee can provide several versions or drafts of covers and ask the class to select one.

Printing and Binding

Many schools have equipment for printing and binding students' works, such as inexpensive comb binding. If available, then you can photocopy and bind the books students create. However, you will need to inform students at the outset whether there are limitations concerning printing and binding. For instance, can you create color copies of the cover? Are there limits on the number of pages per book and the number of books you can produce? If students want additional copies of a book, can you collect money for those copies and reimburse the school for the copies?

If you don't have the necessary photocopy and binding facilities, including sufficient budget, then you can ask students to create a master copy for the class. The publications committee can determine what a copy costs and make copies for students who agree to pay for them.

These procedures can be adapted to various projects, including newspapers, magazines, brochures, and newsletters. For instance, either the entire class or groups within a class can create a newsletter or a brochure using common software packages (e.g., Microsoft Word, Microsoft Publisher, Apple Pages). Such projects may not be bound individually, but a newsletter, for instance, can be a joint effort by the entire class, with particular articles or sections provided by individuals or groups.

Even though many steps in the publishing process for print materials can be used in electronic publishing, it is not the case that a print document can be automatically and easily translated into an electronic document. This is true for several reasons:

1. People read electronic documents differently from print documents (Morkes & Nielsen, 1997). Electronic documents generally are not designed for sustained reading, so if you want your students to produce a book of interviews for the Web, you must recognize that most readers will not want to read every interview beginning with the first one and ending with the last one.

2. An electronic document has different requirements from a print document. Because Web readers expect to have links to other documents and to have choices about what they can read and in what order, you will need to help your students design a Web document.

3. Designing a Web document requires certain skills and knowledge that are not required for print documents. So let's talk about publishing students' work on the Web.

❍ Electronic Classroom Publishing

In electronic publishing, students make their work available in electronic form and for an electronic forum, such as a Web site, blog, or Wiki. Clear rationales have been provided for the value of classroom publishing using the Internet (Bronzo & Simpson, 1998; Kinzer & Leu, 1997; Leu, 1997; Leu & El-Hindi, 1998; Leu & Iannone, 1998; Leu & Leu, 1997; Maring, Wiseman, & Myers, 1997; Shen, 1996), including a positive effect on students' writing. To help students create electronic forums, you need to know three things: (1) how to create electronic products, (2) how to download information from other Web sites, and (3) how to post materials to electronic forums and Web sites.

How to Create Electronic Products

Although an anthology of student work that has been word processed is an electronic product, it does not take advantage of sound, animation, and video, which are components of multimedia publishing. Certainly, students can post a traditional text-only, word-processed book to the Web, but the book will not be a multimedia text and therefore will not have multimedia capabilities. Students can create multimedia books by using tools such as Microsoft PowerPoint, Microsoft Word, Apple Keynote, eZedia, and Microsoft FrontPage. We understand that other electronic products, such as electronic presentations created in Microsoft PowerPoint, also constitute electronic publishing; however, in this section, we are specifically addressing electronic products published through the Internet. In addition, the traditional book, intended as a document that can be read from beginning to end, cannot take advantage of the nonlinear features of hypertext. For instance, in a document with hypertext, readers can follow one idea throughout a text or linked texts without reading all of the text.

Here's an example: Let's say that your class's book of interviews is constructed as a hypertext document. (Remember that the assignment was for each student to interview a member of his or her family who lived at least 30 years ago.) During the planning stage of the book, students would need to think about how readers access hypertexts. In thinking about readers, students would want to consider ways to link the interviews. This could be done, for instance, by each student developing a list of five to 10 index terms for his or her interview. Students would select index terms by considering major themes in their interviews, such as education, leisure activities, cars, clothing, food, and economics. The class or the publication committee would then determine which themes were the most prominent throughout all the interviews. Let's say that the class or publication committee selected education, leisure activities, cars, and family life as the themes most frequently addressed throughout the interviews. Each student would then identify anything in his or her interview related to each of the themes, and the publication committee, using Microsoft FrontPage, would create links that enable readers to follow a theme throughout the entire interview book.

For example, a reader who wanted to know everything the interview book said about family life could start at a designated place (generally the home page for the class or book) and read every entry on that topic. If the class already has a Web page, one hyperlink on the page could be entitled, "Thirty Years Ago: Interviews About Life in the 1970s." A reader would click on that button and read a synopsis of the book, including an explanation of the assignment that generated the book. Then the reader could select a hyperlink for one of the themes and follow that theme throughout the entire book.

Let's say that the students who create the interview book want to do more than provide text-only interview transcripts; they also want to add video and music. One theme of the interviews might be the music of the 1970s, so students decide to include parts of a popular Stevie Wonder song because one of the interviewees said that he particularly liked selections from Motown. In addition to providing a few bars from the selection, the class decides to add a video of Stevie Wonder in concert so that viewers will be able to both see and hear the music. Thus, when readers first read about Motown and Stevie Wonder in the interviews, they will have access to a button that enables them to see and hear Stevie Wonder. Readers can then return to the theme of music in the interviews.

Students also could create a video for their presentation. If, perhaps, a student were vacationing in a place with Motown memorabilia, the student could videotape the memorabilia and use the video as part of the multimedia presentation, capturing the video in a program such as Apple iMovie. Or students could use a scanner to scan pictures of Stevie Wonder and other musicians into a file that is incorporated into the interview book.

How to Download Information from Other Forums

You may want to download information that either (1) is in the public domain or (2) has a disclaimer stating the information can be used freely but needs to be cited or has been approved by the author for public use. Although much classroom use of downloaded information could be covered under the "fair use" provision of the copyright law (meaning that the law allows an individual to copy a certain amount of copyrighted material), you certainly should determine whether your use of such material—especially material that will be distributed outside the classroom—constitutes fair use. Fair use, copyright, and intellectual property are covered in Chapter 5. For now, however, the next issue is how to download information.

1. You can print a copy of the information. You could scan the information into a document you are creating, but a better way is to download the information into a file on the computer's hard drive. Many primary source documents

available on the Web, such as original period sheet music, may be in Adobe Acrobat's portable document format (PDF).

2. You can copy and paste Internet text into a word processing program. Just highlight the text in the Internet document you want to copy, and go to the Edit menu and click on "**Copy.**" The text is ready to be pasted in a word processing document or a multimedia presentation you are creating.

3. You can save graphics by clicking on a graphic you want to download and right-clicking (PC) or control-clicking (Mac) to "**Save this image as . . .**". Then save the image to your hard drive.

4. You must have the appropriate software to download PDFs, audio, and video, so you should check with your local technology coordinator or library media specialist to determine what you need. The coordinator or media specialist may talk to you about plug-ins (software that allows you to download different media). Some files may not be downloadable, such as videos. In this case, you can hyperlink directly to the Web page with the video.

How to Post Materials to Electronic Forums and Web Sites

This type of publishing also can be accomplished by posting or submitting students' documents to other Web sites. That is, students do not have to create a Web site to publish their work. Indeed, they do not have to produce an elaborate multimedia presentation. Rather, they can post or submit their projects to Web sites constructed for the very purpose of eliciting student writing and creating a forum for student writers to view and discuss each other's work.

Two examples of forums for publishing and collaborating are Education Place and Inkspot. Education Place (**http://www.eduplace.com/hmco/school/**) lists Internet writing projects in which your class can participate. You can submit your own writing project, or you can engage in a collaborative writing project with classrooms throughout the United States. Similarly, Inkspot (**http://www.inkspot.com/**) provides resources for students, giving and receiving feedback on their writing. It also provides an electronic bulletin board for posting questions about writing and for finding peer-critique partners. Other examples of such Web sites are listed in Figure 4.6. Most of the sites explain how to submit or post a contribution to the site.

○ Managing Computers in Your Writing Curriculum

Once teachers realize how influential computers are in helping their students use writing to learn and to communicate with audiences, they want to use computers in the classrooms. The first step is to assess your resources. Because of the increased attention to reducing the digital divide and placing more technologies in schools, computers can be

Figure 4.6   Web Sites Where Students Can Publish Their Writing Projects.

- **Candlelight Stories <http://www.candlelightstories.com>:** Publishes students' writing and illustrations.
- **Cyberkids <http://www.cyberkids.com>:** Publishes writing of students ages 7–11.
- **Inkspot for Young Writers <http://www.inkspot.com/~ohi/inkspot/young.html>:** Provides support for writers.
- **KidsPub <http://www.en-garde.com/kidpub/intro.html>:** Publishes all work submitted by students.
- **Kid's Space <http://www.kids-space.org/>:** Provides pictures for which students create a corresponding story.
- **My View <listserv@sjuvm.stjohns.edu>:** Creative writing exchanges for students.
- **Realist Wonder Society <http://www.wondersociety.com/>:** Provides hypertext stories written in different genres that students can respond to online; they can even write a different ending to the stories.
- **The Scoop <http://www.friend.ly.net/scoop/adventure/index.html>:** Provides stories for which students can write their own ending.
- **WAC-L <listserv@vmd.cso.uiuc.edu>:** Focuses on writing across the curriculum.
- **Young Writer's Clubhouse <http://www.realkids.com>:** Provides online chat and bulletin board information about writing contests and advice about writing.

grouped in schools in several ways. We'll highlight three common configurations below, but first we'll provide some examples on how to manage scheduling.

Scheduling Computer Time

Develop a rotation schedule so that students have a guaranteed time on the computer. This is crucial in the one-computer classroom because there is already limited computer integration to a particular stage of the writing process for a particular project. Thus, if every student group is going to have sufficient time to use the computer for keyboarding a handwritten draft during one week, it is important to determine how much time the students need, develop a schedule, and stick to it.

Let's say that you are starting a collaborative writing project. You talk about the project with the students so that they understand what you're expecting. You show them a rubric that you and they will use to evaluate the project, and you ask them if they believe the rubric needs to be modified for this assignment. You set up a schedule for each group to use the computer to keyboard a rough draft, revise it once, and edit it. If the drafting stage takes a week and there are six groups of four in the class and each group should have 15 minutes on the computer each week, you need to schedule time for the groups. Some days you may want to schedule two 15-minute sessions. Other days you may want to schedule no sessions. Or you may want to schedule 30-minute sessions during the revising stage.

While one group is at the computer, the rest of the class should be working on their drafts. They can peer critique another group's draft or work as a group to revise their draft in preparation for using the classroom computer. You may want to schedule individual group conferences about the draft the group members are developing. You need to determine how much time the assignment will take, how long each part of the writing process will be, and how to keep every group involved in the writing process whether that group is actually using the classroom computer or waiting to use it.

A Computer Learning Center in Your Classroom

Some schools have divided a small number of computers, usually between three and five, among classrooms, often referred to as a computer learning center or a computer center. This allows you to integrate computers into your writing curriculum without having to leave the classroom. As described above, you will need to organize a rotational schedule for students to move through the center. With a small number of computers in the classroom, a teacher may choose to conduct whole-group brainstorming sessions to reduce the amount of time students need to be at a computer. Morrison and Lowther (2005) suggest teachers plan three events to smoothly move students through centers: (a) what students do before using the computer, (b) what students do at the computer, and (c) what students do after using the computer. Figures 4.7 and 4.8 provide two examples of managing students with a small number of computers in a classroom.

Computer learning centers may or may not be connected to the school's network or the Internet. Instead, they may only be wired to the printer inside the classroom. Having nonnetworked computers affects the students' access to the Internet and e-mail, which can hinder a student's research and information gathering process. Network technologies, such as the Internet, e-mail, or blogs further students' process writing.

Stationary and Mobile Computer Labs

Two other configurations that are popular in schools are stationary and mobile computer labs. Stationary labs typically have enough computers for a classroom—between 20 and 25—so each student uses a computer individually. Mobile computer labs, sometimes called laptop carts and sometimes called computers on wheels (COWs), allow teachers to bring the computers into their classrooms. With mobile computer labs, teachers do not waste time on "in-school field trips" to stationary computer labs. Mobile computer labs typically have about 15 computers, so small groups or pairs are often used to take advantage of these. Mobile computer labs typically connect to the Internet wirelessly, so students can move into groups and out of groups easily.

Both stationary computer labs and mobile computer labs are networked, so they are linked to each other electronically, and all students can communicate with each other. Thus, students can send their drafts by computer to a peer in the class, and the peer can critique the draft on the computer and send the critiqued draft back to the author. In

Figure 4.7   One Way to Integrate Computer Learning Centers into the Writing Process.

Brainstorming

- The whole class watches the computer monitor as the teacher or a student types the ideas the class is brainstorming. The list of brainstorming ideas can be printed, with copies distributed to each student. Students can work in groups or individually to select a topic. Students begin a first draft by either handwriting it or drafting at the computer.

Writing and Revising

- Individually or in groups (if the paper is a collaborative paper), students can begin to type the written draft into the computer or draft at the computer. For instance, as soon as a person or group is ready to type, that person or group may spend 10 minutes on the computer. While individuals or groups are waiting to use the computer, the teacher can involve them in a related activity, such as reading a selection that fits with the topic the class is writing about.
- After a student or group of students uses their 10 minutes, they print their draft and begin rewriting.
- Once students have revised their draft, they have another 10 minutes to make the changes on the computer.
- If time permits, the teacher can take the students through another cycle of revision.

Reviewing

- Students peer review each other's drafts.

Editing and Proofreading

- On the basis of the peer reviews, the students have time to consider what needs to be changed in the draft; they have 15 minutes to make those changes on the computer.
- The final draft is edited by another student or a parent who has good editing skills, proofread by the author(s), and corrected at the computer before it is printed out and submitted to the teacher for evaluation.

Figure 4.8   A One-Week Writing Project.

Monday: As a class, the students brainstorm while the teacher keyboards the brainstorming ideas so that everyone can see what is typed on the monitor. Alternatively, students could brainstorm, Web, read, search the Internet, interview others, and so forth to collect information and get ready to write.

Tuesday: The teacher divides the class into four groups, one group at each of the four computers. Each group has 30 minutes to prepare a draft. Then each group has 30 minutes to review and revise the draft.

Wednesday: The groups have 30 minutes to make revisions to the draft on the computer, print out a new draft, and pair off (Group 1 with Group 2) to peer review the drafts.

Thursday: The groups have 30 minutes to make revisions to their drafts based on peer reviews, print a new draft, and edit it.

Friday: The groups make the edited revisions and compare (proofread) the edited draft with the new draft to ensure that all the changes have been made, make any changes that weren't made earlier, and print a final copy to be read to the class or published and then turned in to the teacher.

addition, students can communicate with other classes in the same building, across town, or in another state using the Internet.

One of the significant advantages of networked computers is that students can communicate with each other electronically. As the computer becomes increasingly essential to the writing process, students spend more time not only using it to write but also to work through the other stages of the writing process.

COMPUTER CLASSROOM LESSONS

Fortunately, as teachers are more frequently using the computer as a tool to teach literacy (Leu, 1997; Rose & Meyer, 1994), more of their stories are being published (Holland, 1996; Iannone, 1998; Leu & Leu, 1997; Stuhlmann, 1996). Some of the following proven classroom examples are taken from the literature. Each example provides opportunities for students to engage in process writing.

Holiday Stories

Grade Level: Adaptable for K–8

Objective: Students will learn about diversity, gain experience in peer review and getting along with others, learn more about the writing process, and get more practice writing.

Time: 1 week

Problem to Be Solved: Your school has decided to create a time capsule filled with information about today's society, and your class has been assigned to write and publish stories about their favorite holidays using StoryBook Weaver Deluxe CD-ROM. What kinds of stories can you create?

Materials: Paper
Pencil
Computer
Color printer
StoryBook Weaver Deluxe CD-ROM
Projection device, such as LCD projector,
computer connected television, or electronic
SMARTBoard

Steps:

1. Engage students in a discussion of holidays. Ask students to define a holiday and give examples. Ask students to describe favorite holidays and customs.
2. In a whole group setting, present StoryBook Weaver Deluxe to the students, using the projection device.

3. Demonstrate starting a new file, opening a file, printing, and quitting the CD.

4. Demonstrate word processing in a new file. Ask for student volunteers. Model adding graphics to a completed (typed) file. Use student volunteers to add backgrounds, music, people, and objects.

5. Have the students begin writing about their favorite holiday. Tell the students that once a rough draft is completed, the story will be published using StoryBook Weaver Deluxe.

6. Use peer conferences and one formal teacher conference to edit the rough drafts.

7. Assign computer time for students to create their holiday essays using the CD. Color print each completed product.

8. Have students take their stories home for parents, siblings, and friends to read.

Assessment: Use a class-generated rubric. You may give credit for peer-editing feedback.

The Dyadic Paper

Grade Level: 3–8

Objective: The student will think critically about one side of an issue and express the position clearly. The student will demonstrate how e-mail can be used to send text. Students will learn to work as a team.

Time: 1 week

Problem to Be Solved: Carol, a lawyer, needs help demonstrating both sides of an issue. To help Carol, two students will take opposing positions on a topic and write one paper on that topic.

Materials: Computer

Steps:

1. The dyadic paper may be an opinion paper in which students present opposing opinions without research to back up their claims, or the paper may include research (conducted using the Internet). The successful paper represents both sides of an issue equally well. A paper in which one side "wins" is an unsuccessful paper.

2. The format for the paper may vary. It could be a dialogue, a question-and-answer interview, a play in which characters express viewpoints, or a formal report in which the pro (or con) side presents its case and then the con (or pro) side presents its case.

3. If students use two different computers to write their parts of the paper and then combine the parts to revise and edit the final draft, they will need to

know how to transfer text from one computer to another. This could be an opportunity to show how e-mail can be used to send text to another person.

Assessment: The classroom writing rubric should be modified to include whether both sides of the issue were expressed equally and completely. Other criteria should include how well students worked as team members and whether or not there were peer reviews.

Electronic Traveling Journal

Grade Level: Adaptable for 1–8

Objective: Students will communicate and describe their thoughts to an audience unfamiliar with your class environment. Students learn to use a blog (Web log).

Time: 1 day for each student

Problem to Be Solved: Several students in another country are interested in your response to activities in the classroom, so they asked you to keep a traveling journal. A traveling journal offers an opportunity to write personal reactions to a day in the classroom. The journal "travels" from person to person, providing a written history of students' perceptions of the class.

Materials: Word processor
Class blog
Notebook to store daily entries

Steps:

1. At the end of each day, one student is responsible for word processing a traveling journal entry for that day. After the entry has been edited, it is copy/pasted into the class blog space online.
2. To begin class the next day, the student reads the journal entry aloud. The traveling journal gives a forum so that the other students in the class can read an entry and respond electronically to it.

Assessment: The classroom writing rubric should be modified to include details of what happened in the class.

A Dictionary of Slang

Grade Level: Adaptable K–8

Objective: Students identify language changes from one generation to another. Students compile lists of changes. Students gain appreciation for the evaluation of language.

Time: 1–2 weeks

Problem to Be Solved: Adults are often unfamiliar with today's slang terms, so students will brainstorm and define slang terms common in everyday speech. Students then create a dictionary of slang terms.

Materials: Computer
Printer
Web browser (e.g., Internet Explorer,
Netscape Navigator, Safari)
Word processor
Pencil
Crayons or markers

Steps:

1. Engage students in a discussion of language. Discuss the differences in speaking at home and speaking at school. Ask students to think of words or phrases that are considered slang.
2. Using your Web browser, visit **http://www.cbsnews.com/stories/2003/12/04/ earlyshow/contributors/tracysmith/main586911.shtml**. Explain how one class created a slang dictionary.
3. Provide an example of a slang phrase and a definition to get the students started. For example, "chill out" usually refers to calming down or relaxing.
4. Group the students into threes to continue brainstorming slang phrases. Have teams generate definitions for their slang terms or phrases. Be specific about elements to include in each entry, such as part of speech, plurals, and usage in sentence.
5. Using a word processor, have student groups word process their dictionaries.
6. Create the title page of the dictionary. Add clip art if desired.
7. Create remaining pages for slang word entries. Make sure that all slang terms and phrases are defined. Students may add clip art for illustrations or leave blank space for hand drawings.
8. Review slang terms and phrases in a discussion environment. Ask the class to choose one original slang phrase they like best.
9. Compile a list of the 10 most commonly used slang terms from the student dictionaries. Write sentences using the terms, and have students tell the meaning of the sentences.
10. Travel to another class and share the dictionaries with other students. Ask the students to guess the definitions of the terms before telling them. Or you may use the dictionaries as springboards for your students' keypals to learn slang from another part of the country or world.

Assessment: Develop with the students a rubric for the slang dictionary. Be sure to include:

1. Clear definitions and usage;
2. willingness to participate;
3. contribution to group work; and the
4. ability to identify several old and new terms.

An Interactive Writing Adventure on the Web

Grade Level: Adaptable K–8

Objective: Students will identify key elements of plot, construct a Web page, and write a story resolution.

Time: 3 hours

Problem to Be Solved: Read an interactive story on the Internet. Then decide the course of the story by clicking on one of two plot scenarios. Using Microsoft Word, write and publish your own version of the next page in the hypertext story.

Materials: Computer(s) with Internet access (single teacher station, small groups at computers or one computer for each student)
Projection device (e.g., LCD projector, computer connected television, electronic SMARTBoard)
Word processor
Printer
Pencil or pen

Steps:

1. Locate the Web page **http://friend.ly.net/users/jorban/adventure/ page01.html** with your Web browser.
2. Begin reading the interactive adventure.
3. Read several pages, deciding the course of the story by clicking on one of two plot scenarios.
4. Stop the reading of the story at an interesting point.
5. Ask students to imagine what will happen next in the adventure.
6. Invite students to write the next Web page for the interactive story.
7. Provide students with discussion time and individual Internet reading time to generate ideas for their continuations.
8. After brainstorming initial ideas, have students follow the writing process to generate their stories.
9. On the computers, have students word process their stories into products.
10. When all the student products are completed, revisit **http://friend.ly.net/users/ jorban/adventure/ page01.html** and read the continuation of the adventure.

Assessment: A rubric should include:

1. ability to track story plot;
2. willingness to imagine next phase of story;
3. participation in writing Web page; and
4. evaluation of final product for creativity, continuity, grammar, and vocabulary.

◯ Techno-Teacher Tips

Creating Home Pages

Teachers might be concerned about helping students create home pages because in the past, a person needed to know HTML to create a home page. Today, Web page authoring tools, like Microsoft FrontPage, Netscape Composer, and even most word processors, allow easy creation of Web pages. The Web page authoring tools work very similarly to word processors, so you do not have to learn something new. With word processors, when you save the page using "**Save As . . . ,**" check the format at the bottom. You can change this to "**Web page**" to create your own homepage.

Listservs

As discussed in Chapter 1, consider joining a listserv made up of other teachers involved in classroom publishing projects. Listserv members can provide help when you have questions about classroom publishing projects.

Scheduling

Usually the students outnumber the available computers in a classroom. This means that computer time should be scheduled and monitored to ensure that all students receive adequate time to complete their projects. Develop a rotation schedule that allows five to eight students to use the computer in one day. Consider pairing students and doubling their computer time. In this way, students can collaborate as well as use their computer skills for a longer period of time. Require all students to sign a time log when using the computers. Use a kitchen timer to remind students when their allotted time is over. Other schools require signing up to go to the computer lab or signing up to use a wireless laptop cart, so plan ahead to make sure you have access to the computers when you need them.

Software

Many excellent software programs have been developed for writing and publishing. These can enhance the writing process with special features, such as on-screen spell check, word count, thesaurus, clip art, and graphics. However, it is not essential to purchase specialized software titles because most computers already have a basic word processing program developed especially for writing.

○ Frequently Asked Questions

1. **My students are already engaged in process writing and publishing without the use of technology. Will using computers lengthen this process and add to their responsibilities?**

   Yes and no. Initially it will lengthen the processes because students will find handwriting quicker than word processing. But eventually it will actually shorten writing time. As students learn to compose directly into a word processor, the need for a handwritten draft is eliminated. The teacher or peers can edit drafts on screen. Several students can edit a single draft by printing multiple copies. With practice, students (and teachers) can learn to integrate computers into the entire writing process rather than as the final step.

2. **Should every writing assignment employ the entire writing process?**

   No. Students should be allowed, at times, to choose the piece of writing they would like to revise, edit, and publish. To take every writing assignment through the process would be too time consuming. Some writing assignments, such as reflective journals, are not appropriate for the writing process.

3. **How can I ensure that all the students in a group do an equal amount of quality work when they produce a class publication?**

   First, provide students with instruction on individual and group responsibilities. For instance, you might explain that when one student in the group misses a deadline, the other group members fall behind. Second, provide a method for students to evaluate themselves and other group members. Explain the system at the beginning of a collaborative project so that students know they will be responsible for evaluating each other. Third, use peer evaluation and self-evaluation to adjust grades for group projects.

○ References

Anderson-Inman, L., Knox-Quinn, C., & Tromba, P. (1996). Synchronous writing environments: Real-time interaction in cyberspace. *Journal of Adolescent & Adult Literacy, 40*(2), 134–138.

Angeletti, S. R. (1993). Group writing and publishing: Building community in a second-grade classroom. *Language Arts, 70*(6), 494–499.

Atwell, N. (1998). *In the middle: New understanding about writing, reading, and learning* (2nd ed.). Portsmouth, NH: Boynton/Cook.

Baird, R. N., McDonald, D., Pittman, R. H., & Turnbull, A. T. (1993). *The graphics of communication: Methods, media and technology* (6th ed.). Fort Worth, TX: Harcourt Brace.

Baumbach, D., Christopher, T., Fasimpaur, K., & Oliver, K. (2004). Personal literacy assistants: Using handhelds for literacy instruction. *Learning and Leading with Technology, 32*(2), 16–21.

Bronzo, W. G., & Simpson, M. L. (1998). *Readers, teachers, learners: Expanding literacy across the content areas* (3rd ed.). Upper Saddle River, NJ: Merrill.

Butcheri, J., & Hammond, J. J. (1994). Authentic writing makes the difference. *Journal of Reading, 38*(3), 228–229.

Calkins, L. (1986). *The art of teaching writing*. Portsmouth, NH: Heinemann.

Calkins, L. (1990). *Living between the lines*. Portsmouth, NH: Heinemann.

Cohen, M., & Riel, M. (1989). The effects of distant audiences on students' writing. *American Educational Research Journal, 26*(2), 143–159.

Comstock, M. (1993). Writing together, learning together: Collaboration's two-way street. *Quarterly of the National Writing Project and the Center for the Study of Writing, 15*(4), 29–32.

Copeland, J. S., & Lomax, E. D. (1988). Building effective student writing groups. In J. Golub (Ed.), *Focus on collaborative learning: Classroom practices in teaching English* (pp. 99–104). Urbana, IL: National Council of Teachers of English.

DeGroff, L. (1990). Is there a place for computers in whole language classrooms? *The Reading Teacher, 43,* 568–572.

Doolittle, P. E. (1991). *Vygotsky and the socialization of literacy.* (ERIC Document Reproduction Service No. ED 377 473)

Dragga, S. (1988). The effects of praiseworthy grading on students and teachers. *Journal of Teaching Writing, 7*(1), 41–50.

Forman, J. (Ed.). (1992). *New visions of collaborative writing*. Portsmouth, NH: Boynton/Cook.

Fuller, D. (1988). A curious case of our responding habits: What do we respond to and why? *Journal of Advanced Composition, 8,* 88–96.

Fulwiler, T., & Young, A. (Eds.). (1982). *Language connections: Writing and reading across the curriculum*. Urbana, IL: National Council of Teachers of English.

Galegher, J., Kraut, R. E., & Egido, C. (Eds.). (1990). *Intellectual teamwork: Social and technological foundations of cooperative work*. Hillsdale, NJ: Lawrence Erlbaum.

Graves, D. H. (1994). *A fresh look at writing*. Portsmouth, NH: Heinemann.

Holland, H. (1996). Way past word processing. *Electronic Learning, 22,* 24–26.

Hoot, J. L., & Silvern, S. B. (Eds.). (1988). *Writing with computers in the early grades*. New York: Teachers College Press.

Iannone, P. (1998). Just beyond the horizon: Writing-centered literacy activities for traditional and electronic contexts. *The Reading Teacher, 51*(5), 438–443.

Kinzer, C., & Leu, D. J., Jr. (1997). The challenge of change: Exploring literacy and learning in electronic environments. *Language Arts, 74,* 126–136.

Labbo, L., Reinking, D., & McKenna, M. (1995). Incorporating the computer into kindergarten: A case study. In A. Hinchman, D. Leu, & C. K. Kinzer (Eds.), *Perspectives on literacy research and practice, forty-fourth yearbook of the National Reading Conference* (pp. 459–465). Chicago: National Reading Conference.

Le, T. (1989). Computers as partners in writing: A linguistic perspective. *Journal of Reading, 32*(7), 606–610.

Leu, D. (1997). Caity's question: Literacy as deixis on the Internet. *The Reading Teacher, 51*(1), 62–67.

Leu, D. J., & El-Hindi, A. E. (1998). Beyond classroom boundaries: Constructivist teaching with the Internet. *The Reading Teacher, 51*(8), 694–700.

Leu, D., & Leu, D. (1997). *Teaching with the Internet: Lessons from the classroom*. Norwood, MA: Christopher-Gordon.

Leu, D. J., & Leu, D. (1997). Using the Internet for language arts and literature. In *Teaching with the Internet: Lessons from the classroom*. Norwood, MA: Christopher-Gordon.

Leu, D. J., Jr., & Iannone, P. V. (1998). Just beyond the horizon: Writing-centered literacy activities for traditional and electronic contexts. *The Reading Teacher, 51*(5), 438–443.

Long, R., & Bulgarella, L. (1985). Social interaction and the writing process. *Language Arts, 62*(2), 166–172.

Macarthur, C. (1988). The impact of computers on the writing process. *Exceptional Children, 54*(6), 536–542.

Mageau, T. (1992). When technology meets process writing. *Electronic Learning, 31*, 32–34.

Maring, G. H., Wiseman, B. J., & Myers, K. S. (1997). Using the World Wide Web to build learning communities: Writing for genuine purposes. *Journal of Adolescent and Adult Literacy, 41*(3), 196–207.

Marzano, L. (1990). Connecting literature with cooperative writing. *The Reading Teacher, 43*(6), 429–430.

McEachern, W. R. (1986, November). *Group compositions: A model for report writing*. Paper presented at the annual meeting of the National Council of Teachers of English, San Antonio, TX. (ERIC Document Reproduction Service Report No. ED 283 193).

Montague, M. (1990). Computers and writing process instruction. *Computers in the Schools, 7*(3), 5–20.

Montague, M., & Fonseca, F. (1993). Using computers to improve storywriting. In J. J. Hirschbuhl (Ed.), *Computers in education* (pp. 80–83). Guilford, CT: Dushkin.

Morkes, J., & Nielsen, J. (1997). Concise, SCANNABLE, and objective: How to write for the Web. Retrieved June 22, 2006, from http://www.useit.com/papers/webwriting/writing.html

Music, K. (1988). Conquering trauma with group writing. In M. S. Bordner (Ed.), *Strategies in composition: Ideas that work in the classroom*. (ERIC Document Reproduction Service Report No. ED 294 181).

Odell, L., & Goswani, D. (Eds.). (1985). *Writing in nonacademic settings*. New York: Guilford Press.

Paeth, B. (1996). Dear Jenny. *Teachers and Writers, 28*(2), 1–6.

Rose, D. H., & Meyer, A. (1994). The role of technology in language arts instruction. *Language Arts, 71*(4), 290–294.

Sassi, A. (1990). The synergy of cross-age tutoring: A catalyst for computer use. *The Computing Teacher, 17*(5), 9–11.

Shen, V. T. (1996). The role of hypertext as an interactional medium among fifth-grade students. In D. J. Leu, C. K. Kinzer, & K. A. Hinchman (Eds.), *Literacies for the 21ˢᵗ century: Research and practice* (pp. 484–499). Chicago: National Reading Conference.

Smede, S. D. (1995). Flyfishing, portfolios, and authentic writing. *English Journal, 84*(2), 92–94.

Smith, C. (1995). Grandparent pen pals: Authentic writing at work. *Teaching PreK–8, 25*(8), 40–41.

Soloff, S. (1973). The effect of non-content factors on the grading of essays. *Graduate Research in Education and Related Disciplines, 6*(2), 44–54.

Speck, B. W. (2000). *Grading students' classroom writing: Issues and strategies*. ASHE-ERIC Higher Education Report, Volume 27, no. 3. San Francisco, CA: Jossey-Bass.

Speck, B. W. (2002). *Facilitating students' collaborative writing*. ASHE-ERIC Higher Education Report, Volume 28, no. 6. San Francisco, CA: Jossey-Bass.

Speck, B. W. (1998). The teacher's role in the pluralistic classroom. *Perspectives, 28*(1), 19–43.

Spilka, R. (Ed.). (1993). *Writing in the workplace: New research perspectives*. Carbondale and Edwardsville, IL: Southern Illinois University Press.

Stuhlmann, J. (1996). Whole-language strategies for integrating technology into language arts. *Proceedings of the annual National Educational Computing Conference*, Minneapolis, MN. (ERIC Document Reproduction Service No. ED 398 895).

Sullivan, J. (1998). The electronic journal: Combining literacy and technology. *The Reading Teacher, 52*(1), 90–93.

Tsujimoto, S. E. (1988). Partners in the writing process. In Jeff Golub (Ed.), *Focus on collaborative learning: Classroom practices in teaching English* (pp. 85–92). Urbana, IL: National Council of Teachers of English.

Vincent, G. (1993). Just short of paradise: Collaborative writing in middle school. *English Journal, 82*(7), 58–60.

Williams, R. (2003). *The non-designer's design book* (2nd ed.). Berkeley, CA: Peachpit Press.

Yanushefski, J. (1988). Group authorship in the language arts classroom. *Language Arts, 65*(3), 279–287.

Zak, F. (1990). Exclusively positive responses to students' writing. *Journal of Basic Writing, 9*(2), 40–53.

Zukowski, V. (1997). Teeter-totters and tandem bikes: A glimpse into the world of cross-age tutors. *Teaching and Change, 5*(1), 71–91.

Literacy in the Information Age

Chapter 5

"**W**hat's wrong, Greg? You look ashen."

Greg, an English teacher who is also the grade-level leader for eighth grade, holds some papers in his hands that he gives to Mohammed. "Look at this."

Mohammed, after taking the papers and leafing through them for a moment, says with a deadpan expression, "Well, they're certainly not advertising clothing. How do they get that many body parts so tightly woven together?"

Tersely, Greg raises his voice, "This is not a laughing matter. I found these in the computer lab. Did you look at the last page? That's your art assignment from the critical-writing unit we're team teaching."

Mohammed, the only art teacher in Middlebury Junior High, quickly turns to the last page, instantly recognizing the assignment he gave about evaluating artistic statuary. He looks up at Greg. "What's the Web site?" he asks a bit perplexed.

"Don't know," Greg says, shrugging his shoulders, "but I do know that we got problems. I thought the district software would filter this kind of stuff."

"You know the old saying," Mohammed says with a Cheshire grin, "where's there's a filter, there's a way."

"As I said, we have a problem," Greg says flatly.

Mohammed looks again at the beginnings of the art-critique assignment in his hands. "Hmm, interesting," he murmurs to himself. "Ah, so that's how it worked. What deviltry."

"What in the world are you talking about?" Greg asks, with irritation in his voice.

"Look here, Greg," Mohammed says pointing to the assignment. "The student has written down some search terms. One was "statuary". Then, it appears, the terms that came up included "human statuary," so the student clicked on that and a website entitled "live.now.biz" appeared. So far everything looks legit. But click on "live.now.biz" and, I'll bet, one of the pictures we have here was instantly on the monitor."

"I'll take your word for it. In any case, we need to figure out how to help students make critical choices about what to use and what not to use on the Internet."

"Just for the record," Mohammed inserts, "these pictures do not pass many tests of artistic merit. So why do you think the student—students, maybe—printed them?"

"Curiosity," Greg offers quickly. "And I'll wager that the pics were left in a hurry, probably because the student and his or her collaborators were spooked somehow. That's why the assignment was left."

"As we've been talking," Mohammed starts, "I've been thinking about what I could have done to guide students to useful sources. I now notice that my assignment didn't say anything about how to evaluate Internet sources. I don't think it's going to be especially easy to edit this assignment so that students are aware of issues related to authority, authenticity, and bias when they evaluate Internet sources."

"I've been thinking, too," Greg agrees. "I thought evaluating Web sites had been covered long before eighth grade. I didn't think I'd need to cover it in my eighth-grade English class. How do we get around the common notion that one person's trash is another's treasure when it comes to Internet sources?"

"That's a real problem. I hear students say every day that what is right to one person may not be right for another. That rather flimsy approach to life—and to art—means that there are no standards in art, no aesthetic standards to guide our choices of what really is beautiful." Mohammed turns his attention to the pictures he had laid down. Pointing to them, he says, "This stuff is bad art, in so far as it makes any claim to being art at all. But I have no doubt that a diligent student could find something on the Internet, some Web site about the authenticity of this kind of rubbish. A loony may be the author of such a diatribe, but how would students know?"

Greg hesitates but says cautiously, "So are you saying that we need to protect kids from the world out there? What about freedom of expression and all that?"

"We really do need to schedule lunch and talk about this soon," Mohammed says seriously.

"More pressing, I think I know what needs to be added to the agenda for our next grade-level meeting."

○ Expanding the Definitions of Literacy

Over a decade ago, the Secretary's Commission on Achieving Necessary Skills ([SCANS]; Murray, 2003) identified information and technology as two of the five competencies needed for meaningful employment. In the 1990s, other authors (e.g., Tyner, 1998) suggested learning with and from computers required additional literacy skills beyond reading, writing, listening, and speaking. Technology literacy, computer literacy, network literacy (Tyner), Internet literacy (Schmar-Dobler, 2003), information literacy (Bishop, 2003), and media literacy (Aufderheide & Firestone, 1993; Hobbs & Frost, 2003) have all been proposed as requisite literacies for the Information Age, where meaning and interpretations are impacted by sources of information, symbols, and multimedia.

In this chapter, we will examine information literacy and media literacy, which have benefited from research and extensive curricular planning. In addition, we will survey children's safety on the Internet, and finally, copyrights and plagiarism. But first, we provide a Classroom Snapshot by Sonja Bell-Joyner.

Computer Classroom Snapshot

Context

My name is Sonja Bell-Joyner, and I teach fourth through sixth graders at New Hope Christian Academy (NHCA), an independent Christian school located in Memphis, TN. During my third year at NHCA, the school received funding for new laptop computers. The laptops were distributed among our stationary computer lab and the fourth- through sixth-grade classrooms. At that time, NHCA did not have a standardized technology curriculum in place, and the technology teacher was applying lessons based on a technology curriculum created by another independent school in the city.

Using my background in technology integration, I prepared a unit on Internet research to benefit students as they moved on to secondary school. The purpose of this unit was to help address two pressing issues concerning student preparation at New Hope Christian Academy:

1. Incorporating critical-thinking skills into all academic areas, including specialty area instruction (i.e., technology); and
2. Creating a college-preparatory curriculum competitive with other independent schools.

I decided to focus specifically on sixth-grade students, since sixth graders would be moving to other middle schools at the end of the school year.

What I Did and Why

The model used for this lesson's content was the Big 6 Information-Problem-Solving Approach, developed by Mike Eisenberg and Bob Berkowitz. The Big 6

(continued)

provides a step-by-step approach for helping students solve problems that require research using different sources of information. I chose this model for the unit because it satisfied both of the issues mentioned previously: incorporating critical-thinking skills in all curricula and adopting a curriculum that prepares students for other independent schools. Because the problem in this lesson dealt with the students' lack of critical-thinking and computer-researching skills, I focused on providing effective information, seeking strategies to prevent students from adopting poor search behaviors. I believed this method would help not only in reinforcing critical-thinking skills in different subject areas, but also in transferring this new knowledge to future research projects.

Each instructional step of the Big 6 represented a section of the unit, except for Step 5: Synthesis, which was the culminating project. For each section of the unit, I used the following lesson sequence: introduction to the lesson, presentation of new information with examples, guided practice with formative feedback from the teacher, and individual practice with teacher feedback. Prior to beginning a new lesson, I reviewed the previous lessons and conducted any suggested prerequisite activities.

Because the sixth-grade classroom had its own set of laptops, the teacher could discuss the contents of the unit in parts, focusing on the more challenging sections after students reviewed each section of the unit. For example, teachers could concentrate on section one, *identifying the task*, in one day, while the third section, *using advanced search techniques*, might take longer than one day, due to the content. This flexible approach of allocating time to each section provides the teacher with enough time to ensure that each student is learning correctly. The most important reason why I chose this model is that it provided the students with a skill that was transferable to other contexts, such as English, social studies, and history.

What I Learned

When I asked students to express their views on research before starting the unit, they shared both negative and positive aspects. Negative responses included research was "boring," "hectic when procrastinating to complete a project," "avoided when possible," "a waste of time," "hard," and "confusing." Positive responses included research was "interesting," "fun because of the Internet," and "good because it helps you learn more."

After teaching the unit, I noticed that it had a positive influence on the students' learning because it allowed them to honestly evaluate their strengths and weaknesses with regard to research. Students responded that they had more confidence in their knowledge of computers and prediction of performance in future computer classes. They were also interested in learning about other technology units, including Web sites, advanced PowerPoint skills, keyboarding, advanced Internet skills, computer building, basic functions of operating systems, and digital presentations.

However, looking at the students' works indicated that they had difficulty understanding the instruction. At the end of the unit, students should have had a basic understanding of the research process. Most of the activities within the unit required prerequisite knowledge that students had not been exposed to, such as the characteristics of information sources, including differences between periodicals and reference books. Although all students agreed that the practice exercises made learning easier, student performance showed that most exercises resulted in only partial mastery. For example, our students continued to struggle with identifying the subject of a sentence and brainstorming possible synonyms that would be used with keyword searches. These skills were required as part of Steps 1 and 2 in the Big 6 process to determine the focus of the research topic and possible strategies for searches.

In the future, to make the learning process easier and more effective for other students, I will add prelesson activities that will satisfy lesson prerequisites. For example, I plan to create lessons that allow the students to explore the different types of information sources, such as a magazine and encyclopedia scavenger hunt, so that they can contrast the types of information these sources may have. Another example would be to have students use the thesaurus to generate synonyms for their keyword searches and incorporate a supplemental lesson on synonyms. It was also evident that the students needed additional practice exercises at the end of each section. For example, I think students would benefit from evaluating Web sites using a class-generated rubric to judge the quality, accuracy, and bias of sources.

○ Information Literacy

As can be seen from Sonja's illustration above, having students think critically about the types of information they need, possible sources, utility of those sources, and aggregating the information together is not an easy task. These types of skills build on reading and writing abilities typical of traditional literacy. Bishop (2003) defined information literacy as a use of seven skills:

a. recognize the need for information;
b. identify and locate sources;
c. access appropriate information within these sources;
d. evaluate the quality of information from the sources;
e. organize and synthesize the collected information;
f. use the information effectively; and
g. produce new information. (p. 14)

Given the volume of information available digitally (i.e., CD-ROMs, Internet) and in print, this is a tall order for students. These skills include using databases and search engines, choosing appropriate keywords for searches, navigating through electronic systems, downloading, printing or saving various media, using higher-order thinking skills to collate and abstract information, purposefully using the information, and producing new information through the use of other technologies, such as those mentioned in Chapter 2.

Specifically on the Internet, Schmar-Dobler (2003) suggests the sheer quantities of text and information available can be overwhelming. A vast majority of text on the

Internet is expository, so learners must be able to comprehend the text and determine its utility. In addition, using text and media from the Internet requires students to evaluate the features of different organizational structures on Web pages and then determine the usefulness of menu and navigational options. While examining adult readers on the Internet, well-respected "Internet use guru" Jakob Nielsen (2005) found that struggling readers "plowed" through texts online with slow speeds. Moreover, the Children's Partnership (1999) identified literacy and language as barriers to children and adults using the Internet successfully. The majority of online content has been developed for individuals with average or advanced literacy levels. Similarly, an estimated 87 percent of the documents on the Internet are written in English, yet at least 32 million Americans do not speak English as their primary language. So the potential of the Internet is obscured by its textual content and organization. For more information on English-language learners and struggling readers, see Chapters 6 and 7, respectively.

Given the increasing importance of information literacy, Educational Testing Service (ETS) makers and administrators of the SAT and Graduate Record Exam have begun implementing a test of information and communication technology (ICT) (Associated Press, 2006). The test purports to measure both technical skills of using information and communication technology tools as well as critical-thinking skills (Educational Testing Service, 2006).

Standards

While the use of myriad information sources may seem daunting, all teachers are responsible for integrating information literacy into their curricula. In 1998, the American Association of School Librarians (AASL) and the Association for Education Communications and Technology (AECT) proposed three standards for information literacy. The student who is information literate:

1. accesses information efficiently and effectively;
2. evaluates information critically and competently; and
3. uses information accurately and creatively. (Arp & Woodard, 2002, p. 127)

In addition, the widely accepted National Educational Technology Standards for Students (NETS-S) developed by the International Society for Technology in Education ([ISTE], 2000) proposes that students understand ethical, cultural, and societal issues related to technology and information use (Standard 2) as well as use technology to locate, evaluate, and collect information from a variety of sources based on a specific task.

These standards recognize changes in the ways we seek out, research, and use digital information. However, they do not address how we as teachers were taught to access, evaluate, and use information. Most of us in classrooms today were taught to respect and trust specific types of print sources, such as encyclopedias, nonfiction expository texts, and newspapers. In contrast, currently, more and more of us are using digital information from many different sources, such as Web sites, e-mails, and even podcasts. So how do we determine which sources are accurate and reliable? And how do we find these sources to begin with? The standards do little to suggest how we might achieve information literacy. Instead, it is left up to classroom teachers and media specialists to determine the appropriate instruction to meet these standards.

The Big 6

While the standards may suggest a direction for teachers and curricula, the broad language sometimes makes it difficult to integrate into a classroom. To combat this issue at a classroom or school level, Eisenberg, Bekowitz and their colleagues (e.g., Eisenberg, 2003; Eisenberg & Johnson, 2002; **http://www.big6.org**) proposed the Big 6 as a model for information problem solving (see Figure 5.1).

The Big 6, as discussed in the Classroom Snapshot, provides a process for students to follow when solving problems that require the use of information. As the name suggests, there are six steps to follow, which may or may not be linear. See Figure 5.2 for an overview of these steps. Eisenberg (2003) suggests that it is not necessary to teach all the steps at one

Figure 5.1   The Big 6 information skills were created by Mike Eisenberg and Bob Berkowitz to help students and teachers solve information and research problems. The Big 6 Web site is located at http://www.big6.com, and the companion software is located at http://www.Big6TurboTools.com.

Screenshot used with permission.

Figure 5.2   The Big 6 Process for Information Problem-Solving.

1. Task definition
   a. Define the problem.
   b. Identify the information needed.
2. Information Seeking Strategy
   a. Determine all possible sources.
   b. Select the best sources.
3. Location and Access
   a. Locate sources.
   b. Find information within sources.
4. Use of Information
   a. Engage (e.g., read, hear, view).
   b. Extract relevant information.
5. Synthesis
   a. Organize information from multiple sources.
   b. Present the result.
6. Evaluation
   a. Judge the result (effectiveness).
   b. Judge the process (efficiency).

time. More importantly, the Big 6 process should be used in context with appropriate learning activities. For example, task definition and information seeking strategy may be taught while using the Internet with one activity, and later steps may be taught in a different unit.

Because the Big 6 is a process for information literacy, it is not tied to any one particular technology. As such, the process for solving information problems will not become obsolete—even though some of the technologies we use today will.

○ Media Literacy

Like information literacy, media literacy involves analysis, evaluation, and interpretation. Media literacy, moreover, suggests that learners should have the "ability to access, analyze, evaluate, and communicate messages in a wide variety of forms" (Aufderheide & Firestone, 1993 as cited in Hobbs & Frost, 2003, p. 334). Media literacy, in particular, focuses on critical thinking of the media and technology messages we receive from (a) written and oral language, (b) graphics and moving images, and (c) audio and music (Hobbs & Frost).

By integrating media literacy with other types of textual analysis that are part of our language arts curricula, learners will be able to deconstruct the messages in various media with similar elements of traditional curricula, such as meaning, point of view, and literary devices (Hobbs & Frost, 2003). For example, Hobbs and Frost suggest media literacy activities would include:

a. reflect and analyze media consumption;
b. identify author, purpose and point of view;
c. identify the range of production techniques to shape point of view and audience responses; and
d. identify and evaluate quality and bias. (p. 334)

While Hobbs and Frost's research suggests that a sustained media literacy curriculum can positively impact learners' abilities to identify "construction techniques for print news media, audio, and television news" (p. 351), other authors have questioned the impact of media literacy. For instance, Scharrer (2002/2003) reports the limitation of media literacy for helping individuals resist media effects and questions whether we should expect media literacy to impact everyone similarly: Just as the media are not presumed to affect all audience members in a universal way, participation in media literacy should not be presumed to operate similarly for all those involved. (p. 356)

Scharrer suggests the ways that we assess and evaluate media literacy's impact should not be confined to objective measures. Instead, performance measures, such as essays, construction of news media, and critiques of popular culture, television, and music, should be used in an ongoing process.

⊙ Safety on the Internet

With tremendous volumes of information and media available on the Internet, using Internet resources in our classrooms would seem a "no-brainer." But as we've discussed above, determining accuracy, bias, and purpose has made using the myriad digital resources available on the Web tricky. Moreover, it can be precarious. We are all familiar with e-mails similar to the following:

Subject:	Funds Transfer
Date:	May 22, 2006 8:10:19 AM CDT

Dear Sir/Madam:

Do accept my sincere apologies if my mail does not meet your personal ethics. I will introduce myself as William, a staff in the accounts management section of a well-known bank here in South Africa.

One of our accounts with holding balance of $15,000,000 (fifteen million dollars) has been dormant and has not been operated for the past four years.

From my investigations and confirmations, the owner of this account, a foreigner by name Austin Martins, died in August 2000, and since then, nobody has done anything in regards to claiming this money because he has no family members who are aware of the existence of the account or the funds. Also, information from the National Immigration States that he also was single on entry into the SA.

I have secretly discussed this matter with some of the bank officials, and we have agreed to find a reliable foreign partner to deal with. We thus propose to do business

(continued)

with you, standing in as the next of kin of these funds from the deceased, and funds released to you after due processes have been followed.

This transaction is totally free of risk and troubles as the fund is a legitimate and does not originate from drug, money laundering, terrorism, or any other illegal act.

If interested, let me hear from you.

Regards,

William

And ones like this . . .

Subject:	Fw: Fw: PLEEEEASE REEEEEEAD! IT WAS ON GOOD MORNING AMERICA
Date:	Thu, 20 Jul 2006

I had to try this . . . Nothing to lose but a few minutes of my time. Good luck everyone$$$$.

Darlene

——— Original Message———

Sent: Thursday, July 20, 2006 8:24 AM

Subject: Fw: Fw: PLEEEEASE REEEEEEAD! IT WAS ON GOOD MORNING AMERICA

THIS TOOK TWO PAGES OF THE TUESDAY USA TODAY - IT IS FOR REAL

Subject: PLEEEEEEASE READ! ! ! ! It was on GOOD MORNING AMERICA! ! ! ! It was on the news!

Kathy South
Alcoa - EHS Maintenance Coordinator
Phone: 765/771-3547
Pager : 765/420-6575

To all of my friends, I do not usually forward messages, but this is from my good friend Pearlas Sandborn, and she really is an attorney.

(continued)

If she says that this will work—it will work. After all, What have you got to lose? SORRY EVERYBODY. JUST HAD TO TAKE THE CHANCE! ! ! I'm an attorney, and I know the law. This thing is for real. Rest assured, AOL and Intel will follow through with their promises for fear of facing a multimillion-dollar class-action suit similar to the one filed by PepsiCo against General Electric not too long ago.

Dear Friends: Please do not take this as a junk letter. Bill Gates is sharing his fortune. If you ignore this, you will repent later. Microsoft and AOL are now the largest Internet companies, and in an effort to make sure that Internet Explorer remains the most widely used program, Microsoft and AOL are running an e-mail beta test.

When you forward this e-mail to friends, Microsoft can and will track it (if you are a Microsoft Windows user) for a two weeks per time period.

For every person that you forward this e-mail to, Microsoft will pay you $245.00. For every person that you sent it to that forwards it on, Microsoft will pay you $243.00, and for every third person that receives it, you will be paid $241.00. Within two weeks, Microsoft will contact you for your address and then send you a check.

Regards,

Charles S. Bailey
General Manager Field Operations
1-800-842-2332 Ext. 1085 or 904-1085 or RNX
292-1085 Charles_Bailey@csx.com
Charles_bailey@csx.com

I thought this was a scam myself, but two weeks after receiving this e-mail and forwarding it on, Microsoft contacted me for my address and within days, I receive a check for $24,800.00. You need to respond before the beta testing is over. If anyone can afford this, Bill Gates is the man.

It's all marketing expense to him. Please forward this to as many people as possible. You are bound to get at least $10,000.00. We're not going to help them out with their e-mail beta test without getting a little something for our time. My brother's girlfriend got in on this a few months ago when I went to visit him for the Baylor/UT game. She showed me her check. It was for the sum of $4,324.44 and was stamped "Paid in full."

Like I said before, I know the law, and this is for real.

Intel and AOL are now discussing a merger, which would make them the largest Internet company, and in an effort make sure that AOL remains the most widely used program, Intel and AOL are running an e-mail beta test.

When you forward this e-mail to friends, Intel can and will track it (if you are a Microsoft Windows user) for a two week time period.

These types of communications seem very innocuous. The first message, called a "phishing" e-mail because is sent to a large number of individuals hoping to get a "bite" from someone, attempts to solicit your private information. Unfortunately, over a billion dollars are estimated to have been stolen as a result of Internet scams like these (Agence France Press, 2006), while only approximately $2 million have been investigated (National White Collar Crime Center & Federal Bureau of Investigation, 2005). The second message above is one of many Internet hoaxes that have traversed through e-mail for years. Many novice Internet users and individuals with low levels of information and media literacy are drawn to these types of deceptions by forwarding them on and clogging friends and relatives' inboxes. One Web site that has been in existence since 1995 to document these types of scams is Snopes.com (see Figure 5.3). The e-mail hoax in the second message above is documented at **http://www.snopes.com/inboxer/nothing/ microsoft-aol.asp.**

While experienced Internet users may be able to steer clear from phishing expeditions and hoaxes, all children must be protected from the barrage of inappropriate materials, such as graphic and violent images, as well as pornography, that make using the Internet potentially unsafe. Most recently, social networking Web sites, such as MySpace.com, Facebook.com, and Xanga.com, have become magnets for children to express themselves, make friends, and provide personal information unintentionally through blog entries, photos, and responses to friends (Rawe, 2006). During the writing of this text, MySpace.com overtook Google as the most visited site on the Web. One principal has urged parents to supervise what their students are posting onto social networking sites (Bailey, 2006a). As a result of the potential harm to children, schools and districts have implemented three types of interventions to protect students while using the Internet: acceptable use policies, blocking and filtering, and curricular programs.

Acceptable Use Policies (AUPs)

Acceptable use policies (AUPs) offer guidelines for using the technologies available. AUPs—for both teachers and students—are agreements regarding what is appropriate use of technologies, and the consequences for violations (Rader, 2002). Recently, using the Internet with children has provoked concerns about access to obscene materials, contact with pedophiles, and Internet gambling as well as e-mail spam and phishing. These issues are for the protection of children and should also be addressed within an AUP. In addition, software piracy and illegal downloading of music and other copyrighted materials are behaviors that also should be considered for inclusion. AUPs typically cover (a) use of Internet and e-mail, (b) other network applications, such as student information systems, (c) software, such as productivity tools (Mills, 2005), and (d) care with computer hardware.

When teachers begin each school year, they communicate to their students acceptable classroom behavior and academic expectations. These set the groundwork for what is expected and what is acceptable within the classroom regarding behavior, homework,

Figure 5.3 To help document urban legends and Internet hoaxes, Snopes.com collects and verifies potential rumors. This screenshot depicts the Microsoft/AOL giveaway described in the text. When discussing information literacy and media literacy, Snopes.com is a site students can reference to determine validity and authenticity of communications.

Screenshot used with permission from Snopes.com.

assignments, and grades. Similarly, AUPs should be incorporated into this discussion of expectations. Yahoo!'s popular search engine and site for children, Yahooligans (Yahoo! Inc., 2002a), advocates that "AUPs are only as effective as the education that accompanies them," and similar to behavior, they require consistent monitoring and enforcement.

The Web includes a number of sites for examples of AUPs. Yahooligans (Yahoo! Inc., 2002b) provides these guidelines:

1. Define the purpose and educational goals of the technologies and network.
2. Explain what an AUP is and what is included.
3. Describe what access to technology is available when it is available.
4. Define student and teacher responsibilities (dos & don'ts).
5. Describe issues of personal safety and how users should protect themselves.
6. Describe the consequences of inappropriate use.
7. Provide a space for student and parent or teacher consent.

Copies of guidelines are provided to students, parents, and teachers, and signed copies are stored in the school office as documentation of consent. All policies suggest infractions of the AUP result in temporary or permanent loss of access to technologies (Kinnaman, 1995/2003).

Blocking and Filtering

AUPs provide guidelines for responsible and appropriate use while students are on the Internet. However, public law (Children's Internet Protection Act, 2000) and 21 states' laws (National Conference of State Legislatures, 2006) require public libraries and schools to go further. While often used interchangeably, blocking and filtering are two different methods of preventing children from accessing explicit, obscene, or harmful materials and visual depictions.

Blocking means stopping access to Web pages based on their Internet address (i.e., a Web page's Uniform Resources Location, or URL) (Boss, n.d.). Filtering, however, means stopping access based on the specific content of a Web page. Blocks are determined based on a list of "blacklisted" Web addresses. Filtering analyzes the Web page content and compares it against a database of keywords common on risky Web sites (Villeneuve, 2006).

It is important to recognize three issues with regard to blocking and filtering. First, as the Texas Internet Service Providers (ISP) Association (Texas ISP Association, n.d.) notes, all blocking and filtering software are fallible. Parents and teachers are still the most effective means to protect children by educating them, such as with Internet safety curricula, and monitoring children's computer uses. Second, it is also essential to appreciate the cost of using blocking and filtering software: Blocking and filtering software do not always discriminate effectively between acceptable and unacceptable Internet sources. So a person who uses blocking and filtering software may not have access to Internet sources that could be valuable to him or her because, although the sources are perfectly legitimate, for whatever reason they are blocked or filtered. Moreover, there are methods to circumvent blocking and filtering software, which are explained on freely accessible Web pages, which are not blocked (Villeneuve, 2006). Third and finally, blocking and filtering do not apply to all communications technologies (Villeneuve). For example, blocking and filtering do not necessarily affect e-mail, instant messaging or audio and video conferencing. Other security measures are necessary to combat these. But again, the cost of inaccessibility is significant.

Curricular Programs

The final way teachers, schools, and districts can protect students while using the Internet is by integrating Internet safety curricula, like i-SAFE. In addition to access to inappropriate materials, communications on the Internet, such as chat, instant messaging, and e-mail, can be fraught with unsafe activities, such as cyber-bullies and online predators. As described above, students can innocently provide personal information on social networking or other Web sites that require logins.

i-SAFE, supported by the Office of Juvenile Justice and Delinquency Prevention, provides Internet safety curricula (see Figure 5.4). The curriculum for K–4 grades focuses age-appropriate concepts of "safe and responsible Internet use" (i-SAFE America Inc., n.d.,

Curriculum for Kindergarten through Fourth Grades section, para. 1). The fifth through twelfth grades' curricula focuses on four areas through cooperative learning: (a) Internet safety, (b) Internet security, (c) intellectual-property theft, and (d) the Internet community (Curriculum for Fifth through Twelfth Grades section, para. 1). As part of the curriculum, students become advocates for Internet safety with one another. i-SAFE provides free professional development and curricula materials for teachers and schools.

Figure 5.4   Internet safety and responsibility curricula are supplied through i-SAFE, supported through the Office of Juvenile Justice and Delinquency Prevention. Curricula are for students K–12, divided into three grade clusters. See http://www.isafe.org.

Screenshot used with permission.

The Shelby County school system outside of Memphis, TN, has chosen to use i-SAFE aggressively to combat the potential deleterious effects of using the Internet with children and to help prevent unsafe acts and irresponsible deeds, such as meeting online predators and plagiarism (Bailey, 2006a, 2006b).

Protecting Student Privacy

The potential for error is easy: While visiting a link during research on *To Kill a Mockingbird*, a student is asked for her name, e-mail address, and zip code before entering the site. As teachers, administrators, curriculum coordinators, and library media specialists, we must act in the best interest of our children. In this case, we must educate our children about self-disclosing personal information online.

Our students should be instructed not to provide any personal information, such as addresses, telephone numbers, passwords, or social security numbers to sites on the Web (McGraw-Hill Ryerson Limited, 2002), which should be included as part of the education process with AUPs. While Web sites that require registrations are obvious instances where students should be wary, there are less overt sites where students might share personal information. As described above, social networking sites, such as MySpace.com and Facebook.com, offer individuals the opportunity to connect with many others with similar interests. However, students may inadvertently disclose too much personal information in ways that may make them vulnerable. Recently, in the summer of 2006, a teenage girl made national headlines as she secretly flew to the Middle East to meet the man she planned to marry. They met on MySpace.com (Rawe, 2006).

In other chapters of this text, we advocate for publishing student work to the Web, using communications such as e-mail to bring in external audiences to our classrooms, and we propose the use of audio and video recordings to provide authenticity and multiple representations of knowledge. However, we must also encourage teachers and parents to determine how much of this exposure is helpful and how much is potentially harmful to students. Parents, in all cases, must approve photos to be displayed on the Internet, but parents also may need to approve student work before it is posted (McKenzie, 1996 as cited in Wang & Gearhart, 2006; Willard, 2002). The Children's Internet Protection Act (Children's Internet Protection Act, 2000) and the Children's Online Privacy Protection Act (Children's Online Privacy Protection Act of 1998, 2000) provide guidelines for school districts and corporations to follow when posting, collecting, and using personal data about children. So in the same way we teach children to be safe while on playgrounds, we also must educate our children to remain safe while using the Internet.

◯ Teaching and Learning with Digital Sources
Copyright and Fair Use

We have already suggested that students can use materials from other sources to create a multimedia presentation. The perception by many students is that everything that can be copied from the Internet is free to use. Students will illegally download text, images, music, videos, and software because they perceive it to be freely available and in the public domain (Rader, 2002). Most people in fact do not understand that copyright—the exclusive right to one's work—is guaranteed the moment that work is produced. Thus, the first draft of this very chapter, the moment it was written—in fact, *while* it was being written—was copyrighted. Of course, had other supposed authors pirated the chapter in draft form, cleaned it up a bit, and published it, we would have had to decide whether it was worth our time and money to prosecute them. Even though we legally were granted copyright at the moment of production of the chapter, proving our ownership of the chapter is another matter.

The classic way to prove ownership is to file and be awarded a copyright from the U.S. government. Thus, this book has been copyrighted: It displays the copyright symbol together with the year the copyright was awarded. The copyright symbol and date constitute a formal statement of copyright. In fact, the right of copyright precedes the formal statement of copyright. This means that an author's right to control the distribution of his or her work does not require the copyright symbol and date.

What does this have to do with the Internet? We know that original works published on the Internet are the intellectual property of the individual creator, who retains the copyright. When you download a document from the Internet, it may be copyrighted even though it does not carry the copyright symbol and date. We say "may be" because some works—such as government documents—are not copyrighted but are freely available to the public so that people can photocopy or download them without any concern about copyright violation. However, a Web site with instructions about how to evaluate style in writing may very well be copyrighted, and downloading information from that site into your own site, or into a document your students are producing, could be a violation of copyright. At this point in the legal wrangling about copyright, linking your site to another site is not a violation of copyright. So perhaps the best way to deal with many potential and real problems associated with copyright law is to create a hyperlink so that readers can go directly to a related site. In this way you don't have to download information from a site and transfer it to your site. It is, however, *always* appropriate to contact the original site's authors to inform them you will be linking to their site.

While copyright defines ownership of original works, fair use allows teachers and students to use an author's work without prior permission for specific purposes (Johnson & Groneman, 2003). However, fair use is limited in scope. A teacher may use copyrighted works for instructional purposes, but a teacher may not create a collection of works to be copied and distributed to a class. The Agreement on Guidelines for Classroom Copying in Not-for-Profit Educational Institutions (see Johnson & Groneman, 2003 for a summary) is not a law, but it provides an outline for following fair use both in print and electronically: A teacher may create a *single* copy of a work (e.g., chapter of a book, newspaper article, diagram) for use in scholarly research or course preparation.

Wang and Gearhart (2006) provide these guidelines when creating multi- and hypermedia:

1. Students may use portions of copyrighted works if the work is part of a course assignment.
2. There are fair use limits depending on the form of medium: (a) up to 10 percent or three minutes of a copyrighted motion media work; (b) up to 10 percent or 1,000 words of text; (c) up to 10 percent or 30 seconds of music and lyrics; and (d) up to 5 photographic images. (p. 193)

Other sources, such as Web sites and e-mail, are also protected under copyright. The original author or employing company of the work owns the copyright (Wang & Gearhart).

Our students' works should be protected as well. Original student work is also copyrighted. Reflecting the appropriate age level, student and/or parent consent should be considered before publishing student work on the Internet.

Plagiarism

With increasing use of electronic sources of information and the ease of copy/paste commands, plagiarism is a critical concern of writing and literacy in the Information Age. As discussed earlier with copyrights, the illegal use of an author's intellectual property violates copyright. So plagiarism is synonymous with copyright infringement (Johnson & Groneman, 2003). For example, when collecting information for a research paper online, students will often copy and paste the original Web page text into their notes. They may not, however, take the time to paraphrase the text or diligently collect the bibliographical reference. Later, when they are prewriting, students may forget that the text was not paraphrased or simply be too lazy to retrieve the reference. Baron and Crooks (2005) dub this "cut and paste plagiarism." Within the writing process, we need to emphasize the needs for respecting intellectual property, honoring copyrights, and referencing authors' original works whether students are creating word-processed papers, Web sites, or audio recordings.

It is our responsibility to educate our students about appropriate referencing methods and why these are important. An invaluable partner in this endeavor may be your library media specialist. Your media specialist may be able to augment your classroom curriculum with instruction within the library. These individuals may also provide support in your own work to prevent copyright infringement and stay within fair use guidelines. Media coordinators have often been a first alternative for questions regarding fair-use (Mills, 2005).

There are simple methods to aid in preventing plagiarism. Rader (2002) suggests foremost teachers should model ethical behaviors for students, such as avoid using copyrighted works on course handouts, and provide appropriate reference citations. In addition, Rader advocates for discussions about plagiarism. Again, students tend to believe the information available on the Internet is freely available for any use. Second, for your students, it may be necessary to require copies of original source documents when assignments are submitted. Providing the source documents communicates to your students that you respect copyrights. Heberling (2002) suggests a "search in reverse," where the teacher extracts a specific phrase from a student's paper and inserts that phrase into a search engine, such as Google, within quotation marks. Any results to exact matches require additional investigation.

In addition to simple methods to prevent plagiarism, some schools have begun to consider plagiarism detection software as an option to teach students about plagiarism and how to avoid it. Primarily in use in secondary and post-secondary schools, software such as Turnitin.com and SafeAssignment within MyDropBox.com compare submitted student materials and previously submitted papers. Questionable areas are highlighted in an originality report and linked to the original sources. At the University of Memphis, we have begun using Turnitin.com within the past year. Some instructors on campus are allowing students to submit their work prior to due dates, so that the students may revise based on the feedback provided from the software. Other instructors are only using it as a punitive measure to detect plagiarism.

In this chapter, we have discussed a variety of issues and concerns related to literacy in the Information Age. While they do not preclude reading, writing, speaking, and listening, media literacy and information literacy were considered with respect to the traditional forms of literacy and how these new literacies may be impacting how we receive, retrieve, and interpret information messages. In addition, safety on the Internet was discussed. Curricular programs, like i-SAFE, filtering and blocking software are excellent additions, but teachers must be diligent in teaching children how to protect themselves from potentially harmful materials or individuals. Finally, copyright and fair use was surveyed with particular attention to how to work with different media and prevent plagiarism.

COMPUTER CLASSROOM LESSONS

Pinpointing Propaganda

Grade Level: 5–8

Objective: Identify propaganda and persuasive techniques
Analyze different media for purpose, point of view, and bias
Create an advertising or propaganda piece

Time: 3–5 days

Problem to Be Solved: Using different historical and current source media, students will generate an original piece of propaganda

Materials:

Various examples of propaganda from historical documents and current media (e.g., George Tyler WWI Poster Exhibit **http://exhibitions.library.temple.edu/ ww1/index2.jsp**, America's Army video game, or the McDonald's online game **http://www.mcvideogame.com/**)

Internet-connected computers
Various computer production software (e.g., word processor, sound recording, video editing)

Steps:

1. In small groups, provide students with examples and/or links to examples of propaganda or commercial persuasion. Ask students to think about (a) what the authors were trying to accomplish, (b) why they were sending the message, and (c) what types of methods the authors were using to persuade you.
2. Discuss persuasive techniques of Bandwagon, Testimonial, Transfer, Repetition, and Emotional words.
3. Back in small groups, have students identify these techniques in the examples presented earlier. Share their findings with the rest of the class.
4. Still in small groups, have students plan a political or commercial propaganda piece. The piece may be a poster, short radio advertisement, or video commercial. Students will need to brainstorm the purpose of their propaganda piece and which techniques they will use.
5. Students will then produce their piece. A poster may be created on the computer in a word-processing program. For a short radio advertisement, a script will need to be written first, and then it may be recorded into a program such as Audacity or GarageBand. A video commercial will also need a script and plan for different shots. After the video has been captured, it may be edited in a program such as iMovie.
6. Have each student in the group write a short description of the methods their group used in their propaganda piece.

Assessment: Using a rubric, assess the quality of the students' propaganda pieces with regard to (a) planning, (b) purpose, (c) persuasive methods, (d) persuasiveness, (e) difficulty, and (f) creativity. Assess each individual student's descriptive paragraph for accuracy in (a) identifying techniques, (b) defining the technique, and (c) using proper grammar and mechanics.

Quality of Web Site Sources

Grade Level: 6–8 adaptable

Objective: Analyze the accuracy and bias of Web sites
Identify author, purpose, and point of view of Web sites
Identify and evaluate quality of Web sites

Time: 2–3 days

Problem to Be Solved: Using various Web sites, students will analyze these sites using a class-constructed rubric.

Materials: Internet-connected computers

A list of various Web sites to judge author, purpose, point of view, accuracy and bias

Steps:

1. As a whole class demonstration or in a computer lab, show to students one or more of the following sites:
   http://www.malepregnancy.com/
   http://www.improb.com/airchives/classical/cat/cat.html
   http://www.snopes.com/disney/parks/matterho.asp
2. Discuss with students whether a site is real or fake. Make a list on the board of ideas to determine a site's validity. Have students question:
   What methods would you use to determine its authenticity?
   How would you check to see if a site is legitimate?
   What methods do you use to determine the credibility of a Web site? Is the author an authority?
3. If not already covered, extend your class discussion to include:
   Bias
   Purpose
   Currency
   Coverage of a topic
4. As a class, distill the list to create possible criteria to judge Web sites. Convert the list of criteria into an evaluation checklist. You may retype the list, providing students with a copy for each site they will visit later. Or have students copy the list into their notebooks and create a chart for each of the sites they visit.
5. In a computer lab, with a laptop cart, using rotations in your classroom, or in small groups, have students visit three to five Web sites. Have them use the class-generated rubric to judge the legitimacy and quality of the sites.
6. In dyads or small groups, have students compare and discuss answers.
7. As a whole class, tally the responses from each student's rubric onto a class chart (either on the board or LCD computer projector). Discuss each site, its authenticity, and its quality. Be sure students understand methods to determine the reliability of information they find on the Internet.

Assessment: Use whole class teacher questioning to assess understanding of accuracy, bias, author, point of view and quality in different Web sites. During questioning, propose scenarios that students should consider when viewing a Web site as a source of information. Review student Web site evaluations for (a) analysis of accuracy and bias within Web sites; (b) identification of author, purpose, point of view, currency, and coverage of topic; and (c) evaluation of overall quality of Web site to provide reliable information.

○ Techno-Teacher Tips

Working at Home

Some teachers use their personal computers and Internet connections at home to locate Internet resources and evaluate Web sites for students to use. A number of teachers have related to us that they spent hours researching Web sites for their students at home only to discover the school computers blocked many of the sites. Since filtering is typically managed centrally at a district or state level, it can be difficult to unblock Web sites teachers have identified as useful. Teachers typically have to submit the Web site to a district- or state-level technology coordinator with a justification as to why the site should be unblocked. As a tip, be sure to check any Web sites you may have located at home on a school computer prior to teaching the lesson.

Preventing Unauthorized Access

Many Web sites that require logins with passwords will also have an option to save your login ID and/or password as a convenience so you don't have to enter it each time. If you're on your own personal computer at home, this is fine. However, if you or your students are using computers at school, particularly where many people share the computer, such as in a computer lab, be sure to leave this unchecked. Your login information is stored in a "cookie" on the computer hard drive itself, and the next person who visits that Web site will be able to login as you, because the computer will supply the login and password for them.

When using computers that are shared, be sure to quit or exit completely from Web browsers when you have visited Web sites that require logins and passwords. Many sites keep you logged in even if you visit another Web site. So the next person who uses the computer and visits the same site would still be logged in as you. This can be critical when you have multiple class periods that follow the same lesson plan. For example, when Period 2 students come in to visit the Web site you have planned, if your Period 1 students have not logged off properly, the Period 2 students may already be logged in as Period 1 students.

○ Frequently Asked Questions

1. **Wikipedia seems like a great online encyclopedia. Why doesn't everybody use it?**

    Wikipedia is an open, collaborative site, where anyone can contribute. As such, it is a work in progress, where some topics may include misinformation, opinion, or vandalism. Wikipedia suggests that their older articles typically are the most accurate, reliable, and comprehensive (Wikipedia Foundation Inc., 2006a). However, their newer topics often represent the most current information and research. In addition, because of the way Wikipedia relates with other information sources on the Web, you should be wary of other online sources that may corroborate information in Wikipedia; these sources, instead, may just be reproductions of previous Wikipedia versions. In fact, Wikipedia suggests you keep in mind three simple rules for information searches:

○ Always be wary of any one single source or of multiple works that derive from a single source.
○ Where articles have references to external sources (whether online or not), read the references and check whether they really do support what the article says.
○ Many times, an encyclopedia may not constitute an acceptable source for a research paper. (Wikipedia Foundation Inc., 2006b)

2. **I would really like to include something like the Big6 information problem solving model in my curriculum, but it seems like it would take too long. Is that true?**

Having students initially work through the Big6 model could take a week or more, depending on the depth of searching and research. But it's important to note that the whole model does not have to be accomplished—beginning to end—to be effective. Instead, it is possible to divide parts of the process into chunks and have students work on these sections separately at different times of the year with different projects. For example, it is possible to have students complete Step 1: Task Definition and Step 2: Information-Seeking Strategies as part of another unit, similar to the lesson plan "Quality of Web Site Sources" described above. In another unit, you may want students to practice library skills and searching for scientific information, so you may have them complete Steps 1 and 2 and then add Step 3: Location and Access to include both print and digital resources. With students comfortable with these steps, you may have students complete a full research assignment continuing through all six steps.

3. **I help tutor elementary-age students in an after-school care program at a neighborhood community center. We don't have any filtering software on our computers. Is there a way I can help protect our children from inappropriate Web sites?**

In addition to having supervised computer time, which is a must, you can change the preferences in your search engine to increase the filtering options. For example, in Google, you can go to the Google preferences (**http://www. google.com/preferences?hl5en**) and select "Use strict filtering," which will filter out explicit text and explicit images. As described above, no filter is 100 percent accurate, so supervising computer time with the children is essential.

◯ References

Agence France Press. (2006). *500-plus nabbed in global Internet scams:* U.S. Retrieved August 18, 2006, from LexisNexis Academic database.

Arp, L., & Woodard, B. S. (2002). Recent trends in information literacy and instruction. *Reference & User Services Quarterly, 42*(2), 124–132.

Associated Press. (2006, February 6). *New exam measures technical literacy.* Retrieved February 6, 2006, from http://www.foxnews.com/story/0,2933,183773,00.html

Aufderheide, P., & Firestone, C. (1993). *Media literacy: A report of the national leadership conference on media literacy.* Queenstown, MD: Aspen Institute.

Bailey, T. (2006a, January 20). Bullies swagger onto Web. *The Commercial Appeal,* pp. B1–2.

Bailey, T. (2006b, January 14). Mom did well in capture of sex offender. *The Commercial Appeal,* pp. B1–2.

Baron, J., & Crooks, S. M. (2005). Academic integrity in Web based distance education. *TechTrends, 49*(2), 40–45.

Bishop, K. (2003). What in the world is happening with information literacy? *Knowledge Quest, 31*(5), 14–16.

Boss, R. W. (n.d.). *Meeting CIPA requirements with technology.* Retrieved June 26, 2006, from http://www.pla.org/ala/pla/plapubs/technotes/internetfiltering.htm

Children's Internet Protection Act, 20 U.S.C. (2000).

Children's Online Privacy Protection Act of 1998, 15 U.S.C. 6501 (2000).

Educational Testing Service. (2006). ETS® ICT literacy assessment overview. Retrieved September 6, 2006, from http://www.ets.org/portal/site/ets/menuitem.1488512ecfd5b8849a77b13bc3921509/?vgnextoid5fde9af5e44df4010VgnVCM10000022f95190RCRD&vgnextchannel5cd7314ee98459010VgnVCM10000022f95190RCRD

Eisenberg, M. B. (2003). Technology for a purpose: Technology for information problem-solving with the Big6. *TechTrends, 47*(1), 13–17.

Eisenberg, M. B., & Johnson, D. (2002). Computer skills for information problem-solving: Learning and teaching technology in context. *Emergency Librarian, 21*(2), 8–16.

Heberling, M. (2002). Maintaining academic integrity in online education. *Online Journal of Distance Learning Administration, 5*(1), Retrieved August 20, 2006, from http://www.westga.edu/~distance/ojdla/spring2051/heberling2051.html

Hobbs, R., & Frost, R. (2003). Measuring the acquisition of media-literacy skills. *Reading Research Quarterly, 38*(2), 330–355.

i-SAFE America Inc. (n.d.). i-SAFE and educators working together to build a safer USA [Promotional flyer]. Carlsbad, CA: author.

International Society for Technology in Education. (2000). National educational technology standards for students. Retrieved August 17, 2006, from http://cnets.iste.org/students/s_stands.html

Johnson, K., & Groneman, N. (2003). Legal and illegal use of the Internet: Implication for educators. *Journal of Education for Business, 78*(3), 147–152.

Kinnaman, D. (1995/2003, August, 2003). *Critiquing acceptable use policies.* Retrieved June 26, 2006, from http://www.io.com/~kinnaman/aupessay.html

McGraw-Hill Ryerson Limited. (2002). *P.O.W.E.R. learning: Privacy and safety.* Retrieved June 22, 2006, from http://www.mcgrawhill.ca/college/feldmanPower/webresearch/privacy.mhtml

Mills, L. B. (2005). Read any good technology policies lately? *School Administrator, 62*(1), 8.

Murray, J. (2003). Contemporary literacy: Essential skills for the 21st century. *Multimedia Schools, 10*(2), 14–18.

National Conference of State Legislatures. (2006, January 20). Children and the Internet: Laws relating to filtering, blocking and usage policies in schools and libraries. Retrieved June 26, 2006, from http://www.ncsl.org/programs/lis/cip/filterlaws.htm

National White Collar Crime Center, & Federal Bureau of Investigation. (2005). *IC3 2005 Internet crime report: January 1, 2005–December 31, 2005.* Washington, D.C.: Author.

Nielsen, J. (2005). Low-literacy users. *Jakob Neilsen's alertbox–March 14, 2005.* Retrieved March 16, 2005, from http://www.useit.com/alertbox/20050314.html

Rader, M. H. (2002). Strategies for teaching Internet ethics. *The Delta Pi Epsilon Journal, 44*(2), 73–79.

Rawe, J. (2006, July 3). How safe is Myspace? *Time, 168,* 35–36.

Scharrer, E. (2002/2003). Making a case for media literacy in the curriculum: Outcomes and assessments. *Journal of Adolescent and Adult Literacy, 46*(4), 358.

Schmar-Dobler, E. (2003). Reading on the Internet: The link between literacy and technology. *Journal of Adolescent and Adult Literacy, 47*(1), 80–85.

Texas ISP Association. (n.d.). Internet content filtering information: Net filters and tools to block objectionable material. Retrieved June 26, 2006, from http://www.tispa.org/info/kinnaman/filtering.htm

The Children's Partnership. (1999, March). Online content for low-income and underserved Americans. Retrieved March 24, 2004, from http://www.childrenspartnership.org/pub/low_income/index.html

Tyner, K. (1998). *Literacy in a digital world.* Mahwah, NJ: Lawrence Erlbaum Associates.

Villeneuve, N. (2006). The filtering matrix: Integrated mechanisms of information control and demarcation of borders in cyberspace. *First Monday, 11*(1), Retrieved June 26, 2006 from http://firstmonday.org/issues/issue2011_2001/villeneuve/index.html

Wang, H., & Gearhart, D. J. (2006). *Designing and developing Web-based instruction.* Upper Saddle River, NJ: Pearson Merrill Prentice Hall.

Wikipedia Foundation Inc. (2006a, August 18). Wikipedia: About. Retrieved August 24, 2006, from http://en.wikipedia.org/wiki/Wikipedia:About

Wikipedia Foundation Inc. (2006b, August 21). Wikipedia: Researching with Wikipedia. Retrieved August 24, 2006, from http://en.wikipedia.org/wiki/Wikipedia:Researching_with_Wikipedia

Willard, N. (2002, June 28, 2002). Ensuring student privacy on the Internet. *Education World.* Retrieved July 14, 2006, from http://www.education-world.com/a_tech/tech120.shtml

Yahoo! Inc. (2002a). Yahooligans! teachers' guide: Acceptable use policies: What next? Retrieved June 26, 2006, from http://yahooligans.yahoo.com/tg/aup6.html

Yahoo! Inc. (2002b). Yahooligans! teachers' guide: Acceptable use policies: What to include. Retrieved June 26, 2006, from http://yahooligans.yahoo.com/tg/aup4.html

Chapter 6

Technology-Enhanced ESL Instruction and Learning in K–8 Classrooms

by Anita Pandey

Runo looks intently at the computer screen as he considers which verb ending he wants to use in a sentence he is writing about his native food. Bill is also writing about his native food, hamburgers, and he pauses at the keyboard for a moment to consider Runo's intent gaze at the computer screen.

"Hey, Runo, what food are you writing about?"

Runo, without looking away from the screen, replies, "Fatagas."

"Huh?" Bill replies "What's a fatwayga?"

"Fa-ta-gas," Runo corrects. He now looks at Bill. "A fataga is a like a tortilla but it is harder and not so easy to roll. Momma puts a mix of lamb, rice, and something like the red sauce for noodles . . ."

Bill looks quizzical. "You mean spaghetti sauce?"

"Yes, that's it. And adds other spices. She cooks all that and it is what you put over the fataga."

"I've never eaten lamb," Bill says, not even sure where a person would buy lamb. "Do you pick up the fataga and eat it like a sandwich?"

"You can, but we eat it with a fork." Then Runo says, "Why don't you read about fatagas in my writing?"

"Yeah, good idea. Just send me your draft, and I'll look at it. Do you want me to do a peer review form on it?"

"Not yet," Runo replies. "I want to work on it some more first, but maybe you can help me with some verb endings."

"Sure I can do that," Bill responds, "but you know you can go to endings.net and get lots of help. I use that site sometimes when I'm having trouble with verb endings."

"Endings.net? Never heard of it."

"It's great! They've got games you can play to figure out which verb ending works. You don't just look up an answer when you go there. You have to play a game to answer the question you have. It's neat. I hate grammar with a capital *H,* but endings.net makes the whole mess of verb endings fun."

"Wow. Thanks," Runo says gratefully. Then, remembering he needs to send his research report to Bill, he says, "Here it goes. You should have it soon."

In a few seconds, Bill says, "Got it." Then after a brief pause, "I'll bet there's a Web site about fatagas, or at least one about your native food. You ought to Google fatagas."

"I already did," Runo responds, "and I found one recipe, but it didn't look very good. Not like my mother makes. By the way, what are you writing about?"

"Hamburgers," Bill says proudly.

"Oh, German food!" Runo says with a bit of superiority.

"German!" Bill spouts, aghast, and then retorts, "American!"

"Well, it sounds German. My father is German, and he says Hamburg is where hamburgers came from."

Bill sits stunned. Then he brightens. "I'll Google hamburgers. We'll see if your dad is right."

"My dad is always right. Just ask him," Runo says with a broad smile.

"OK," Bill plays along, "but how are his verb endings?"

○ Technology in ESL: The Time Is Now

The value of technology is not always immediately apparent, particularly given the global digital divide. My personal experience is exemplary. Some might be surprised to hear that it wasn't until I was 19 that I first used a computer. Having grown up in predominantly rural Zambia and Nigeria, I was lucky if I had access to a photocopying machine. Computers were rarely visible in those parts in the 1970s, and even in the late 1980s when I worked on

my bachelor's thesis. At the university I attended, computers were reserved for computer science students. So I typed my 205-page undergraduate thesis (required of all students) on an electric typewriter and was pretty proud of it, until I saw what computers and laser printers could do. Naturally, I had no idea what e-mail meant until I came to the United States for graduate work. By then, I was so afraid of being technologically ignorant that I developed a computer phobia. If it hadn't been for a professor who required that all our papers be turned in on diskettes, I probably would not have dared to venture near those "computer creatures" for quite a while. I owe that professor many thanks. Because of my personal experience, I endorse computer technology in the teaching of English as a Second Language (ESL), so this chapter illustrates the value of technology-enhanced ESL instruction and learning and explains how best to use current technology to teach ESL in K–8 classrooms.

Why exactly, is it important for all teachers to have facility in teaching ESL? Current census figures point to a noteworthy change in our school-age population: ESL students are flocking to schools all across the country, making up the fastest growing group (see Rumbaut, 1998; Fulignii 2001; Lee, 2003; Jelinek, 2005; Pandey, forthcoming). The growth in the number of ESL students requires teachers to use computer technology to provide these students with a quality learning experience. In fact, the variety of instructional technologies currently available is astounding. About 13 years ago, around 10,000 instructional software packages were commercially available (Franklin & Strudler, 1989). Today, thousands more are readily available. Indeed, the time has come for all of us—not just ESL teachers—to be equipped with basic second-language and literacy-enhancing knowledge and skills to meet the needs of our diverse student body (Cookson, 2006).

To show how teachers can meet the literacy needs of ESL students through computer technology, first I provide a Computer Classroom Snapshot as an example of how Ginger Joe, an elementary teacher, uses the computer to help ESL students create a family book. Next, I outline some benefits of using technology to teach ESL and literacy to K–8 students in targeted grades before providing guidelines for its effective use. The kinds of language-literacy instructional technologies currently available are examined. Then recommendations are provided for their use in class and beyond, as well as strategies for K–8 instructors to keep up with advances in ESL instructional technology.

◥ Computer Classroom Snapshot

Context

Welcome to the demanding world of an elementary classroom teacher. Going into my 28th teaching year, I speak from experience as a regular classroom teacher and a special-education teacher. My name is Ginger W. Joe, and I am currently an instructional resource teacher in an urban Title I school serving students in grades K–5. Our school has a computer lab and a classroom set of laptops on a rolling cart. My classroom has five Windows computers, one Macintosh computer, and three printers. My largest group of students at any time could be as many as 13, and what I am beginning to see lately is the influx of ESL students in my special-education classes. Finding myself searching for a more efficient way to reach these type of students, I turned to computers.

What I Did and Why

I was challenged to develop a program that accepts and respects the language and culture of ESL students and empowers them to feel confident enough to risk getting involved in the learning process, which includes making mistakes. The following activity describes a way in which I worked with culturally and linguistically diverse students to create such an educational climate. It also validates and reinforces the importance of students' cultures and knowledge of their backgrounds.

I identified that these students had anxiety with writing and trouble with structured activities related to writing. To address this issue and create a situation where students could start with their strengths, rather than be faced with their weaknesses, I tried something different. I had my students create an electronic presentation about themselves, their families, and the things that are important to them. Rather than force the students to fill out a storyboard in writing, I decided to start with oral communication. I printed the questions from the storyboards onto index cards. Each storyboard became one index card and each group of two students was given a set of index cards. The students read each question on the cards. Then they audio recorded their answers on the computers by speaking into the computers' microphones. In this way, the audio track in the electronic presentation was created

(continued)

before anything else was done. Students took turns recording the answers to each card. When they were done with the complete audio track, I helped them import the digital pictures of family photos and traditions in their cultures found on the Internet and matched the pictures with the soundtrack they had already recorded.

What I Learned

This project was a great success with the class. Computers and technology provided several distinct advantages for the ESL learners. Computer-based technologies provided a medium for students to engage in and interact with at their own level and speed. The multimedia projects created on the computer brought together graphics, video, audio, and text, providing students a variety of ways in which they could express themselves creatively.

This technology-based project allowed ESL students to draw on their cultural strengths and background experiences, which might otherwise have gone unnoticed. Creative projects incorporating visual and aural media addressed different learning styles and modalities. By constructing knowledge from learning artifacts, students became active learners, researchers, and producers, and they took pride in the end results. A well-developed multimedia project provides avenues for teachers to delve into their students' background experience and to draw on the knowledge of these students' families and communities. The process of creating such projects gives students the opportunity to stretch their imaginations and reach for the words to express themselves, providing an enjoyable and interactive way to achieve language learning goals. I am already planning my next project to include a digital video!

◯ Why Technology-Enhanced ESL Instruction and Learning?

NCATE, TESOL, NCELA, NABE, ISTE's National Educational Technology Standards (NETS), the National Center for Educational Statistics (see their 2000 report), and other veritable academic organizations as well as researchers (Johnson et al., 2000), advise technology integration. Not to utilize technology, given our access to it (Cuban, 2001), constitutes a disservice to our students and to the profession. Technology provides affirming and enriching instructional-learning environments and lends itself well to individual use and collaboration (Briggs, 1998), for example e-mail, story cocreation, instant messaging, and WebQuests (Egbert, 2005). Given that emerging technologies are most readily embraced by our children and young adults, it makes sense to use technology in instructing our K–8th graders. In fact, early introduction to technology, just as early introduction to language, has an added value—it equips learners with creative ways to engage themselves with language (not just the target language), thereby producing—and very likely ensuring—task-based language acquisition.

Technology-enhanced language acquisition is also more effective for teachers, and, in the long run, less time consuming. Most would agree that preparing for class—making lesson plans that only utilize resources such as books and teacher or student talk—is far more time consuming and cumbersome than adopting the role of a facilitator who monitors students' language progress as students interact with language through a variety of technological tools and software packages. Moreover, technology constitutes a vital component of professional development today, and instructional technologies of value abound in practically every field. Not surprisingly, TESOL, the largest ESL professional organization, mandates the use of technology in its pre-K–12 ESL Standards (**www.tesol.org/ standards**). In-service and preservice teachers, including early childhood educators or care providers, would, therefore, do well to familiarize themselves with these standards and periodically consult them for updates.

Technology alone, however, is not sufficient for teaching ESL students. Teaching ESL requires an innovative teacher with sound knowledge of second-language acquisition theory and of approaches to teaching ESL (Bhatia & Ritchie, 1996; Larsen-Freeman, 1986), an appreciation for crosscultural differences (Clayton, 1996), a desire to continue learning (Pandey, forthcoming), and the capability of using a variety of engaging tools that can ensure continued learning (Bush & Terry, 1997; Egbert 2005, 1997; Levy, 1997; Nunan; 1996). Additionally, it's a good idea to put ESL students in charge of their own language learning. As Freeman and Freeman (1992, p. 233) observe, "Faith in the learner expands student potential." In fact, research in second-language acquisition shows that interactive and experiential learning is far more effective and advisable than an approach in which teachers attempt to "deposit" knowledge in student "banks" (Cummins, 1989). Dunkel (1991) reminds us, "Although they may not be able to express themselves in English, the young ESL children you are meeting are, in fact, experienced language users" (p. 1). Thus, ESL students are capable language learners.

Computer-Assisted Language Learning

To help these language learners, teachers will need to become familiar with ESL computer technology. Common acronyms for technology-enhanced language instruction (not just English) include CALL (computer-assisted language learning), CELL (computer-enhanced language learning), TELL (technology-enhanced language learning), and CRI (computer-supported reading instruction). In what follows, I will focus on CALL, an umbrella term that encompasses a variety of technologies subsumed in the other acronyms.

CALL is essentially learner centered, minimizing the distinction between traditional instruction and learning, providing for whole language learning (Freeman & Freeman, 1992, p. 4). Via e-penpaling, videoconferencing, sound files, and streaming media-oriented Internet sites, CALL exposes children to authentic language, a prerequisite for effective second language and literacy acquisition (Brown, 1994; Diaz-Rico & Weed, 1995; Gass & Selinker, 1995). CALL also provides the language learner with a steady source of "comprehensible input" (Krashen, 1996), a linguistic prerequisite for successful language acquisition.

For the most part, research points in favor of CALL. Grosse and Leto (1999) argue that technology can be extremely useful in teaching ESL "if used correctly" (p. 1).

They observe, "Electronic learning breaks down traditional time and space constraints on learning" and instructors interact with more students "than they would have through the traditional classroom format" (p. 7). They cite examples of interactions in virtual English classrooms that allowed for meaningful real-time exchanges. These days, participants in such classrooms—like those enabled by Blackboard—can use the "white board" for illustrative purposes, which is, in fact, far more accessible and visible than the chalkboard. Such venues simulate free writing, and the documents students create can be saved easily and accessed later for review and assessment.

CALL has, in fact, changed the very definition of language, learning, and teaching (Bush & Terry, 1997; Dunkel, 1991; Gardner & Garcia, 1996; Little, 1996; Voller & Pickard, 1996). For example, Levy (1997) envisions three roles for technology, namely, that of tutor, teacher, and tool. While Egbert (2005) views it as a tool (arguably, many software programs are excellent tutors, as well), the fact remains that current CALL technologies have variable instructional-learning capabilities. Last but not the least, CALL's sustainability enables language-instruction learning outside the traditional classroom. Once we determine the age-appropriate and grade-specific content to be covered (NCATE and TESOL-sanctioned), it is easy to integrate appropriate technologies in the instruction-learning process, as will be illustrated.

As with other students, we should strive to provide our ESL students with an instructional-learning environment conducive to language and literacy development (Egbert, 2005). The ESL child's basic content needs are, in fact, no different from those of any monolingual English-fluent child's, so suitable instructional-learning technologies that simultaneously advance the ESL child's English language and literacy skills can make a difference (Ovando et al., 2005). The following conditions, which can be achieved effectively by CALL, ensure greater success in second language and literacy acquisition:

- ◯ Participants feel empowered and validated (Freire, 1970; Pandey, forthcoming);
- ◯ Participants take an active role in the process (i.e., learner-centered pedagogy enables them to actually switch between facilitator and learner roles);
- ◯ They receive continued comprehensible input in the target language and in their primary language (Schecter & Bailey, 2002; Schecter & Cummins, 2003);
- ◯ They have ample opportunities for meaning negotiation (Gass & Selinker, 1995);
- ◯ They are immersed sociolinguistically, having the benefit of multiple instructional media (i.e., technology), a versatile and sustained instructional-learning environment, and varied input and feedback sources.

In addition, ESL students are provided with cogent explanations, are motivated, have ample time to complete designated tasks, and are not intimidated or otherwise psychologically stressed (Egbert, 2005; Krashen, 1996). Of note is the fact that technology usage readily satisfies all of these conditions and aligns well with the pre-K–12 TESOL Standards.

Where ESL children currently make up a relatively small percentage of each grade level, which is increasing, you would do well to create self-instructors of these learners—in short, to prepare and encourage your students to take advantage of the autonomous language learning that computer-based technology enables. By so doing, you empower both your students and yourself (Freeman & Freeman, 1992; Freire, 1970; Higgins, 1991; Pandey, 1999), reinforcing one-on-one and face-to-face lessons with CALL. ESL students at different grade levels can then acquire English through meaningful interactions with the language—as they are successfully enabled by the multiple technological resources available today.

Effective Technology Use in ESL Instruction and Learning: Some Guidelines

Diaz-Rico and Weed (1995) observe, "A critical aspect of any lesson is the proper selection and use of materials" (p. 121). Technology is no exception. Regardless of which specific technology you use with your ESL children (and others), make sure that it is goal driven. This will ensure that you are employing it effectively. In short, curricular objectives—and often, too, assessment—should drive technology selection. Technology should not be employed merely for its own sake (Egbert, 2005). Additional selection criteria include: (1) Are the content objectives for the lesson adequately presented by the material? and (2) Is the material comprehensible and purposeful? The second is probably less of a concern with Web sites, which are generally multipaginal and multidimensional, catering to different learning styles. For additional guidelines on selecting and recommending sites, consult Healey and Jackson (1999) and Egbert (2005). Criteria for the evaluation of ESL instructional resources also can be found in the Foreign Language Framework of California's Department of Education (California State Department of Education, 1989).

○ Technology-Enhanced ESL per Grade Level

It helps to remember that "children learning ESL are, first of all, children" (Ashworth & Wakefield, 1994, p. 33). Displaced from their comfort zones—from their primary cultural milieus—ESL children often feel twice removed from their "home" (Clayton, 1996; Rodriquez, 1980), so it is necessary to be sensitive and genuinely attentive to them. Because language and culture are intertwined (McKay & Hornberger, 1996; Romaine, 1994), the ESL teacher has to be careful not to disregard or negate a child's home culture. Given cultural differences in literacy practices (Edwards, 2004; Pandey, forthcoming), sustained exposure to print-rich environments and practices (reading, including daily reading in the home and in the child's primary community) will acquaint all ESL students, not just those in the primary grades, with the Western literacy styles and preferences (i.e., the primacy of print over speech). Today's technology, being engaging and multimodal, is perfect for ensuring this while simultaneously appealing to variable learning styles and preferences. We will examine three grade clusters to see how best to integrate technology with ESL students in age-appropriate ways: (a) kindergarten, (b) first through third grades, and (c) fourth through eighth grades.

Kindergarten

ESL students already constitute a sizeable majority in kindergartens (Cohn & Bahrampour, 2006). Research shows that an early academic start increases a child's likelihood for success in the later years. For this reason, as well as the rapidity with which this segment of our population is growing, pre-K and kindergarten has received considerable legislative attention in the past three years. National initiatives such as the ECEPD grant (in which a clear English language acquisition plan is an invitational priority) attest to the visibility and importance of our ESL pre-K/K. Some states are even considering making preschool mandatory. Since academic success is contingent upon high quality and research-grounded instruction in early (oral) language, (pre)literacy, numeracy, and overall social-interactional skills, we should strive to provide environments rich in these skills. Technology is perfect for ensuring this. For those who believe in assessment-driven instruction, the most frequently employed preschool assessments, including the ELLCO (Smith & Dickinson, 2002) and the ECERS, specifically gauge the quality of the language and literacy environment, and resources and activities employed. Once again, proper technology use is likely to yield higher scores.

For ESL pre-K and kindergarten, bilingual and biliterate technologies are highly recommended for instruction, learning, and assessment, given research findings of a positive correlation between first and subsequent language and literacy success (Schechter & Cummins, 2003). We should employ manipulatives, print, and digital resources that stimulate a child's linguistic senses, specifically those of sight (for orthographic recognition), touch (for social-interaction-based language), and hearing (for receptive and expressive language). Most technological resources provide these vital aural, visual, and tactile components. Phonics software programs, such as Rock 'N Learn are currently available and have been found to effectively teach ESL students the English alphabet, both in isolation and in combination with paper-based sources, such as flashcards, board games (like Phonics Adventure), and even songs and other oral mechanisms. Since oral language precedes writing and is actually a prerequisite for this secondary literacy (Snow et al., 1991), technology can be employed to engender verbal (re)tellings of stories and relationships. Needs assessments should help you determine which resources will be most facilitative for each ESL child and how best to utilize them (i.e., through individual or collaborative use). Figure 6.1 is an example of the types of technology that can be employed with this group. Similar curriculum-driven technology selections could be devised for each grade level and subsequently updated, based on one's experience, consultations with one's colleagues and other professionals, and students (highly advisable and in synch with technology-friendly, learner-centered pedagogies). The objectives in Figure 6.1 are not ranked, and some overlap. The overarching goal is to develop strong school-readiness skills.

Figure 6.1 Aligning Curricular Goals and Technology.

Objectives/Focal Areas	Applicable Technology
1. Enriching receptive	Graphics depicting literacy instantiations, Webcasts, videos, language sound files (including online radio files).
2. Expressive language	Digitized, bilingual storytelling using self-created, coauthored, or tech-prompted stories or verses (with an older child or adult as annotator/writer), picture books, or digital books (available on the Internet and DVDs such as *Dora* & *Diego*).
3. Phonological awareness	Keyboard stimulation, word processing with letters, CDs, e-nursery rhymes (with recall-facilitative visual accompaniments), PowerPoint projections, visual simulation (repetitive).
4. Alphabet recognition	The keyboard, clip art, word art (Lindroth, 2006), word processing with letters, CDs, applicable software (e.g., creating alphabet tables in MS Word).
5. Social-interactional language (e.g., uses culturally appropriate speech acts—salutations, leave-taking,praise/ appreciation, apologies, etc.)	E-books and Web sites like Dorena.
6. Age-appropriate cognitive skills (object comparison—opposites, variable sizes, etc.)	E-books and Web sites.
7. Bilingualism and bicultural awareness	Bilingual or code-mixed e-books, digitized (ethnographic) videos, DVDs, and Web sites that depict variable cultural and linguistic practices (i.e., the oral tradition as well as reading habits, including library visits and bedtime stories).

First Through Third Grade

Curricular objectives for this level are essentially extensions of those outlined above. In using technology to cover content areas for the sake of the ESL students in your class, you could emphasize the language as much as the content or employ content-area teaching, such as those described in Chapter 3, as a means to an end, namely, vocabulary and grammar comprehension and expansion. "It takes a village to raise a child," and it takes a collaborative effort—that is, interested staff, students, and community—to make ESL enjoyable, meaningful, and effective. Therefore, do not rely solely on the designated ESL teacher to assist the ESL students in your classes.

First-grade teacher Ginger Joe, who wrote the Classroom Snapshot in this chapter, had the following to say about the utility of computer-based phonics programs:

> Ever since I started using them with not just my ESL students, but with all the students in my class, I've noticed a remarkable improvement. It's amazing how quickly they learn the alphabet and how to correctly pronounce words that I used to have such a hard time teaching them. I highly recommend the use of technology. I've also had great success with Kid Pix and Kid Works. It makes me sad to see the brand new computers sitting idle in some classrooms; the teachers just don't use them. Imagine all the extra ESL-learning activities I could do in my class if I had those computers!

Kid Works is a graphic arts program that children find very engaging. It is great for preliteracy priming, for drawing/art, for developing motor skills (like introductory word processing), and for other learning tasks. For instance, ESL children could be taught umbrella words like animals, flowers, and birds, and asked to sort and classify members of these groups by using the visuals the program contains. To use Kid Works, schools simply have to secure a license. Another beneficial software program that can be downloaded is Roxie's ABC Fish, which teaches the alphabet by using music and songs. It is an excellent interactive program for pre-K–3 ESL students in particular.

Kid Pix Deluxe is an exciting, interactive computer program of great value to first through third graders. For examples of its use with ESL (and other) children, refer to **http://marilee.us/kidworks.html#myproj1st**. Students develop their preliteracy skills by handling writing instruments and tools, and, in the process, they learn how to do so properly. The computer responds by reading (often backward) whatever they enter. The computer alerts you to nonsense and misspelled words. Both Kid Pix and Kid Works are ideal for autonomous, out-of-class learning with pre-K–4 ESL students. Beautiful Dorena, featuring soundscapes, motion detector art, and live video art, is a new paint program for the early years (see **http://www.pixelpoppin.com/dorena/index.html**) and worth testing.

Since comprehension precedes production or expressive language (Brown, 1994), the use of colorful and informative CDs, such as the ones from Discovery or National Geographic, are good for developing the listening comprehension skills of ESL children. Second- and third-grade teacher Laura Constance highly recommends these for use with pre-K–4 ESL students. In her words, "I have found that it greatly enhances the learning experience for pretty much every child. Some of these CDs, are even brighter than T.V.! My kids are absolutely transfixed, even when I pause for comprehension checks and explanations. They just love them." ESL teacher Christina Mo also recommends the use of media stories (CDs/DVDs, even VHS) as stories in movie mode help develop a child's imagination and language skills (listening/comprehension, and expression, including vital culture-specific nonverbal language) and can also be used to encourage ESL children to share their life stories with classmates. Numerous nursery rhymes and songs—excellent cultural vignettes—are now available in DVD format and can also be used to teach vocabulary, cultural elements, and phonics to pre-K–3 ESL pupils.

Living Books (**http://www.livingbooks.com**) like the classic *The Cat in the Hat* are now readily available. They run the literary gamut in titles and are absolutely delightful, even for adults. One of the things I find fascinating is that they're realistic and interactive. The oral narrative is accompanied by visual displays of the words and sentences. If you click on any of the highlighted words, you're immediately treated to a delightful medley of colorful images, new scenes in the story, songs, music, dance, and dialog-added incentives. It is probably easier and quicker for children "reading" or viewing these stories to make the connections between (1) the sounds and words used in various dialects of American English and (2) the words and sentences in context. Also, the International Children's Digital Library (**http://www.childrenslibrary.org**; see Figure 6.2) provides original books in multiple languages from around the world. See Chapter 7 for more examples of electronic books.

Figure 6.2   The International Children's Digital Library (http://www. childrenslibrary.org) provides full-color, full-text children's books from around the world in a number of different languages. Pages from the copyrighted books have been scanned with permission, so teachers should not download and print these pages.

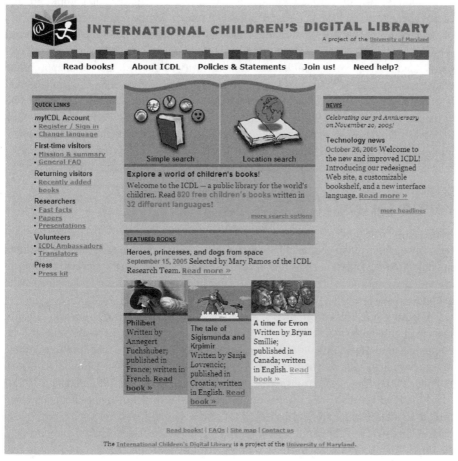

Screenshot used with permission.

A variety of CD-ROMs is currently available for ESL students of variable ages and proficiency levels. Examples include the following from **www.altaesl.com**:

- ○ *Dynamic Classics* (e.g., *Robin Hood, Alice in Wonderland*)
- ○ *Delta ESL Phonics Series*
- ○ *Clifford Songs and Chants*
- ○ *E-Blocks*
- ○ *What a World: Amazing Stories from Around the World*
- ○ *Let's Talk English*
- ○ *New Dynamic English*, which provides video footage, dialogues, and speech recognition technology to make it especially interactive.

An attention-getting tool for use with lower-level ESL students is a large display monitor or LCD panel. In this way, cooperative learning can take place, because all computer images, including Internet searches of sites intended for or possibly even created through the collaborative effort of an elementary school class, can be projected on a T.V. monitor for general viewing. Words and images are enlarged and amplified, and each student does not have to have an individual screen. Moreover, students who are not old enough or responsible enough to do a useful Web search are not made to do so, yet they can learn many sight words in this manner (Gibbons, 1991). Web surfing is not recommended for very young children, as their curiosity might lead them to inappropriate adult sites. Instead, if Web searches are to be used, it's a good idea to prescreen and bookmark a few sites of value and to have students browse these and select one or two to focus on for tasks. It is also not advisable to assign out-of-class Web surfing exercises to pupils in grades K–4, as parental involvement and plagiarism could constitute a problem. This does not mean, however, that ESL students and their parents should not be made aware of the many ESL acquisitional opportunities the Internet provides.

Fourth Through Eighth Grade

With intermediate grades, much more can be accomplished through CALL. CD-based stories can be employed in conjunction with the same or similar movies so that ESL children in grades four through six can be introduced to new vocabulary items, especially idioms in context, and students in grades seven and eight can master comparison and contrast (vital analytic tools).

Focusing ESL students in grades four through six on word processing will advance them in English literacy development. A number of studies have illustrated that students who compose and revise on PCs write better papers and generally have a more positive attitude toward writing than those who do not (Roblyer, Castine, & King, 1988; Grant, Ross, Wang, & Potter, 2005). This is also true of ESL students (Neu & Scarcella, 1991; Phinney, 1991).

In particular, Web sites offer a number of possibilities for upper-elementary and middle grades. Teachers could have ESL students surf the Web for topics covered in class (Gibbons, 1991; Sperling, 1999), so that they come to class prepared to report their findings. They could also make a running list of field-specific jargon (words and expressions) they came across and compile individualized e-dictionaries, inserting contextualized examples of their own. They could even rate the sites individually or in pairs or groups. Also, teachers can engage students in WebQuests, as discussed in Chapter 3, instead of supplying them with topics to write about. In fact, Egbert (2005) finds WebQuests to be more instructive for self-directedness and self-regulation.

In addition, Web sites can help develop the reading comprehension and paraphrasing skills of your ESL students. For instance, students can summarize articles or stories, promoting task-based second-language acquisition (i.e., students learn by doing), and then they can e-mail their summaries to you, along with an attachment of the article they selected, to guard against what we consider "plagiarism" (this term has culturally variable interpretations). E-mail and other technologies can be employed in a variety of ways (Levy & Stockwell, 2006; Warschauer, 1999). Your students can keep personal dictionaries in word processors, spreadsheets, or databases and construct sentences using newly learned words in context. Once a Web site engages an ESL learner, language learning is inevitable, and focused browsing is one means of ensuring whole language learning (Healey & Jackson, 1999; Robinett, 1999; Sperling, 1999). To make the learning experience more fruitful, a Web search exercise could be accompanied by a set of questions or information retrieval prompts. Keep in mind that a site does not have to be targeted at ESL learners to be language-literacy instructional. Simply learn to think beyond the textbook and challenge your students by creatively incorporating online resources both inside and outside your classroom, and you may be pleasantly surprised.

A variety of online ESL texts are now available for ESL learners, both children and adults. One that contains samples of authentic dialogues recorded in different contexts, glossaries, and exercises is the *Online ESL Conversation Textbook* (**http://deil.lang. uiuc.edu/students/r-li5/book/**). I wrote the unit on shopping, and, like other units in this "text," it is suitable for ESL students in sixth through eighth grades. Figure 6.3 includes Web sites that pre-K–8 teachers could use with their students. Keep in mind that the Internet addresses might change, but keyword searches should help you relocate them. Many of these sites invite teachers to share ideas with other professionals, and most provide links to other instructional pages and contact information. The last few are useful for independent ESL learning and practice. Of particular note, Ex*Change, recipient of the Magellan 4-star award for creativity and language teaching, was one of the first sites for ESL learners (Li & Hart, 1996). The Internet for English Learners rated it as the best Internet site for ESL students. Different search engines (e.g., Lycos, Yahoo) are likely to yield other relevant sites and CALL resources.

Most instructional Web sites have bulletin boards and chat rooms in which teachers could employ synchronous and asynchronous language-literacy learning/teaching. Even ESL sites intended for adult ESL students, such as Paolo Rossetti's Online English, can be adapted for use with fourth through eighth graders. Two other Web-based technologies offer promise for ESL. Keypals (via e-mail, text and instant messaging, for instance) is highly recommended for seventh and eighth graders, as it gets students in the habit of writing in academic and nonacademic English and also encourages them to establish new friendships. If your ESL students have American conversation partners and

Figure 6.3   Resource Sites for ESL Teachers.

1. **http://www.tesol.edu/** and **http://polyglot.lss.wisc.edu/lss/staff/erica/CALL** (Membership connects you to a global group)
2. **http://www.ncela.gwu.edu/resabout/literacy/** (National Clearing House for English Language Acquisition and Language Instruction)
3. **http://www.eslpartyland.com/teach3.htm** (Karin's ESL PartyLand: resources for teachers)
4. **http://iteslj.org/** (The Internet TESL Journal—for both instructors and ESL students)
5. **http://www.everythingESL.net/** (Source for educational software)
6. **http://www.csun.edu/~hcedu013/** (Online resources for social studies)
7. **http://www.itec.sfsu.edu** (Papers about online learning)
8. **http://www.csun.edu/~hcedu013/eslplans.html** (ESL lesson plans for older students)
9. **http://iac.snow.edu/faculty/dogden/vis/tesollistserve.html/** (TESOL's video interest section)
10. **http://members.xoom.com** (Features various Web tools)
11. **http://www.eslcafe.com/idea/index.cgi?Internet:** (Dave's ESL café internet cookbook)
12. **http://www.englishclub.com/pronunciation/index.htm**
13. **http://cmsu2.cmsu.edu/~jdt82860/ESL%20Links.htm** (ESL Web links)
14. **http://www.ohiou.edu/esl/english/index.html** (English resources for students)
15. **http://www.iei.uiuc.edu/student_internet_res.html/** (A link to Internet English resources, divided into language areas, such as listening, oral communication, etc.)
16. **http://w3.byuh.edu/academics/lang/EIL_World/** (ESL Student Writing)
17. **http://www2.hawaii.edu/~ashea/etec442/cnn.html** ("CNN Newsroom & Worldview for ESL," a site containing vocabulary and grammar exercises)
18. **http://www.iei.uiuc.edu/web.pages/readinglist.html** (ESL literacy resources)
19. **http://towerofenglish.com** (Tower of English, "the ESL Guide to the Internet")
20. **http://www.esl-lab.com/** (Randall's ESL Cyber Listening Lab)
21. **http://www.npr.org/** (National Public Radio)

Webpals, they are likely to learn American culture much more quickly through their exchanges. In turn, Americans become more knowledgeable global citizens. Teichmann (1994) discusses how German and American children were effectively linked via e-mail and videoconferencing. The resultant exchange, conducted in English, was cross-cultural and of value to both sides. The Classroom Snapshot in Chapter 2 with Candace Pauchnick's classroom described a similar experience. We could invite our fifth- through eighth-grade ESL students to listen to Internet radio broadcasts and view Webcasts at their convenience, giving them multiple opportunities to listen and instantly replay authentic narratives and exchanges.

The e-Lective Language Learning System (Cummins, 1998) is another valuable resource. Well suited to meet the needs of older ESL students, it provides a variety of texts (poems, stories, plays) in electronic form, accompanied by visuals and sound effects, so that it is more "authentic" than traditional formats. ESL teachers could also employ interactive programs like Daedalus Interchange or First Class, both readily available and widely used in writing programs.

◯ How to Keep up with ESL Instructional Technology

There are many ways to keep up with instructional technology of direct value to pre-K–8 ESL students. One is to subscribe to *The TESOL Journal*, which features articles on the utility of new technology, book notices, ads for CALL resources, and Christine Meloni's helpful tips for Net surfing, appropriately dubbed "Wandering the Web" in *TESOL Matters*.

It's also a good idea to subscribe to the NCELA newsletter, the TESL-List, and the Linguist List, as you can learn about ESL-instructional resources that other professionals have employed, and you can post questions. Levy (1997) and Levy and Stockwell (2006) list other CALL-related listservs. Subscribing to such sources also enables you to participate in a variety of discussions. You can learn about new resources, ongoing projects, conferences, and e-journals that put out calls for abstracts and contributions.

Many schools provide teachers with professional development incentives, including taking one or more courses, obtaining ESL certification, or even an MA in TESL, which is more valuable than a certificate. Courses in ESL instructional technology are increasingly available in isolation as well as through the core graduate curriculum. It would be good to take advantage of such opportunities. You could even apply for one or more federal- and state-funded technology grants so your school can invest more in current instructional technology. It helps to be an avid user of the technology, so that apart from being able to anticipate your students' reactions to it, you get a good feel for how best to use it. We all know that mastering academic language and literacy takes time, effort, and encouragement (Collier, 1998; Snow et al., 1991). We have to constantly remind ourselves that linguistic miracles are rare and that second-language acquisition does not occur in a linear series of well-defined stages. For this reason, I endeavor to pay more attention to the *message* (versus the *form*).

With technology as your *carefully chosen* tool, you can considerably enhance your curriculum, and often, too, make it self-instructional. Yet some fundamental questions necessitate further research. For example, what is known about the process of language learning that suggests the learning environment provided by current technology *could* and actually *does* have a positive impact for both facilitators and learners? Could we potentially overuse technology? How has our use of technology changed our beliefs—about instruction, learning, and assessment, including ESL-instruction learning? To what extent has technology measurably strengthened ESL (and/or other) students' academic and sociolinguistic knowledge? How have family involvement and our instructional style or pedagogy changed as a consequence of our use of technology? Clearly, answers to these and other questions can only be found if we unhesitatingly employ CALL with our students both inside and outside the classroom. As Garrett (1996) observes, "[T]he sharpest questions raised by our attempts to understand the role of technology in language learning are really not questions about technology but about language learning itself, and the most significant advantage of technology is its potential to catalyze and to focus our attention on these fundamental issues" (p. xv).

COMPUTER CLASSROOM LESSONS

Teaching ESL Students the Use of Idioms and Slang in the English Language

by Jim Kelley

Grade Level: 4–6

Objective: Identify phrases such as idioms and slang and discuss how these phrases differ in English compared to other languages.

Time: 2 school days. 2 hours to teach a lesson on idioms and slang, show a short film, and discuss the slang and idioms used in the film. The following school day will involve the students discussing idioms and slang that they found for homework on television, radio, computer, etc.

Materials: Television
VCR/DVD
Current age-appropriate short film
Computer with Internet

Steps:

1. The teacher will introduce the lesson by explaining what idioms and slang are and how they are used in English.
2. The students will watch a short film in which idioms and slang are used.
3. The class will discuss the different examples of idioms and slang observed in the film and what they mean.
4. The students are assigned homework to find examples of idioms or slang used on television, radio, computer games, Internet, Internet streaming media, etc.
5. The next day the students share their homework examples with the class.

Assessment: Students receive credit for contributions and participation in both the class discussion after the film and the following day's discussion of the homework. Students also receive credit for examples brought to class for homework.

The Tortoise and the Hare: Bilingual Vocabulary

Grade Level: 2–4

Objective: Identify 5–10 words in a language that is different from their native one.

Time: 1 school week. 1 hour to read the story; 30 minutes a day for four days to practice for assessment.

Materials: One computer

Living Books: The Tortoise and the Hare by Broderbund

Steps:

1. The teacher can introduce the assignment by having the story read aloud to the students in Spanish and in English.
2. Students who have never seen a Living Book will need to be shown how to click on a word with the cursor to have it read aloud.
3. Students will be placed in groups with both Spanish and English native speakers. The students will select five words they do not know (from a list provided by the teacher) and will have to identify and pronounce the words in both Spanish and English. The native speaking students will assist the non-native speaking students with pronunciation.
4. Daily activities can be used to reinforce the new words. Some activities can involve reading the story on computer or reading the book. The "Play with Me" feature allows for student interaction. The teacher's guide has several worksheet activities that can be modified to include words from both English and Spanish. Students can develop their own study aids, such as creating flash cards and generating quizzes. For cooperative groups, a teacher can design four activities that the students rotate to on different days to practice the words.
5. The students are assessed in groups on the final day. The number of correct words in the native and non-native language is assessed.
6. Groups that learned different words should share them with the class.

Assessment: Students should receive credit for the words they learned in the other language and for the success of their group members. Each student receives points for the words his or her group members learned as well as for his or her own words. This promotes the cooperative aspect of the lesson.

○ Techno-Teacher Tips

Communicating with Peers

Due to their estrangement from their country of origin, culture, and language, ESL students are constantly looking for avenues to communicate with other youth like themselves. Encourage them to make friends with keypals and other bilingual youth who could help their English acquisition. See Chapter 3 for appropriate keypal Web sites.

Using Search Engines

Popular search engines, such as Google and Yahoo!, are now capable of being used in multiple language formats. This tool may be very helpful for ESL students when searching for information in your class. You can do this by changing the preferences, usually under Advanced Features. Make your students aware of this option prior to working with search engines.

○ Frequently Asked Questions

1. **I'd like to be able to devote more time to my ESL students, but my class size and schedule don't permit me to. I don't want to neglect my non-ESL students. Are there any specific technologies I can employ to occupy and simultaneously instruct these students?**

   Indeed. Refer to the resources listed in this chapter. The Classroom Snapshot is helpful and presents an exercise that simultaneously serves as a needs assessment and instructional instrument for us teachers. In the upper grades, you could have English-fluent peers gather and/or present ESL classmates' stories and vice versa. This way, everyone is involved and you provide more opportunities for fruitful meaning, negotiation, and cross-cultural exchange. Also, researcher Stephen Krashen's I+1 is a very good strategy, where I stands for comprehensible input, a necessary ingredient, and 1 represents the catalyst or acquisitional incentive—the greater fluency of the peer with whom the language learner is paired. Additionally, at one of your staff meetings—or even via e-mail—try to collaborate with other teachers to create a survival technology kit of sorts for use with your ESL students (especially useful for new teachers). You could include cross-grade activities—highly advisable.

2. **Could the use of the Internet, Webcasts, podcasts, television, etc., in ESL-instruction, learning impede rather than enhance language acquisition due to slang and improper usage?**

   The use of real-life examples in teaching ESL learners is very important in teaching a more conversational English as opposed to simply teaching textbook English. The use of these resources in the classroom gives the ESL learner a chance to see and hear genuine English conversations and exchanges.

○ References

ALC. (1996). *The Internet for English learners.* Seoul: ALC Press.

The Arc. (1994). *How to evaluate and select assistive technology.* Arlington, TX: Arc. (ERIC Document Reproduction Service No. ED 376 664).

Ashworth, M., & Wakefield, P. (1994). *Teaching the world's children: ESL for ages three to seven.* Markham, Ontario: Pippin.

Bhatia, T., & Ritchie, W. (Eds.). (1996). *Handbook of second language acquisition.* New York: Pergamon Press.

Bitter, G. G. (1993). *Using a microcomputer in the classroom* (3rd ed.). Needham Heights, MA: Allyn & Bacon.

Briggs, D. (1998). *A class of their own: When children teach children.* Westport, CT: Bergin & Garvey.

Brosnan, P. A. (1995). *Learning about tasks computers can perform.* Columbus, OH: ERIC Clearinghouse for Science, Mathematics, and Environmental Education. (ERIC Document Reproduction Service No. ED 380 280).

Brown, H. (1994). *Teaching by principles: An interactive approach to language pedagogy* (3rd ed.). Englewood Cliffs, NJ: Prentice Hall.

Bush, M., & Terry, R. M. (1997). *Technology-enhanced language learning.* Lincolnwood, IL: National Textbook.

California State Department of Education. (1989). *Foreign language framework.* Sacramento, CA: Author.

Casey, J. M. (2000). *Early literacy: The empowerment of technology.* Englewood, CO: Libraries Unlimited.

Clayton, J. B. (1996). *Your land, my land: Children in the process of acculturation.* Portsmouth, NH: Heinemann.

Cohn, D. V., & Bahrampour, T. (2006, May 10). Of U.S. children under 5, nearly half are minorities: Hispanic growth fuels rise, census says. *Washington Post,* pp. 1, A14.

Collier, V. P. (1998). *Promoting academic success for E.S.L. students: Understanding second language acquisition for school.* Calverton, MD: Macro International.

Cuban, L. (2001). *Oversold and underused: Computers in the classroom.* Cambridge, MA: Harvard University Press.

Cummins, J. (1989). *Empowering minority students.* Sacramento, CA: CABE.

Cummins, J. (1998, Spring). e-lective language learning: Design of a computer-assisted text-based ESL/EFL learning system. *TESOL Journal,* 18–21.

Daiute, C. (1985). *Writing and computers.* Reading, MA: Addison-Wesley.

Diaz-Rico, L., & Weed, K. Z. (1995). *The crosscultural, language, and academic development handbook: A complete K–12 reference guide.* Boston, MA: Allyn & Bacon.

Dunkel, P. (Ed.). (1991). *Computer-assisted language learning and testing: Research issues and practice.* New York: Newbury House.

Edwards, P. (2004). *Children's literacy development: Making it happen through school, family, and community involvement.* Boston: Pearson.

Egbert, J. (2005). *CALL essentials: Principles and practice in CALL classrooms.* Alexandria, VA: TESOL, Inc.

Franklin, S., & Strudler, S. (1989). *Computer-integrated instruction inservice notebook: Elementary school.* Eugene, OR: International Society for Technology in Education.

Freeman, Y. S., & Freeman, D. E. (1992). *Whole language for second language learners.* Portsmouth, NH: Heinemann.

Freire, P. (1970). *Pedagogy of the oppressed.* New York: Continuum.

Fulignii, A. J. (2001). A comparative longitudinal approach to acculturation among children from immigrant families. *Harvard Educational Review, 71*(3), 566–79.

Gardner, D., & Garcia, R. B. (1996). (Ed.). Interactive video as self-access support for language learning beginners. In R. Pemberton et al. (Eds.), *Taking control: Autonomy in language learning* (pp. 219–232). Hong Kong: Hong Kong University Press.

Gass, S., & Selinker, L. (1995). *SLA: An introduction.* Mahwah, NJ: Lawrence Erlbaum.

Gibbons, P. (1991). *Learning to learn in a second language.* Portsmouth, NH: Heinemann.

Gómez, E. L. (2006). *Parent guide to the ESL standards for pre-K–12 students.* Teachers of English to Speakers of Other Languages, Inc.

Grant, M. M., Ross, S. M., Wang, W., & Potter, A. (2005). Computers on wheels (COWS): An alternative to 'each one has one.' *British Journal of Educational Technology, 36*(6), 1017–1034.

Grosse, C. U., & Leto, L. J. (1999). Virtual communications and networking in distance learning. *TESOL Matters, 9*(1), 1–7.

Hayes, J., & O'Loughlin, J. (1999, Summer). Meeting the challenge of content instruction in the pre-K–8 classroom. *TESOL Journal*, 18–21.

Healey, D., & Jackson, N. (Eds.). (1999). *1999 CALL interest section software list*. Burlingame, CA: Alta.

Higgins, J. (1991). *Fuel for learning: The neglected element in textbooks and call*. Paper presented at the meeting of TESOL, New York.

Higgins, J. (1995). *Computers and English language learning*. Oxford: Intellect.

Jelinek, P. (2005). Hispanics are fastest-growing minority. *Associated Press and WBAL*, June 9, 1:51 PM EDT.

Johnson, D. L., Maddux, C. D., & Liu, L. (Eds.). (2000). *Integration of technology in the classroom: Case studies*. New York: Haworth Press.

Krashen, S. (1996). *The natural approach: Language acquisition in the classroom (Language Teaching Methodology Series)*. (2nd ed.). United Kingdom: Bloodaxe Books, Ltd.

Larsen-Freeman, D. (1986). *Techniques and principles in language teaching*. New York: Oxford University Press.

Larson-Freeman, D., & Long, M. (1991). *An introduction to second language acquisition research*. New York: Addison-Wesley.

Levy, M. (1997). *Computer-assisted language learning*. Oxford: Clarendon Press.

Levy, M., & Stockwell G. (2006). *CALL dimensions: Options and issues in computer assisted language learning (ESL & Applied Linguistics Professional Series)*. Mahwah, NJ: Lawrence Erlbaum Associates.

Li, R. C., & Hart, R. S. (1996, Winter). What can the World Wide Web offer ESL teachers? *TESOL Journal*, 5–9.

Lindroth, L. (2006). WordArt Resources. *Teaching pre-K–8: The Magazine for Professional Development*. Retrieved September 14, 2006, from http://www.teachingk-8.com/archives/online_extras/wordart_resources_by_linda_lindroth.html.

Little, P. (1996). Freedom to learn and compulsion to interact: Promoting learner autonomy through the use of information systems and information technologies. In R. Pemberton et al. (Eds.), *Taking control: Autonomy in language learning* (pp. 203–218). Hong Kong: Hong Kong University Press.

Madsen, H. (1991). Computer-adaptive testing of listening and reading comprehension: The Brigham Young University approach. In P. Dunkel (Ed.), *Computer-assisted language learning and testing: Research issues and practice* (pp. 237–258). New York: Newbury House.

McKay, S., & Hornberger, N. H. (Eds.). (1996). *Sociolinguistics and language and language teaching*. Oxford: Oxford University Press.

Neu, J., & Scarcella, R. (1991). Word processing in the ESL writing classroom: A survey of student attitudes. In P. Dunkel (Ed.), *Computer-assisted language learning and testing: Research issues and practice* (pp. 169–188). New York: Newbury House.

Nunan, D. (1996). Towards autonomous learning: Some theoretical, empirical, and practical issues. In R. Pemberton et al. (Eds.), *Taking control: Autonomy in language learning* (pp. 13–27). Hong Kong: Hong Kong University Press.

Olsen, S. (1980). Foreign language departments and computer-assisted instruction: A survey. *Modern Language Journal, 64*(3), 341–349.

Ovando, C., Combs, M., & Collier, V. (2005). *Bilingual and ESL classrooms : Teaching in multicultural contexts with PowerWeb*. New York: McGraw-Hill.

Pandey, A. (Forthcoming). *Bridges over ESL country: A child-facilitated approach to language and literacy development*. Boston: Information Age Publishing.

Pemberton, R., Li, E. S. L., Or, W. W. F., & H. D. Pierson, (Eds.). (1996). *Taking control: Autonomy in language learning*. Hong Kong: Hong Kong University Press.

Phinney, M. (1991). Computer-assisted writing and writing apprehension in ESL students. In P. Dunkel (Ed.), *Computer-assisted language learning and testing: Research issues and practice* (pp. 189–204). New York: Newbury House.

Robinett, T. (1999). *Frameworks for teachers: A self-paced Internet training program and resource guide specifically designed for teachers*. Burlingame, CA: Alta.

Roblyer, M. D., Castine, W. H., & King, F. J. (1988). Computer applications have "undeniable value," research shows. *Electronic Learning, 8*, 38–47.

Rodriquez, R. (1981). Aria: Memoir of a bilingual childhood. In *Hunger of memory: An autobiography, the education of Richard Rodriquez*. Boston: D. R. Godine.

Romaine, S. (1994). *Language in society: An introduction*. Oxford: Oxford University Press.

Schecter, S. R., & Bayley, R. (Eds.). (2002). *Language as cultural practice: Mexicanos en el Norte*. Mahwah, NJ: Lawrence-Erlbaum Associates.

Schecter, S. R., & Cummins, J. (2003). *Multilingual education in practice: Using diversity as a resource*. Portsmouth, NH: Heinemann.

Siegel, J., Good, K., & Moore, J. (1996). Integrating technology into educating pre-service education teachers. *Action in Teacher Education, 17*(4), 53–63.

Smith, M. W., & Dickinson, D. K. (2003). *Users guide to the ELLCO toolkit*. Baltimore: Paul H. Brookes Publishing.

Snow, C., Barnes, W., Chandler, J., Goodman, I., & Hemphill, L. (1991). *Unfulfilled expectations: Home and school influences on literacy*. Cambridge, MA: Harvard University Press.

Sperling, D. (1999). *Dave Sperling's Internet guide: For English language teachers*. Burlingame, CA: Alta.

Stevenson, J., & Gross, S. (1991). Use of a computerized adaptive testing model for ESOL/bilingual entry/exit decision making. In P. Dunkel (Ed.), *Computer-assisted language learning and testing: Research issues and practice* (pp. 223–236). New York: Newbury House.

Teichmann, D. (1994). Connecting through e-mail and videoconferencing. *Technology and Learning, 14*(8), 49–66.

Venkatagiri, H. S. (1995). Techniques for enhancing communication productivity in AAC: A review of research. *American Journal of Speech Language Pathology, 4*(4), 36–45.

Voller, P., & Pickard, V. (1996). Conversation exchange: A way towards autonomous language learning. In R. Pemberton et al. (Eds.), *Taking control: Autonomy in language learning* (pp. 115–132). Hong Kong: Hong Kong University Press.

Warschauer, M. (1999). *E-mail for English teaching: Bringing the Internet and computer learning networks into the language classroom*. Burlingame, CA: Alta.

Chapter 7

Using Technology to Teach Literacy to Struggling Readers

by Janna Siegel Robertson

Rorie is drawing a replica of a pyramid on a computer screen using a special keyboard that allows him to overcome motor coordination problems due to cerebral palsy. Rorie is able to accomplish quite a bit with the keyboard, but he teams up with Phillipe to write text for the story. He and Phillipe are creating a piece about the "Mysterious Pyramid," as they call it. Phillipe helps Rorie type text and Rorie helps Phillipe (a non-native speaker of English) fix verb endings, because Phillipe sometimes confuses singulars and plurals.

As their teacher, Mr. James, watches Rorie and Phillipe work together, he recalls the days when Rorie would have been in a class with other "special ed" students. Yet today Rorie and Phillipe are working together to create a book that they will read to the class. *And the book*, Mr. James says to himself, *will be a professional product because the computer is incredible, simply incredible.*

Mr. James looks around his sixth-grade classroom and sees other student teams—some with special needs students, some with ESL students, some with students who have great facility with computers, some with students who are eager to use the computer but quite unpracticed in its use. He is again considering the technological magic of computers when he hears Phillipe saying something loud in Spanish. Mr. James turns toward the workstation where Rorie and Phillipe are collaborating and sees Phillipe shaking his fist at the computer screen and speaking rapidly in Spanish. Rorie is laughing.

Mr. James approaches Rorie and asks, "What's the problem?" Rorie blurts out, "Phillipe accidentally pushed the 'Delete' key and our words are gone, so he's angry with the computer." Phillipe, out of words and face flushed, realizes that the class is watching him, so he looks a bit sheepish with embarrassment. Rorie, not at all bothered by the missing texts, explains to Phillipe how to bring back the words by using the mouse and cursor to click "Undo Delete" on a pull-down menu. Phillipe's eyes are big when the words reappear, and Rorie says, "I guess this really is a mysterious pyramid." Both Rorie and Phillipe laugh and continue working on the story they will present to the class in a couple of days.

Rorie and Phillipe are busy adding text to their book, and Mr. James, smiling, thinks to himself, *Computers are incredible. We just brought back the pyramids from oblivion.*

○ Struggling Readers Today

In the educational climate of integrating students with special needs into the general education classroom, teachers have found it challenging to instruct special-needs students who have significantly different reading and writing abilities from other students. In fact, even special-education teachers face challenges in broadening the literacy of special-needs students. Fortunately, as Karen Anderson's Classroom Snapshot illustrates below, computer-assisted instruction provides opportunities for students to access computers regardless of the students' physical or sensory disabilities. In addition, the Internet provides information and classroom activities for teachers who work with special needs students.

Karen Anderson, a longtime teacher of special education, gives an example of how she uses technology in her classroom.

⩜ Computer Classroom Snapshot

Context

Multimedia software allows the user to create slide presentations. Students can illustrate their stories by selecting the scene, images, and sounds. They can also use text-to-speech that lets them hear their creation read aloud. This activity encourages creativity, cooperation, planning, and research. It allows the teacher the opportunity to meet each student's learning style. It gets the students engaged in the lesson, and the knowledge gained stays with the learners because they have an active role in the end product, so they feel pride in their creations, and learning becomes fun.

Some of this software also incorporates animation in the images. One of the first producers of multimedia software was Roger Wagner Publishing with Hyper-Studio. Stanley's Sticker Stories by Edmark (now part of Riverdeep), Storybook Weaver by the Learning Company, and the Amazing Writing Machine by Riverdeep

(continued)

are other examples of such software. PowerPoint also has the capability of creating slide show presentations, as do many other word-processing programs.

What I Did and Why

I was a teacher of children with special needs for 22 years. During this time, I was fortunate to be part of a state-funded project that put $20,000 worth of computer technology in my classroom. This equipment included a teaching station that was composed of a 32-inch television, a Macintosh computer, a laser disc player, and a video recorder. It was from this station that my class created numerous multimedia projects related to various units of study.

I used computer technology, particularly multimedia technology, in my classroom because all the students could get involved. Use of computers in the classroom can improve academic performance, motivate students to learn, enable them to accomplish things that they wouldn't otherwise be able to do, and build self-esteem. I have seen the student with special needs show typical students how to do something on the computer. One way to look at computer technology, in relation to the special-needs child, is as an "equalizer."

In one of my favorite activities, I used Kid Pix Studio Deluxe by Riverdeep to write a language experience story about a field trip to the zoo. From this first slide, students had to re-create the trip in sequential order. Everyone was actively involved in selection of the backgrounds, pictures, sounds, and narration of their creation. I allowed each of them, using text-to-speech, to read a page of the story. If the child had difficulty with reading, I coached him or her prior to the recording. After we were finished, we viewed our slide show. What a great way to get everyone involved and to build self-esteem! When they heard their voices on the computer, the faces of the children were priceless. This slide show was also used at an open house, where the parents were just as excited to hear their child's voice on the computer. I also printed the story to include in the class storybook and place on the bookshelf in the reading corner. The children loved reading this compilation of their stories during free reading time. Copies of our story were also sent home to the parents with the assignment of having their child read to them. All the children could read the stories, regardless of their reading level.

I used multimedia presentations in various other ways, including book reports, science or social studies projects, and journal writing. We usually kept a class journal, and on Friday mornings we recapped the week.

What I Learned

Multimedia instruction gets the students excited about what they are doing. It teaches much more than content. The students learn proper social skills. Some take leadership roles. They develop necessary planning skills because they have to know what they are doing before they get started. Everyone participates and becomes actively engaged in the project. For the child with special needs, learning can be frustrating and therefore not motivating. But using the computer in school has been proven to be a motivator for *all* children. Multimedia is one way of getting everyone involved.

⊙ Using Technology to Teach Literacy with Struggling Readers: Strategies

As Karen illustrated, the variety of software applications that can be used to motivate and excite children is widely available, both commercially and through educational vendors. Multimedia in particular offers students opportunities to access multiple senses with learning. As we examine strategies to integrate technology with literacy instruction, we will concentrate on four areas: (a) computer-assisted instruction, (b) the three-tier model and schoolwide literacy programs, (c) assistive technology, and (d) literacy development and students with disabilities. Finally, we will survey the research literature, aggregating many studies and authors' findings on integrating technology with literacy instruction and struggling readers.

Computer-Assisted Instruction

Special-needs students can be aided by computer-assisted instruction because these programs are often self-paced and individualized for each student's needs. For instance, computer-assisted instruction programs allow for assessment, drill and practice, instruction, simulation, or creative productions, all to suit the individual needs of the students (Siegel, Good, & Moore, 1996). In fact, researchers have evidence that computer-assisted instruction motivates, teaches, and empowers special-needs students, helping them to improve their communication skills (Bitter, 1993; Cochran & Bull, 1993; Holzberg, 1994). Furthermore, nonverbal or limited-verbal individuals have used computers as a major component of communication (Bigge, 1991).

Computers create a context for instruction that can provide stimulus (text, audio, and visual) for interaction between instructors and students (Giordano, Leeper, & Siegel, 1996). Indeed, schools are now using the Internet, CDs, and software that include interaction with audio and video elements. In some cases, teachers can program questions or directions into the video to create an interactive activity customized for their students and their curriculum (Brosnan, 1995). Several different software programs, available in language, reading, and writing development, are designed to accommodate students with cognitive, physical, or sensory disabilities.

Two concerns are related to computer-assisted instruction. One is that it may cause teaching to become more and more automatized, and as a consequence, students may socialize less with peers. Considering the current isolation problems of individuals with disabilities, practitioners, in their enthusiasm for embracing exciting instructional opportunities for students with disabilities, should not segregate special-needs students in computer labs (Siegel, 1999). Rather, such students should be integrated into computer lab activities with general-education students. This can be done with a "buddy" system or with cooperative learning groups.

The second concern is that computer-assisted instruction will be used too much for skill-and-drill. Woodward and Gersten (1992), for instance, reviewed research studies indicating that special-needs students and their nondisabled peers spent comparable amounts of time on computer-assisted instruction, but the special-needs students' computer-assisted instruction use was significantly more in the area of drill and practice programs. Technology is available to help special-needs students go beyond mere skill-and-drill, so teachers should consider using that technology with them.

Students with physical and sensory disabilities sometimes require additional software or hardware modification. Software programs with modifications can be sorted into three categories: Electronic/Animated Books, Tutorials/Drill and Practice, and Creative/Multimedia Programs. Software in all three categories has accommodations for students of different skill levels and abilities.

Electronic/Animated Books. As described in Chapter 2, lower-level readers can read these books at their own pace and have particular words or passages repeated as many times as needed. Because the pictures are animated, there are opportunities for context clues for beginning readers. For example, Riverdeep is one publisher of interactive books. In its *Living Books* series, the developers select favorite children's books, such as *Green Eggs and Ham* by Dr. Seuss, and include a "Let Me Play" feature, so when a student clicks on the word *ham*, a voice says "ham" and the program reveals a picture of a green ham. Whenever a student clicks on illustrations, a short animation is initiated. For teachers who have trouble showing reluctant readers that words are fun, the *Living Books* series provides highly motivating and rewarding material. Some of the animations can become distracting, interrupting the flow of comprehension, so teacher supervision is sometimes necessary for optimum learning.

Many Internet examples of hypermedia books are available online. Starfall, StoryPlace, and the International Children's Digital Library (see Figure 7.1) are three free online sites that have motivating books for young children. See Figure 7.2 for links to these and other online resources.

Tutorials/Drill and Practice. Some computer-assisted instruction programs teach oral reading, phonics, fluency, comprehension, word attack, grammar, and spelling. Often these programs can be modified for the struggling reader, allowing for improved programmed instruction.

One example is the Laureate series for language development for special education and ESL. For instance, in its program First Verbs, the animations allow the verbs to come alive. The teacher controls the content and format and can modify the program to either teach verbs or test a student's understanding of verbs. This instructional method allows for continuous repetitions with attractive animations and no negative feedback (only prompts for correct answers until the student's response is correct). The positive feedback cartoons are amusing and motivating to students.

Figure 7.1   At the International Children's Digital Library (http://www.childrens library.org), teachers and students can search for full-text books in a number of languages.

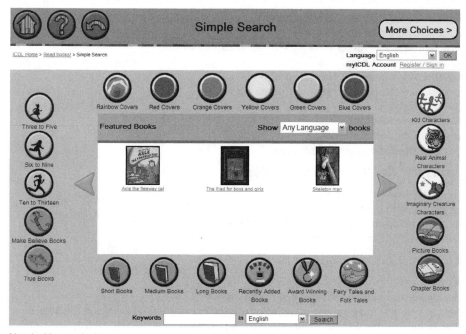

Used with permission.

Online tutorials and videos and practice parts at Starfall are also available. Some of the best drills and practice are found at game sites, such as Funbrain and GameGoo. See Figure 7.2 for links to these and other online instructional tools.

Creative/Multimedia Programs. The creative "writing to read" programs are some of the most easily adapted to all levels of literacy ability. Programs such as Don Johnson's PixWriter enable students to select pictures to write a story of their own. This is a great tool for young children or for those who cannot yet write or type. Other creative software leaves much more up to the student. Most software packages include a language experience approach where students read their own writing (so it is automatically modified to their level).

Some classic multimedia software programs are Bailey's Book House and the Imagination Express series from Edmark (Riverdeep). They not only enable students to write, illustrate, and publish their own stories, but also to animate them at a high level of sophistication, making students' books look quite professional. For example, if a student

Figure 7.2   Internet resources for struggling students and their teachers.

Companies with Software and Hardware for Readers with Special Needs

Don Johnston: **http://www.donjohnston.com/index.htm**
Enablemart: **http://www.enablemart.com/**
Laureate: **http://www.laureatelearning.com/professionals602/index.html**
Marblesoft: **http://www.marblesoft.com/**
Mayer-Johnson Co.: **http://www.mayer-johnson.com/**
Premier: **http://www.premier-programming.com/home.htm**
Riverdeep: **http://www.riverdeep.net/**
Sunburst: **http://www.tomsnyder.com/**
Texthelp: **http://www.texthelp.com/home.asp?**
Tom Snyder Productions: **http://www.tomsnyder.com/**

Reading Programs for Tier 2 and 3 Instruction

Failure Free Reading: **http://www.failurefreeonline.com/**
Lexia: **http://www.lexialearning.com/**
READ 180: **http://teacher.scholastic.com/products/read180/**
Waterford: **http://www.waterford.org/index.jsp**

Free Software for Teachers and Students

CNET: **http://www.cnet.com/**
Owl & Mouse: **http://www.yourchildlearns.com/owlmouse.htm**
The Screen Magnifiers Homepage (downloads): **http://www.magnifiers.org/links/Download_Software/**
StudyDog (free software for low income): **http://www.studydog.com/**
TRACE Software Toolkits: **http://trace.wisc.edu/world/computer_access/#three**
TUCOWS: **http://www.tucows.com/**
ZDNet downloads: **http://downloads-zdnet.com.com/**

Internet Accessibility Information and Tools

Apple Accessibility: **http://www.apple.com/accessibility/**
Color Blindness Image Correction: **http://www.vischeck.com/daltonize/**
Cynthia Says: **http://www.cynthiasays.com/**
Microsoft Accessibility: **http://www.microsoft.com/enable/**
The Wave: **http://www.wave.webaim.org/index.jsp**
WebABLE: **http://www.webable.com/**
WebPage Backward Compatibility Checker: **http://www.delorie.com/web/wpbcv.html**
WebXACT(formerly Bobby): **http://webxact.watchfire.com/**

Information for Teachers on Special Needs and Literacy

ABLEDATA: **http://www.abledata.com/**
Alliance for Technology Access: **http://www.ataccess.org/**
Blue Web'N: **http://www.kn.pacbell.com/wired/bluewebn/**
CAST: **http://www.cast.org/index.html**
Discovery School: **http://school.discovery.com/**
Education World: **http://www.educationworld.com/**

(continued)

Figure 7.2 Continued.

Internet4Classrooms: **http://www.internet4classrooms.com/**
Internet Public Library: **http://www.ipl.org/kidspace/browse/ref0000**
LDOnline: **http://www.ldonline.org/**
LDResources: **http://www.ldresources.com/**
MarcoPolo: **http://www.marcopolo-education.org/home.aspx**
NIMAS: **http://nimas.cast.org/**
Online Books Page: **http://digital.library.upenn.edu/books/**
Universal Design for Learning: **http://www.cast.org/teachingeverystudent/**

Free Literacy Sites for Student Computer Assisted Instruction

Edu4Kids: **http://www.edu4kids.com/**
FunBrain: **http://www.funbrain.com/**
GameGoo: **http://www.cogcon.com/gamgoo/gooy.html**
Literacy Center: **http://www.literacy-center.net**
NoteStar: **http://notestar.4teachers.org/**
PersuadeStar: **http://persuadestar.4teachers.org/**
ProjectPoster: **http://poster.4teachers.org/**
PowerProofreading: **http://www.eduplace.com/kids/hme/k_5/proofread/**
Starfall: **http://www.starfall.com**
StoryPlace: **http://www.storyplace.org**
ThinkTank: **http://thinktank.4teachers.org/**
VerbViper: **http://arcademic.altec.org/**

writes a story using the Pyramids program from Edmark, he or she can write about exploring ancient Egyptian ruins and animate and narrate the story, allowing readers to interact with the text by clicking on pictures that use animation or audio.

Another type of creative software is organization and concept mapping software, such as Inspiration. As discussed in Chapter 2, Inspiration and Kidspiration allow students to produce graphic organizers for note taking or writing development (see Figure 7.3). These strategies are especially beneficial for struggling readers who need support in organizing their thoughts and information. Free online organization tools (such as ThinkTank and NoteStar) can be found at 4teachers.org. See Figure 7.2 for links to these and other tools.

Three-Tier Model and Schoolwide Literacy Programs

Many large-scale programs are being adopted by school districts under No Child Left Behind, Reading First, and Response to Intervention initiatives under IDEA. Most of these scientifically based research programs subscribe to the National Reading Panel's

Figure 7.3 Students can use concept-mapping software such as Kidspiration (shown here) to make connections among ideas, brainstorm, or create an outline for a writing assignment.

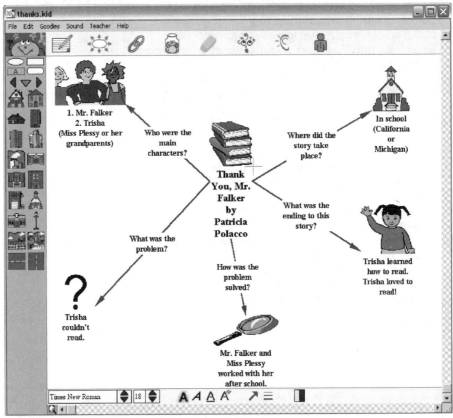

Diagram created in Kidspiration® by Inspiration Software®, Inc.

recommendations. As detailed in Chapter 3, the National Reading Panel recommends programs that have explicit instruction in the following areas:

Alphabetics
○ Phonemic Awareness
○ Phonics
Fluency
○ Guided Oral Reading
○ Independent Silent Reading
Comprehension
○ Vocabulary
○ Text Comprehension

Though the research supports these as the main components of teaching reading, a dilemma exists for students who experience difficulty with learning to read. For example, some students cannot process words phonologically. So even though reading programs that use National Reading Panel suggestions may be successful overall, some readers still may not respond to some of the strategies, such as explicit phonemic instruction. No one program is successful with all learners. Students who have difficulty reading when using a scientifically based reading research program are referred to as "treatment resistant" (Torgeson, 2000).

The core reading program adopted by a school is referred to as "Tier 1." Most students are successful learning to read using the core reading program adopted by a school. But for students who are struggling to learn to read or write, there are Tier 2 and Tier 3 interventions (Good, Kame'enui, Simmons, & Chard, 2002). Tier 2 interventions usually involve some extra small-group instruction, tutoring, after-school programs, or designated Title 1 programs. Tier 3 is even more intensive and usually is provided by or in conjunction with special-education personnel.

Allington (2006) cautions about schools adopting different reading programs for Tiers 1–3. He states that struggling readers will only be confused by different programs. Most students learn reading the same way, but struggling readers usually need more intensity or supports rather than an entirely new program. But there are exceptions. Some students do learn in different ways and may not be successful with a specific program. In that case, the student's program should be changed rather than a new one added. Allington (2006) gives the following example:

> However, we cautioned that any intervention had to build primarily around students' instructional needs. For instance, if students struggled because they did not use effective comprehension strategies, then expanding comprehension strategy instruction in the intervention lessons would seem a good idea. If students struggled because they did not self-monitor, then that would become one focus of the intervention lessons. Designing effective intervention requires that a student's specific instructional needs be identified. (p. 20)

Below are examples of a few scientifically based reading research programs designed for struggling readers at Tier 2 and/or Tier 3 levels. All use computer-assisted instruction that is helpful for two reasons. It ensures the fidelity of the instruction and helps to standardize the implementation of the program. The main reason research-based reading programs do not work is due to poor execution from the teacher. Having parts or all of these programs computer based allows for some or all of the program to remain as originally designed. See Figure 7.2 for more information about these programs.

Waterford Intervention is a software-based curriculum. Waterford Early Reading Program from Pearson Digital provides three levels of full-year instruction: Level One for emergent readers through Level Three for developing fluency. The program presents an explicit and systematic instruction based on Reading First's five essential reading components. It uses daily 15-minute computer lessons individualized to the student's progress. Though designed for all learners, it has been successful with struggling readers as well.

Lexia reading programs for ages four through adult build strengths in phonemic aware-ness, sound-symbol correspondence, decoding, fluency, phonics, and vocabulary—areas researchers have identified as essential to comprehension. Based on the Orton-Gillingham method of reading remediation, Lexia software provides a structured approach to mas-tering reading skills that correlates easily with lesson plans and curriculum standards and aligns with federal guidelines. Lexia has been used in special education programs for years due to its individualized approach.

READ 180 from Scholastic is a comprehensive reading intervention program designed to meet the needs of students in elementary to high school whose reading achievement is below the proficient level. The program's multimodal approach provides significant advantages for all students, mixing video software, Universal Access provisions, audio books, and paperbacks to ensure that all students, regardless of learning modality pref-erence, are able to benefit. It is based on brain research and universal design for learn-ing principles of differentiated instruction.

Failure Free Reading is a nontraditional program for all ages that does not focus on phonics. Developed to be successful with "phonetically deaf children," the program fo-cuses on elements found to be successful with struggling readers. Failure Free Reading presents age-appropriate materials within a multisensory format using practices based on direct instruction and metacognitive strategies. The materials incorporate the princi-ples of cumulative learning and stress the therapeutic necessity of (1) repetition within multiple instructional contexts, (2) control for syntax and semantics, and (3) immediate performance feedback. It has been used for Tier 2 and Tier 3 students as well as for ESL students, and it is available online rather than through software that is installed.

Assistive Technology

Even though software programs are essential to provide special needs students with a variety of approaches to literacy education, those students sometimes need additional software or hardware to access educational technology. That is, they need assistive tech-nology. For instance, augmented keyboards, touch pads, voice commands, and other as-sistive devices help students with physical and sensory disabilities to master the physical requirements of computers (Siegel, Good, & Moore, 1996). Individuals with disabilities use assistive technology in several ways: communication, environmental control, mo-bility, education, daily living, employment, and recreation. Teachers, however, have fo-cused on assistive technology that is necessary for literacy (see Figure 7.4).

The comprehensive list in Figure 7.4 includes both "low-tech" options, such as a larger pen for a student who has trouble writing, and "high-tech" solutions, such as speech synthesizers and hardware and software necessary for individuals with sensory and phys-ical impairments to access computers. In addition, several programs built into the cur-rent operating systems of Macintosh and Windows can be used for students with visual

Figure 7.4   Examples of Assistive Technology for Literacy.

Literacy Area	Purpose of Assistive Technology	Assistive Technology Equipment
Listening	■ Enhances sound and speech reception	■ Hearing aid, cochlear implant, assistive listening systems
	■ Converts speech to text	■ Captioning of videotapes and T.V., computer-assisted real-time captioning, computer-assisted note taking, computer-generated speech output
Speech Language	■ Enhances speech production	■ Speech amplifier, speech clarifier
	■ Supplements/replaces speech with text or graphics that communicate	■ Communication board/book, typewriter, portable word processor, computer, or communication device
	■ Supplements/replaces speech production with alternative speech	■ Artificial larynx, tape-recorded speech and computer-generated speech output with a variety of input, storage, and retrieval options
Reading	■ Enhances standard text and graphics	■ Corrective lenses, highlighting, color overlays, manually or electronically changing spacing, screen color/contrast adaptations, pictures/graphics, symbols, sign language cues
	■ Enlarges text and graphics	■ Large-print books, handheld and screen magnifiers, closed-circuit T.V., screen enlarging software
	■ Converts text and graphics to speech	■ Talking dictionary, talking word processor, screen-reading system, video description

(continued)

Figure 7.4 Continued.

Literacy Area	Purpose of Assistive Technology	Assistive Technology Equipment
	■ Converts text and graphics to Braille or other tactile symbols	■ Braille translation software and Braille printer, refreshable Braille computer output, tactile graphic display systems
Writing	■ Enhances standard writing utensils and supports	■ Adaptive grip, larger size, rubber grips, or adaptive writing tool; splints or wrist supports; special paper with wider lines, texture; writing guides; slanted, larger or no-slip writing surface
	■ Replaces standard writing utensils and supports	■ Typewriter, electronic note taker, portable word processor can have Braille input, keyboard enhancements, alternative keyboard, alternative input such as switches with scanning, word prediction, and macros; computer with voice dictation input
	■ Enhances the composition of written expression	■ Dictionary or thesaurus (talking), spell checker, grammar checker, abbreviation expansion, word prediction, or macros, voice dictation input, multimedia software

Note: From *Assistive Technology in Special Education: Policy and Practice* (pp. 40–41), by D. Golden, 1998, Reston, VA: Council for Exceptional Children. 1998. Used with permission.

impairments. For instance, the size of the screen view can be enlarged to allow students even with severely limited vision to read text and see graphics. Fewer accommodations are available for individuals with hearing impairments because computers are mainly visual, but there are visual cues rather than the "beep" the computer usually makes to get one's attention (Buggey, 1999). For students with motor difficulties, several tools are available to change the sensitivity and speed of the keyboard and mouse. They can be found in the control panel settings under Accessibility Options or Original Setup Options on most computers. See Figure 7.2 for Internet sites with links to additional information.

Following is a list of accessibility options available on most computers at no cost. Many of these accommodations not only assist students with sensory or motor difficulties, but they can also be useful for students with lower cognition or learning disabilities (Eorgrave, 2002). Typical accessibility features and their definitions are listed below.

Tools for Visual or Reading Disabilities

○ Screen Magnifier: Enlarges the screen or portions under the mouse cursor.
○ Visual Cursor Enhancer: Enlarges the cursor.
○ Scanning Software: Highlights each item on a page for mouse/switch interactions or speech to text.
○ Keyboard Audio Feedback: Gives spoken feedback for keys that are used.
○ Scanning Software: Highlights each item on a page for mouse/switch interactions or speech to text.
○ Screen Reader: Reads screen to either voice or Braille outputs.
○ Voice Output Application or Text to Speech: Speaks aloud text and graphical items on computer screen.
○ Braille Utilities: Convert text to Braille (requires a Braille printer).

Tools for Motor or Writing Disabilities

○ Mouse Enhancer: Allows all mouse functions to be accomplished by single clicks or the keyboard.
○ Onscreen Keyboard: Allows all keyboard functions to be accomplished by a mouse or switch.
○ Abbreviation/Expansion: Allows macros for words (using fewer keystrokes).
○ Word Prediction/Completion: Allows for fewer keystrokes for typing by giving the writer a list of predicted words.
○ Scanning Software: Highlights each item on a page for mouse/switch interactions or speech to text.
○ Voice Input Application: Allows speech input to control computer functions, writing, and/or communicating through computer audio communications.
○ Keyboard Modifications and Shortcuts: Allows a variety of keyboard modifications to accommodate individual needs.

Occasionally the tools provided in a typical computer are not sufficient to accommodate a person with very severe disabilities. In these cases, assistive technology provides extra equipment. For example, Braille writers and touch-response mice are available for individuals with little or no sight. Alternative keyboards with touch windows and switches are available for students with limited motor control. Also, infrared "head mouse" options, eye-gazing tools, and other innovative technologies enable special-needs students to access computers. Several software publishers, such as Edmark (Riverdeep), Don Johnson, and Laureate, incorporate simple controls so that the program will automatically scan, highlighting an object on the screen (often at a speed the student can select), allowing the student to click with the mouse, touch the screen, or push a switch to choose the option. With scanning, students can access simple tutorial or drill-and-practice programs or even learn to write compositions using on-screen keyboards or word predication software. Often the style of on-screen keyboards or alternative keyboards follows the models used for augmentative alternative communication (AAC) devices.

AAC makes use of two broad methods of inputting information into communication devices or computers. One is random selection of letters, words, symbols, or options; the other gives access to two choices, and the individual must choose one. To accomplish this input, communication boards offer symbols, pictures, or words to accommodate a student's needs. Often current keyboard layouts are not suitable for input by students with physical or cognitive limitations. Augmented keyboards may include rearranged keys in more efficient layouts, reduced keys for fewer physical demands, and expanded keys for additional message options. Encoding alternatives also are available with the following options:

- pictures or symbols in which one symbol or picture may have many possible meanings, depending on keys pressed;
- alphabetic encoding, in which one alphabet letter has several meanings;
- enlarged key keyboards;
- abbreviation expansion, in which a few letters allow the whole word to be spoken or written; and
- lexical predication, in which a list of likely options is provided after each letter typed.

The output can be written or spoken. Spoken output is usually provided by computerized voices (speech synthesizers), which are now faster, less mechanistic sounding, and more age and gender appropriate than older versions (Tinker, 2001).

In 2004, the U.S. Department of Education endorsed the National Instructional Materials Accessibility Standard (NIMAS). This voluntary standard guides the production and electronic distribution of flexible digital instructional materials, such as textbooks, so that they can be more easily converted to Braille, text-to-speech, and other accessible formats.

Although the Internet provides a multitude of free instructional resources to students and teachers, not all pages are accessible to individuals who use assistive technology (Robertson, 2002). Section 508 of the 1998 Rehabilitation Act gives specific guidelines to Web page developers for making information accessible to individuals using assistive technology devices. Many pages have accessibility features built in, such as text-only features, descriptions of all graphics, and captions or transcripts, to accompany digital videos (Robertson, 2002; Robertson & Harris, 2003).

A variety of issues need to be considered when a teacher is deciding which assistive-technology device to use. Figure 7.5 is the SETT Framework developed by Joy Zabala to help teachers, families, and individuals in making this important decision

Figure 7.5   SETT Framework.

A Brief Updated Introduction to the SETT Framework (2002)

Joy Smiley Zabala

The SETT Framework is an organizational tool to help collaborative teams create Student-centered, Environmentally useful, and Tasks-focused Tool systems that foster the educational success of students with disabilities. The SETT Framework is built on the premise that to develop an appropriate system of assistive technology devices and services, teams first must gather information about the students, the customary environments in which the students spend their time, and the tasks that are required for the students to be active participants in the teaching/learning processes that lead to educational success. It is believed that the elements of the SETT Framework, with minor adjustments, also can be applied to non-educational environments and service plans.

Critical Elements of SETT

- Collaboration
- Communication
- Multiple Perspectives
- Pertinent Information
- Shared Knowledge
- Flexibility
- Ongoing Processes

It must be remembered that SETT is a framework, not a protocol. The questions under each section of the SETT Framework are expected to guide discussions rather than to be complete and comprehensive in and of themselves. As each of these questions is explored, it is likely that many other questions will arise. The team continues the exploration until there is consensus that there is enough shared knowledge to make an informed, reasonable decision that can be supported by data.

The Student

- What is the functional area(s) of concern? What does the student need to be able to do that is difficult or impossible to do independently at this time?
- Special needs (related to area of concern)
- Current abilities (related to area of concern)

The Environments

- Arrangement (instructional, physical)
- Support (available to both the student and the staff)
- Materials and Equipment (commonly used by others in the environments)
- Access Issues (technological, physical, instructional)
- Attitudes and Expectations (staff, family, others)

(continued)

181

Figure 7.5 Continued.

The Tasks

- What SPECIFIC tasks occur in the student's natural environments that enable progress toward mastery of IEP goals and objectives?
- What SPECIFIC tasks are required for active involvement in identified environments? (related to communication, instruction, participation, productivity, environmental control)

The Tools

In the SETT Framework, Tools include devices, services, and strategies—everything that is needed to help the student succeed. Analyze the information gathered on the Student, the Environments, and the Tasks to address the following questions and activities:

- Is it expected that the student will not be able to make reasonable progress toward educational goals without assistive technology devices and services?
- If yes, describe what a useful system of assistive technology devices and services for the student would be like.
- Brainstorm Tools could be included in a system that addresses student needs.
- Select the most promising Tools for trials in the natural environments. Plan the specifics of the trial (expected changes, when/how tools will be used, cues, etc.).
- Collect data on effectiveness.

It is expected that the SETT Framework will be useful during all phases of assistive technology service delivery. With that in mind, it is important to revisit the SETT Framework information periodically to determine if the information that is guiding decision-making and implementation is accurate, up to date, and clearly reflects the shared knowledge of all involved.

(Zabala, 2002). However, because assistive-technology selection can be confusing, most school districts hire specialists or contract with outside consultants.

Literacy Development and Students with Disabilities

The most important aspect of incorporating technology in the teaching of beginning literacy is to support the natural developmental sequence of learning to communicate, including listening, speaking, reading, and writing. All the computer-assisted instruction and AT tools discussed previously can support children with or without special needs. But because children with disabilities often miss many opportunities, supporting successful early literacy allows these struggling readers to reap the literacy benefits other children enjoy.

Figure 7.6, which illustrates general developmental needs displayed by all young children to promote initial concept development, values, and skills, lists ways that teachers can make a difference using technological and nontechnological activities. Most important, the majority of these activities provide solutions to children's problems with literacy whether or not they have disabilities. All students benefit from a well-rounded literacy curriculum, and students with disabilities are no exception.

Figure 7.6 Developmental Needs of Children with Disabilities.

What Children Need	What Children with Disabilities May Experience	What To Do	Activities
Opportunities to explore and play	Fewer opportunities to learn through active exploration and play because of limited ability to see, move, hear, or communicate	Plan space allowing for special needs; provide materials and experiences that provide input through the senses; make appropriate adaptations to environment	Visit museums, schedule play groups, use computer games, play with adaptive toys with proper positioning
Lots of opportunities to interact with print materials	Limited access to print materials	Provide large print materials, assistive technology, computer technology, language experiences; give family information	Kitchen activities, turn on the closed captioning on the television, adaptive writing instruments, text-to-speech software
Many opportunities to observe the functions of print, especially at home	Fewer opportunities to see the functions of print modeled	Opportunities to engage children with print; functional classroom settings	Read the newspaper, e-mail friends on the computer, create multimedia books, write journal entries, take roll at school, conduct lunch count in class
Belief that learning to read and write is important	Less emphasis placed on learning to read and write compared to concerns about physical needs and learning self-help skills	Plan to provide appropriate literacy experiences and opportunities to address needs related to the disability; educate families	Make the computer accessible, use adaptations for pencils, find some sort of graphic output

(continued)

Figure 7.6 Continued.

What Children Need	What Children with Disabilities May Experience	What To Do	Activities
Expectations that child has the ability to read and write	Lowered expectations that child will learn to read and write	Model high expectations for family; provide videos and stories about individuals with disabilities	Computer accessibility, educational software, note takers
Many opportunities to communicate with peers and adults in interactive situations	Fewer experiences interacting and communicating with others	Provide a means of communication for the child; provide opportunities for interaction	Electronic communication devices, manual communication boards
Knowledge of how sounds in language relate to alphabet	Fewer opportunities to hear sounds, see symbols, and say sounds	Plan activities that engage in learning sound-symbol relationships, play oral and board games, experiment with writing and reading	Computer software, educational, text-to-speech tape recorders, imitation games

When teachers use technology to teach literacy, all students—including those with special needs—benefit, particularly because technology can be modified to help them read and write. Assistive technology also enables special-needs students to access computers. As more and more accommodations are built into computer hardware and software, all students can benefit from easy access to technology. For example, once speech-to-text input is easy to do, wouldn't we all love to dictate our writing rather than type! Think of how technology can enable all types of students to have equal access to computers, making them a truly user-friendly tool that one day will take no more thought to use than a telephone. As computers become increasingly easy to use, educators will be able to employ them to enhance learning for all students.

◯ Using Technology to Teach Literacy with Struggling Readers: What the Research Has to Say

While in previous sections we've explored strategies to augment our pedagogy, we can now turn our attention to what the research literature has to say about integrating technology into literacy instruction with struggling readers. In a thorough research review, MacArthur, Ferretti, Okolo, and Cavalier (2001) found that computers were an effective medium for literacy instruction for students with reading difficulties. The following is a summary of their findings, other more recent studies and reviews, and an explanation of how teachers should interpret the research for their classroom instruction. Only limited research was done on some aspects of literacy, so more research is needed to be able to truly know the impact of computer literacy programs on struggling readers and writers.

Word Identification

Computer-assisted instruction was effective in teaching phonics and/or sight words in five studies reviewed by MacArthur et al. (2001). Additional studies conducted more recently also found that computer-based reading instruction (both software and Internet-based) was successful for students with reading disabilities to learn phonics, word identification, and definitions (Magnan & Ecalle, 2006; Lee & Vail, 2005; Englert, Zhao, Collings, & Romig, 2005). Even students with significant disabilities, such as autism, had success using computer-assisted instruction to learn decoding and word identification (Coleman-Martin, Heller, Cihak, & Irvine, 2005). The researchers noted that no studies examined whether students' improved identification and decoding of words transferred to improved reading comprehension.

The use of speech feedback where words were broken into syllables also was successful in improving word recognition skills. The research studies did not establish whether the use of speech feedback worked better than other methods of instruction (MacArthur et al., 2001; Wong, 2001).

Even for students with lower cognitive abilities, computer-assisted instruction was successful in teaching students functional reading skills. For example, one program taught students how to read the signs and locate items in a grocery store (Mechling, Gast, & Langone, 2002).

Reading Comprehension

The research review by MacArthur et al. (2001) examined the use of electronic texts to promote comprehension using digital speech (recorded) or speech synthesis. Electronic texts are a popular use of computers for literacy since having text read aloud is essential for some students with visual, cognitive, or learning disabilities. Screen reading had mixed results; two studies showed positive impact while three studies did not show significant improvement. The researchers concluded that the impact of using speech synthesizers or digital recordings of electronic texts may depend more on the characteristics of the student than on the specifics of the computer program.

The use of speech synthesis/digital recordings was not only for reading texts, but also for explaining graphics. They may be used for adding embedded definitions, paraphrasing, and providing hints and tips while a student is reading. Only a few of the research studies reviewed examined these other uses for speech output, but they found these features were sometimes helpful, depending on the students (MacArthur et al., 2001; Wong 2001).

Cognitive-mapping software was successfully used by students with behavior disorders and reading problems (Blankenship, Ayres, & Langone, 2005). With these students, the cognitive maps enabled successful reading comprehension of content areas without additional assistance from the teacher.

Fluency

No studies examined fluency with the use of technology and special-needs children. But using taped or electronic books can assist with fluency if teachers or the software programs use practices that have been effective in teaching fluency, such as speed drills, rapid word recognition, choral reading or neurological impress method, and/or repeated readings (Mather & Goldstein, 2001).

Writing

To be successful, word processing requires instruction for students with reading and/or writing difficulties. (MacArthur et al., 2001; Gersten & Baker, 2001). Only one study had evidence that word prediction assisted with writing, and no studies examined the use of speech synthesis on writing. Also, the use of typing instruction or voice input with struggling writers has not been examined.

Hetzroni and Shrieber (2004) found success with using a word processor for middle school students with writing disabilities. They had improved spelling, increased word usage, fewer reading errors, and overall improvement in organization.

Two additional studies (Mastropieri, Scruggs, & Graetz, 2003; Sturms & Rankin-Erickson, 2002) have examined the use of organization software on students' writing and understanding and found positive results. Students with learning disabilities learned more from using the concept-mapping software and had a strong preference for using the software (Mastropieri et al., 2003).

Additional Research

One interesting study looked at using Internet-supported reading instruction for students (Forbes, 2004). The author described the importance of Internet reading skills and explained how using Web-based bookmarks was helpful to students with reading difficulties. Forbes described how Web-based bookmarks provided students with special needs a way of organizing the topics and content of their work.

Solan, Shelley-Tremblay, Ficarra, Silverman, and Larson (2003) found that attention therapy improved reading comprehension. After 12 weeks of attention therapy, 30 sixth-grade students with moderate reading disabilities had significant improvement in reading comprehension and attention.

Additional research is needed on the use of computers in the instruction of literacy, though the existing studies are mostly positive (MacArthur et al., 2001; Wong 2001). The future is bright for technology enhancement. Voice recognition is continuing to improve, and pronunciation recognizers are better at interpreting accents and speech difficulties (Tinker, 2001).

Though the research is not conclusive, there are many reasons why computer-assisted instruction, assistive technology, and Internet resources are helpful to teachers who are teaching literacy to struggling students and students with individual needs.

COMPUTER CLASSROOM LESSONS

Writing About the Pyramids

Grade Level: 5–8

Objective: Students will create and print a 5–10 page book using Imagination Express.

Time: 1-hour introduction, 1-hour to create a rubric with students, then 30 minutes a day for 5 days to complete. After completion, 3 more hours for critique, revision, and presentation will be needed.

Problem to Be Solved: The students are to create children's books for younger students showing what they have learned in the unit on Ancient Egypt.

Materials: Computers
Imagination Express Pyramids by Edmark (Riverdeep)

Steps:

1. The teacher can introduce the assignment by showing the sample e-book to the class.
2. For students who have never created a book using Imagination Express, one hour of instruction may be required on how to add text, backgrounds, and pictures to the story. All students should be encouraged to add animation and sound to their stories as well.
3. Criteria will be set in a rubric co-constructed with students. These criteria may include the number of sentences, correct grammar and spelling, a title to the story, characters being given names and interacting with each other, and points for including material from the unit on Ancient Egypt. Usually in rubrics, more points are given for students who develop their story more fully than those who follow the minimum criteria.
4. Students will create their stories with assistance and reminders about items in the rubric. If any students do not have an idea for a story, they should listen to the ideas in the story idea section.
5. After completion, students should evaluate their stories in small groups using the rubric.

6. After being given feedback, students will spend one more hour improving their stories.
7. The stories will then be presented orally to the class to demonstrate sounds and animations. These will be presented to younger children as deemed appropriate by the teacher.

Assessment: In the writing rubric, usually no more than five criteria are identified. Students are assigned one to three points for minimal, average, and excellent achievement of the criteria. The grades are determined by the teacher only on the final product, not on the intermediate feedback given by other students.

Modifications for Students: The best aspect of writing stories is that they are easily adapted for students. A student with writing difficulties may write simpler sentences but can improve his or her story with more animation. Another student may need modifications to the rubric but can still participate with the class. For students with motor problems, assistive technology (AT) can be used with Touch Windows or switches. If AT is not available, a student with motor difficulties can also instruct another student on what to put in the book. Even a student with significant developmental delays can enjoy having the stories read to him or her and clicking on the animations.

"Zac the Rat" at Starfall.com

Grade Level: K–2

Objective: Students will identify and make words that have the short "a" sound in the "-an" and "-at" word endings.

Time: One school week. One hour to read the story; 30 minutes a day for four days to practice for assessment.

Materials: One or more computers
Go to "Zac the Rat" story at **http://www.starfall.com/n/short-a/sa/load.htm?f**
The two word family "Make a Word" practice sites are at
http:// www.starfall.com/n/make-a-word/an/load.htm?f
http://www.starfall.com/n/make-a-word/at/load.htm?f
All of the "Zac the Rat" materials are at **http://www.starfall.com/n/N-info/scope.htm#01**

Steps:

1. The teacher can introduce the assignment by having the story read aloud to the students. The story is animated with text to speech. Teachers can print a black-and-white book and give it to the students for additional practice.

      1. Zac is a rat.

      2. Zac sat on a can.

      3. The ants ran to the jam.

      4. Zac had a pan.

      5. Zac had a fan.

      6. The ants ran and ran.

      7. Zac had a nap.

2. Students who have never seen a Starfall book will need to be shown how to click on a word with the cursor to have it read aloud.

3. Students will be placed in groups with both typical-achieving students and with those with special needs.

4. Daily activities can be used to reinforce the new words. Some activities can involve reading the story on the computer or in a book. The story allows for student interaction. The teacher's guide has several worksheet activities that can be modified for students with special needs. Students can develop their own study aids, such as flashcards, to quiz themselves. For cooperative groups, a teacher can design four activities that the students rotate to on different days to practice the words.

5. There is an interactive worksheet to practice the "-an" and "-at" word families. These worksheets are called "Make a Word." They give additional practice to students who need it.

6. The students are assessed in groups on the final day. The number of correct words in the "-at" and "-an" word families is assessed.

7. A short alphabet video to show to the class for review is at **http://www. starfall.com/n/skills/alphabet/load.htm?f**

Assessment: Students should receive credit for the words they learned in the "-at" and "-an" word families and also for the success of their group members. Each student receives points for the words his or her group members learned as well as his or her own points. This promotes the cooperative aspect of the lesson.

⊙ Techno-Teacher Tips

Licking the Keyboarding Problem

A number of special-needs students have disabilities that keep them from successfully using a keyboard. The answer to their problem may be voice-activated computer or voice-activated software available for existing computers. Remember that this solution is only good for quiet classrooms and for students who are patient and willing to train the computer to recognize their voice. For other students who have difficulty with keyboards, there are online keyboards (that only need a mouse click) and modified keyboards for students who have the use of some hand movement.

Computer Supervision

Getting enough hardware is only the first challenge for schools. For most teachers, the hard part is organizing, supervising, and helping struggling students succeed with information technology. Points to consider:

1. You, the teacher, must keep up to date with your software knowledge. The choices for effective software to support literacy are multiplying. Keeping students interested and challenged at the same time requires that you be in a continual upgrade mode. Luckily, good online sites keep you up to date, such as Children's Technology Revue (**http://www.childrenssoftware.com/**) and Superkids Educational Software Review (**http://www.superkids.com/aWeb/ pages/reviews/reviews.shtml**). Remember that some good online options are also available for your students as well.

2. Have backup projects waiting in the wings for two reasons: the unpredictable nature of computers to crash, and the waning interest of some students as they get tired with tasks or finish early.

3. Remember that as lucky as you may be to have a paraprofessional working with your students with special needs, your job is to keep the paraprofessional up to skill level with computer use. This could take extra time, but it is well worth the effort.

◯ Frequently Asked Questions ─────────────

1. **I have a student with a visual impairment that uses JAWS for Windows so she can hear what is on a computer at home and at school. Is that the same program I should use for a student with a severe reading disability?**

 JAWS or Window-Eyes are the best text-speech programs for students who are blind. But for learning disabilities, a student may not need all the features these programs have, nor would they want the high cost associated with them. Though there is no harm in using the same program for both students, if you are buying additional software, many screen readers work just as well and cost less if the person can see where to click and how to do simple commands. The screen readers I have used are Texthelp and products from Premier Assistive Technology.

2. **I teach English literature at a middle school, and I give extra credit points to students who read additional books. Though I can order ahead of time and get digital class books for my student who uses a screen reader, how can he find books to read for extra credit?**

 Several good online sites with free digital books are perfect for use with screen readers. My favorite is the Online Books Page at **http://digital.library. upenn.edu/books/.** I also have used the books at Project Gutenberg at **http://www.gutenberg.org/** that are also described in Chapter 2. A worthwhile class service-learning project for extra credit may be to have your students edit pages or work on digitizing (usually word-processing) a classic book that is not yet in electronic format. Both sites have links on how to volunteer.

3. **I have only a few computers in my classroom, so when the students work on them, they usually work in groups. In cooperative groups I encourage students to work together, but I keep seeing my more able students actually doing the work for some of my students with special needs. How can I get the students to help rather than do it for them?**

   A great idea from Lorrie Jackson (writer at Education World and educational technology specialist) suggests using "Hands-Off Helping." Teach students to help without taking on the task. Make it a class rule that students can help one another, but they cannot ever touch another student's computer. That way, you can be sure that learning occurs even when students help one another.

○ References

Allington, R. L. (2006). Research and the three-tier model. *Reading Today, 23*(5), 20.

Bigge, J. L. (1991). *Teaching individuals with physical and multiple disabilities* (3rd ed.). New York: Macmillan.

Bitter, G. G. (1993). *Using a microcomputer in the classroom* (3rd ed.). Needham Heights, MA: Allyn & Bacon.

Blankenship, T. L., Ayes, K. M., & Langone, J. (2005). Effects of computer-based cognitive mapping on reading comprehension for students with emotional behavioral disorders. *Journal of Special Education Technology, 20*(2), 15–23.

Brosnan, P. A. (1995). *Learning about tasks computers can perform.* Columbus, OH: ERIC Clearinghouse for Science, Mathematics, and Environmental Education. (ERIC Document Reproduction Service No. ED 380 280).

Buggey, T. (1999). Assistive technology for learners with special needs. In G. R. Morrison, D. Lowther, & L. Demeulle, *Integrating computer technology in the classroom* (pp. 114–115). Upper Saddle River, NJ: Prentice Hall.

Coleman-Martin, M. B., Heller, K. W., Cihak, D. F., & Irvine, K. L. (2005). Using computer-assisted instruction and the non-verbal reading approach to teach word identification. *Focus on Autism and Other Developmental Disabilities, 20*(2), 80–90.

Cochran, P. S., & Bull, G. L. (1993). Computers and individuals with speech and language disorders. In J. D. Lindsey (Ed.), *Computers and exceptional individuals* (2nd ed., pp. 143–158). Austin, TX: PRO: ED.

Englert, C. S., Zhao, Y., Collings, N., & Romig, N. (2005). Learning to read words: The effect of Internet-based software on the improvement of reading performance. *Remedial and Special Education 26*(6), 357–371.

Forbes, L. S. (2004). Using Web-based bookmarks in K–8 settings: Linking the Internet to instruction. *The Reading Teacher, 58*(2), 148–153.

Forgrave, K. E. (2002). Assistive technology: Empowering students with learning disabilities. *Clearing House, 75*(3), 122–126.

Gersten, R., & Baker, S. (2001). Teaching expressive writing to students with learning disabilities: A meta-analysis. *Elementary School Journal, 101*(3), 251–272.

Giordano, G., Leeper, L., & Siegel, J. (1996). Computer assisted literacy programs. In G. Giordano (Ed.), *Literacy: Programs for adults with developmental disabilities* (pp. 83–104). San Diego: Singular.

Golden, D. (1998). *Assistive technology in special education: Policy and practice.* Reston, VA: Council for Exceptional Children.

Good, R. H., Kame'enui, E. J., Simmons, D. S., & Chard, D. J. (2002). *Focus and nature of primary, secondary, and tertiary prevention: The CIRCUITS model* (Tech. Rep. No. 1). Eugene, OR: University of Oregon, College of Education, Institute for the Development of Educational Achievement.

Hetzroni, O. E., & Shrieber, B. (2004). Word processing as an assistive tool for enhancing academic outcomes of students with writing disabilities in the general classroom. *Journal of Learning Disabilities, 37*(2), 143–154.

Holzberg, C. S. (1994). Technology in special education. *Technology and Learning, 14*(7), 18–21.

Kajder, S., & Bull, G. (2003). Scaffolding for struggling students: Reading and writing with blogs. *Learning and Leading with Technology, 31*(2), 32–35.

Lee, Y., & Vail, C. O. (2005). Computer-based reading instruction for young children with disabilities. *Journal of Special Education Technology, 20*(1), 5–18.

MacArthur, C. A., Ferretti, R. P., Okolo, C. M., & Cavalier, A. R. (2001). Technology applications for students with literacy problems: A critical review. *Elementary School Journal, 101*(1), 273–301.

Magnan, A., & Ecalle, J. (2006). Audio-visual training in children with reading disabilities. *Computers and Education, 46*(4), 407–425.

Mastropieri, M. A., Scruggs, T. E., & Graetz, J. E. (2003). Reading comprehension instruction for secondary students: Challenges for struggling students and teachers. *Learning Disability Quarterly, 26*(2), 103–116.

Mather, N., & Goldstein, S. (2001). *Learning disabilities and challenging behaviors: A guide to intervention and classroom management.* Baltimore: Brookes Publishing Company.

Mechling, L. C., Gast, D. L., & Langone, J. (2002). Computer-based video instruction to teach persons with moderate intellectual disabilities to read grocery aisle signs and locate items. *Journal of Special Education, 35*(4), 224–240.

Robertson, J. S. (2002 July/August). Making online information accessible to students with disabilities. *The Technology Source.* Available at: http://technologysource.org/article/making_online_information_accessible_to_students_with_disabilities/

Robertson, J. S., & Harris, J. W. (2003 January/February). Making online information accessible to students with disabilities: Part II. *The Technology Source.* Available at: http:// technology source.org/article/making_online_information_accessible_to_students_with_disabilities_part_ii/

Siegel, J. (1999). Utilizing technology for the inclusion of individuals with mental retardation. In P. Retish & S. Reiter (Eds.), *Adults with disabilities: International perspectives in the community* (pp. 287–308). Mahwah, NJ: Lawrence Erlbaum.

Siegel, J., Good, K., & Moore, J. (1996). Integrating technology into educating pre-service education teachers. *Action in Teacher Education, 17*(4), 53–63.

Solan, H. A., Shelley-Tremblay, J., Ficarra, A., Silverman, M., & Larson, S. (2003). Effect of attention therapy on reading comprehension. *Journal of Learning Disabilities, 36*(6), 556–563.

Sturm, J. M., & Rankin-Erickson, J. L. (2002). Effects of hand-drawn and computer-generated concept mapping on the expository writing of middle school students with learning disabilities. *Learning Disabilities: Research & Practice, 17*(2), 124–139.

Tinker, R. (2001). Future technologies for special learners. *Journal of Special Education Technology, 16*(4), 31–37.

Torgeson, J. K. (2000) Individual differences in response to early interventions in reading: The lingering problem of treatment resisters. *Learning Disabilities Research and Practice, 15*(1), 55–64.

Wong, B. (2001). Commentary: Pointers for literacy instruction from education technology and research on writing instruction. *Elementary School Journal, 101*(3), 359–369.

Woodward, J., & Gersten, R. (1992). Innovative technology for secondary students with learning disabilities. *Exceptional Children, 59*, 407–421.

Zabala, J. S. (2002). A brief updated introduction to the SETT Framework. Retrieved June 27, 2006, from http://sweb.uky.edu/~jszaba0/SETTupdate2002.html

Chapter 8

Assessing Students' Work

"Leroy, I can't understand why my students' writing doesn't show growth in their electronic portfolios," Jo Ann laments as she looks at the rubrics she just completed.

"I know the feeling," Leroy says, "but I think I now know more about how to help students be successful."

"What do you mean?"

"Well," Leroy begins slowly, "let me just repeat: I know the feeling. You mark a set of papers and your disappointment grows with each paper. You wonder how in the world the students could have done so poorly, and you start to blame them. You even blame yourself a little, but you're really at a loss in trying to figure out what went wrong."

"Yeah, I'm with you," Jo Ann agrees, wondering what Leroy will say next.

"But," Leroy pauses enough to show that he's about to drop a shoe, "we don't blame ourselves enough." Then he quickly adds, "Just think about it, Jo Ann. If so many students mess up an assignment, shouldn't we logically consider whether it's the students' fault after all? Perhaps, just perhaps, the teacher bears a heavy part of the failure."

Jo Ann, a bit feisty, replies, "It's a good thing you and I are friends, Leroy, or else I might just be a tad bit insulted right now."

Leroy, smiling broadly at Jo Ann's response, returns, "Yes, it *is* a good thing we're friends, or I wouldn't have ventured to go beyond our joint lamenting of poor student writing. But now that I've broached the subject," Leroy begins . . .

"Wait a minute my friend. Please don't launch into yet another lecture on the glories of assessment."

"How about a mini-lecture?" Leroy teases. "I really can't help myself. I've gotten so excited about assessment since taking Dr. Alberts' course. She really makes assessment come alive. I always thought assessment was just a labor-intensive activity that had to be done so I could turn in evaluations of my students, but I have learned better."

"Ok, you're past the introduction to the mini-lesson. Can we stop now?"

Leroy, sensitive to Jo Ann, kindly says, "If you want to."

"You know that I've heard some of your lecture before," Jo Ann demurs to back away from her irritation. "And," she continues thoughtfully, "I probably know what you say is right, but I'd have to change the way I teach if I really, really agree with you."

"Well, maybe you can just really agree with me and leave the really, really agreeing for another time," Leroy says to reach a compromise.

Jo Ann, after looking down at the stack of rubrics, looks Leroy in the eye and says, "I really do have to at least agree with you. I can't continue breaking my own heart over my students' poor progress. Something has got to give, and it looks like I'm the one who has to make some changes."

"I know the feeling," Leroy says. "I had to make adjustments that were painful at first. I had to give up some of my authority as a grader to get another kind of authority as a mentor."

"Yep, there'll be changes alright," Jo Ann says with a sense of commitment.

"But, hey, I don't have to give you the mini-lecture. Let me give you a few articles that really helped me see the light about assessment. You don't have to go it alone. We can talk about changes that will help your students—and you—become more successful. It's really great when you can see students grow as writers."

"I hope I get to know that feeling," Jo Ann says smiling.

"You will," Leroy says encouragingly. "You will."

◯ Facilitating Assessment

The word *assessment* is often linked with grading or giving a student a final evaluation of his or her work. Assessement, however, entails much more than final or summative evaluation. In fact, assessment starts when an assignment is created, because students' successful completion of an assignment requires them to know at the outset in specific and unambiguous terms what success will require. Thus, assessment begins with the construction of an assignment, includes the teachers' role as mentor throughout the assignment to nurture formative assessment, and is complete when the student is given a letter or numeric grade. In fact, assessment refers not only to the teachers' evaluation of students' learning, but also to teachers' evaluation of their own assignments.

Although we will provide information that will help you think more critically about assessment, the literature on assessment is rich and we recommend that you consult it when you have time (e.g., Anderson & Speck, 1998; Angelo & Cross, 1993; Applebee, 1984; Banta, Lund, Black, & Oblander, 1996; Greenberg, 1988; Harp, 1993; Henning-Stout, 1994; Peterson, 1995; Speck, 1998a; Tierney, Carter, & Desai, 1991; White, 1985; White, Lutz, & Kamusikiri, 1996; Zak & Weaver, 1998). For our part, we will discuss a philosophy of assessment, review methods of assessment, and talk about when to use various types of assessment. Let's begin with David Paige's use of assessment to help his students become better writers.

Computer Classroom Snapshot

Context

Motivating students is a challenge for all teachers, particularly writing teachers, and most particularly for special-education writing teachers. I'm David Paige, and I teach language arts to middle-school students with reading and writing disabilities. I was having a difficult time getting sixth-grade students excited about writing, and I was taking "academic chances" that resulted in students reaching a new plateau in their writing abilities. This particular class was composed of 14 African-American students, all with reading and writing disabilities. I decided that I needed to create some excitement that would get the students' attention and help motivate them in their writing attempts. Integrating technology with assessment seemed to be a natural fit.

What I Did and Why

With this in mind, I decided that I would take a chance by turning a simple rubric for writing into a spreadsheet program that could be displayed on a laptop projector. In the sixth grade, my students have extreme difficulty composing simple sentences, organizing their writing, and providing details when telling a story. To help them put these steps together in the writing process, I designed the spreadsheet rubric so they could refer to it as they wrote. The rubric was very simple, with four categories: topic sentence, supporting details, grammar, and creativity. Across the spreadsheet were columns for scores from one through five. The final column on the right totaled the grade for each of the four categories. On the bottom of the spreadsheet was a cell that gave the grand score, out of a possible 20, for all categories.

Although my students do not write well, they are competitive and each one thinks he or she can be the best. My plan was to have each student write a persuasive article from a classroom-developed topic list. If the topic list was not adequate, students were free to use their own topic. The rubric would be displayed throughout the writing process, so each student could refer to it while writing. I explained that after each student was finished, we would each read our writing aloud to the class, and class members would then be responsible for agreeing on a score for each category in the rubric. I told the class that I would first read my article for them to grade so they could see how the process would work. My overall goal in designing the spreadsheet assessment was to help students see, in a creative and interesting way, how to improve their writing through a peer-review process.

After everyone had finished his or her article, I read mine to the class and intentionally included content and grammatical errors that I knew the class would spot. As the class gave me a score for the first category, topic sentence, I entered it into the spreadsheet displayed on the projector. After the class graded my paper and the computer totaled the score in the bottom cell, the class let out a collective "ah" of amazement. I now knew that they had the idea, and I had their interest.

My initial concern was that the class would grade each other very "roughly," maybe even with some cruelty, and that I would need to contribute strong guidance during the process. With this in mind, I used the strategy of substituting numbers for students' names on their papers. I read aloud for the class what students had written, instructing them to write quick notes when they heard something that they liked or that interested them. I again reviewed the rubric and suggested to the class that they listen keenly for evidence of the categories in the rubric and how each writer addressed them.

Once the reading was completed, I introduced the first category in the rubric and began gathering opinions from the class on what they liked and what didn't quite make sense to them. "Did the writer have a topic sentence that was clearly stated?" A couple of students offered their opinions, and I read the topic sentence again. I asked the class, "From this sentence, can you tell what the writer's opinion is?" After a couple more minutes of discussion, we agreed on a score of 4 out of a possible 5 for "topic sentence." We were off!

We completed the rubric for the first piece of writing, a good score of 17. The rest of the class went very smoothly, and I had happy students feeling good about their writing by the end of class. This went better than I expected, and my risk yielded a big return.

What I Learned

I learned several lessons from this idea of integrating technology with assessment, and the first involved student motivation. Most of my students had never seen a spreadsheet application program operate, and this provided a high degree of interest and intrigue. As my students watched the program total their writing scores on the rubric, the novelty of the spreadsheet program quickly changed into the realization that technology is a tool that can make routine tasks easy and even fun.

Another aspect of this technology application was the competitive environment that it provided as each student watched scores being evaluated on the overhead rubric. Every student wanted a good score that would be better than everyone else's, and this competitive atmosphere helped to raise each student's motivation.

(continued)

Still another area of learning for me was how involved the students became in the evaluation of each piece of writing and the air of suspense that surrounded the eventual score. This suspense operated to keep students interested in paying attention to the critique that was taking place in the classroom. The critique functioned as a "coaching" opportunity between the student, the class, and the teacher and was at the heart of helping students to learn how to self-assess their writing. Here again, the spreadsheet-rubric was the glue that held the interest of the class, surging the learning forward.

The final lesson I learned was that applying technology into lessons can be a creative process that melds several different facets important to student learning. In this lesson, technology functioned to engage the students and heighten interest in what I was teaching. This, in turn, led to increased motivation and more on-task behavior from the students, resulting in an environment where productive discussions could take place and lead to new learning and skill building. In the end, taking well thought-out assessment risks can be great for both the teacher and the student.

◯ A Philosophy of Assessment

Whereas in David's Classroom Snapshot above the assessment was more explicit for his students, assessment is a complex activity that may seem capricious for many. For instance, a student or parent can challenge a grade, asking how the teacher derived it. The teacher's explanation may seem strained if he or she simply says, "In my judgment . . . " Those who challenge a grade may not be willing to bow before the authority invested in a teacher and accept his or her judgment as valid. Indeed, challengers may ask for evidence beyond professional judgment. Although the teacher does indeed need to provide such evidence (and thus keep good records), what challengers may not understand is that teacher judgment is central to assessment. Even before adding up scores to determine a final grade, teachers decide how much weight to give to a particular component of an assignment. Thus, teacher judgment is critical to assessment (Speck, 1998c).

This does not mean, however, that teacher judgment is absolute and indisputable. After all, teacher judgments may contradict each other. For instance, two or more teachers might give a full range of grades to the same student's business letter (Dulek & Shelby, 1981; Wilkinson, 1979) or other written projects (Edwards, 1982). Thus, their formal authority as teachers cannot be the sole justification for the assessments they give. However, the problem of reliability among teachers' grades when assessing students' products suggests the benefit of teachers talking to each other in formal ways about grading. Teachers can mark one or two student papers independently and then get together to discuss their approaches to and reasons for marking as they did. Out of a dialogue about assessment, teachers can begin to develop local standards.

In appealing to formal authority, which is granted to teachers as representatives of an educational institution, teachers should ensure that their professional judgments, which are somewhat subjective, are in line with more objective measures. There should be evidence of how a grade was derived, and part of that evidence should include various types of grading instruments (which we discuss shortly). Our philosophical position requires teachers to share their authority with students, not to establish themselves as the sole authority in the classroom. Rather, they are facilitators of authority. They help students learn to use authority effectively by ensuring that students participate in the grading process (Speck, 1998b).

The notion that students should participate in the grading process may be a bit frightening, because traditionally, teachers have been the sole proprietors of grading, from producing assignments to giving a final grade for a course. However, the traditional approach fails to consider the need for students to participate actively in the education process, including assessment. Students have to internalize evaluative standards so that they can apply them not only to their own work, but also to that of their peers and, later in life, their subordinates. Indeed, if one of the primary purposes of evaluation is to promote improvement, those being evaluated must be able to understand not only what has to be improved, but also how it can be improved. The evaluation process, therefore, should be open to investigation by colleagues, students, parents, and other interested parties.

In short, assessment is not a private affair. Assessment is a community concern that should include not only the teacher but also students in the assessment process, and students should not merely be seen as the recipients of assessments, but students should be actively engaged in learning how to assess.

We have presented an all-too-brief philosophy of assessment, but refer to Figure 8.1 and to the literature on assessment cited at the end of this chapter so that you can consult in-depth resources on the philosophy and practice of assessment. Also, it is important to address the types of assessments that you could use to promote student learning, so we now turn to that topic.

○ Methods of Assessment

Throughout much of this text, we have advocated for teachers to use constructivist approaches within literacy instruction, particularly with writing and publishing. With constructivist pedagogy, assessments are performance based and often built in collaboration among teacher and students (Hirumi, 2002). To present the most accurate depiction of how teachers are using technology for instruction, we would be remiss if we did not address the current culture of standardized tests and objective assessments. To this end, we will discuss both types of classroom assessments, objective and performance-based, identifying where technology can be used with each method.

Objective Assessments

Ojective assessments are indicative of the state-mandated tests students take each year. Objective assessment items are very familiar to all of us. They include the selected- or

Figure 8.1 Comparison of philosophical beliefs and theoretical assumptions of traditional and alternative assessment.

Traditional Assessment		*Alternative Assessment*
Universal assessment	**Knowledge**	Multiple meanings
Passive process	**Learning**	Active process
Separates process from product	**Process**	Emphasizes process and product
Discrete, isolated bits of information	**Focus**	Focuses on inquiry
To document learning	**Purpose**	To facilitate learning
Cognitive abilities as separate from affective and conative abilities	**Abilities**	Connects between cognitive, affective and conative abilities
Views assessment as objective, value-free and neutral	**Assessment**	Views assessment as subjective and value-laden
Hierarchical model	**Power and Control**	Shared model
Learning as an individual	**Individual vs Collaborative Process**	Learning as a collaborative process

From Anderson (1998), Jossey Bass. Used with permission.

constricted-response items, such as multiple choice, true-false, and matching; they also include fill-in-the-blank types of questions.

The selected-response type of assessment items are effective when you want students to be able to identify, define, discriminate, select, locate, evaluate, and judge from recognition. For example, identifying parts of speech, selecting the correct verb tense, and evaluating the effectiveness of three different persuasive paragraphs are common uses

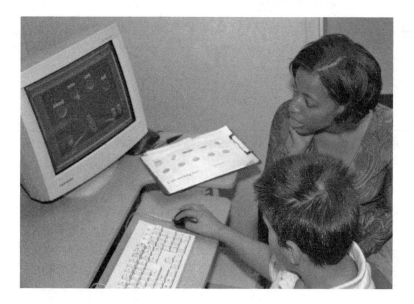

for these types of objective assessments. Fill-in-the blank test items, similarily, allow learners to identify, select, solve, and discriminate by inserting from memory the correct answer (Dick, Carey, & Carey, 2005).

The attractiveness of objective assessments is twofold. First, in general, they are quick for students to complete. Second, they are typically quick for teaches to grade. In particular, selected-response items can be graded through optical scanning and computer-based testing. Fill-in-the-blank items, however, require teacher judgement to determine an answer's accuarcy. So they must be graded by hand.

Using Technology with Objective Assessments. Because selected-response assessment items do not require teacher judgement for grading, except to determine the initial key, these items take full advantage of a computer's ability to process repetitive tasks quickly. Computer-based testing grades objective test items efficiently for the teacher and provides reports of student achievement. These reports can be used to make data-driven decisions about student progress. As one example, Quizstar (see Figure 8.2) was developed for teachers through funds from the U.S. Department of Education and is part of the 4teachers.org Web site. Accelerated Reader, as described in earlier chapters, makes use of computer-based testing to gauge student reading levels with comprehension. Other more sophisticated integrated learning systems that combine instruction and assessment include PLATO, CompassLearning, and READ180. Moreover, many schools are using PDAs to gather objective assessment data (Honey, Culp, & Spielvogel, 1999). Again, these types of software are designed to help teachers make decisions about student achievement. For more sample Web sites for creating online quizzes, see Figure 8.3.

Figure 8.2   QuizStar, a companion to RubiStar, allows teachers to create quizzes students take online. Teachers must register and log in, and students must register and log in as well. QuizStar creates objective assessments in a variety of formats.

Figure 8.3 Web Sites for Generating Objective Tests and Quizzes.

QuizStar

http://quizstar.4teachers.org/
RubiStar's online quiz companion. It's free. You do have to create an account and your students do, too.

Hot Potatoes

http://hotpot.uvic.ca/
Free for teachers, even though it looks like it might not be. You can create quizzes as Web pages. With a simple search, there are other sites that tell you how to "hack" Hot Potatoes quizzes to make more robust quizzes.

Questionmarker

http://www.questionmarker.com/home.htm
You can create tests and edit them for free. But you have to pay a subscription to access the gradebook where the scores are stored.

Discovery's Custom Classroom Quiz Center

http://school.discovery.com/quizcenter/quizcenter.html
You first have to create a custom classroom account, and then you can create a quiz or puzzle and save it.

Performance-Based Assessments

The second method of assessment is performance based, and the primary types of performance-based assessments include checklists, rubrics, and portfolios. As we discuss these types of assessments, remember that their full use incorporates students in the process of creating them. A checklist, for example, loses some of it power as an instrument for student learning when students merely use it without having consultative powers in its creation. Because performance-based assessments require teacher judgement, it is extremely difficult to integrate technology with these assessments, except in their creation.

Checklists

A checklist is just what it purports to be: a list of requirements that students and teachers can check, or check off, to determine whether the students have fulfilled the formal conditions of an assignment. Checklists include two columns beside each criterion for an assignment (Dick, Carey, & Carey 2005). The two columns typically are labeled "Yes" and "No" or "Included" and "Not included." Checklists simply identify whether a criterion was observed or not observed. Checklists can be used with very young children, replacing the "yes/no" labels with a "smiley face" and a "frowny face." Checklists either should be provided at the outset of an assignment, when the assignment is given to students, or soon after the assignment if students are involved in creating a checklist. As David Paige demonstrated in his Classroom Snapshot, students can be led to articulate standards that they already know. In other words, students have prior knowledge that can have a positive influence on creating effective assessments. In developing a checklist, the teacher can tease out that prior knowledge and show its relationship to a particular assignment.

The checklist, once created jointly by teacher and students, should be used as a quality anchor throughout the process of completing the assignment. The teacher, instead of answering questions about what is acceptable for the assignment, can refer students to the checklist so that they become accustomed to consulting it as the benchmark for evaluating their efforts. As they refer to the checklist to answer questions about what is appropriate quality for an assignment, they internalize the quality standards and not only have those standards available to evaluate their own work, but also the work of their peers.

There are three benefits to using checklists as an assessment instrument. First, a large number of criteria can be assessed rather quickly. Second, the criteria increase assessment reliability across students. Finally, an overall score can be obtained quickly. On the other hand, checklists are also limited in their assessment power. A learner who receives a "no" check on criterion neither knows why he or she received that score nor receives any further details related to the topic (Dick, Carey, & Carey, 2005).

Using Technology to Create Checklists. Checklists can easily be created using a table in a word processor or even in a spreadsheet. A good place on the Web to create a checklist is PBL Checklist at **4teachers.org.** This site is one of the few assessment sites on the Web that is suitable for early elementary students' assignments. See Figure 8.4 for an example of a checklist created at PBL Checklists.

Rubrics

Rubrics, scoring guides that clearly delineate criteria and corresponding rating values to evaluate students' performance (Sadler & Andrade, 2004), are another performance-based method to promote student learning (see an example in Figure 8.5). Rubrics can provide transparent evaluative standards at the beginning of an assignment, throughout the formative assessment process, and during summative assessment. A rubric establishes the evaluative criteria when an assignment is introduced to students, or shortly thereafter, and then becomes the instrument the teacher and students use for assessing not only progress during the project, but also the completed project. As previously stated, a rubric should be developed at the outset of a project *or shortly thereafter* because sometimes students may need to become involved with the project before they have an adequate understanding of how it should be evaluated. Additionally, this is not

Figure 8.4 A beginning writing checklist from PBLChecklist@4teachers.org. For each criterion, you can open another window to select specific assessment items to include.

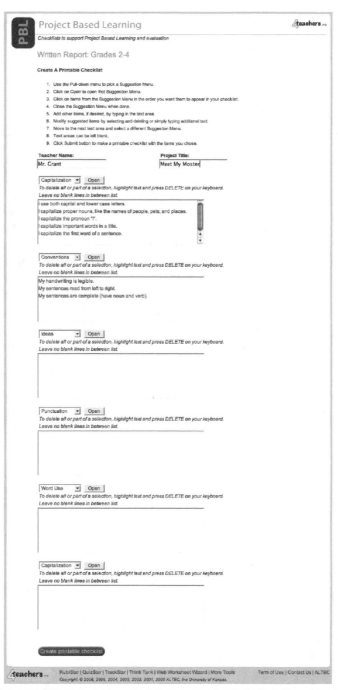

Figure 8.5   A sample rubric for a series of similes produced in an electronic presentation modeled after *Quick as a Cricket* by A. Woods.

Similes Presentation			
Criteria	☺	☹	☹
Story Creativity	Imaginative.		Unoriginal.
Similes	Follows simile forms of "like" or "as."		Does not follow simile forms of "like" or "as."
Slide Show	There is a title slide and five or more slides in the presentation.	There is a title slide and three or four more slides.	A title slide is missing or there are fewer than three slides.
Title Slide	Includes author and illustrator's names.		Does not include both author and illustrator's names.
Artwork	Uses clip art on every slide to illustrate simile.	Uses clip art on several slides that mostly illustrate simile.	Few slides include clips art to illustrate simile.
Spelling	One or no spelling errors.	Two or three spelling errors.	More than three spelling errors.
Capitals and Periods	All sentences start with a capital letter and end with a period.	One or two sentences do not start with a capital letter or end with a period.	More than two sentences do not start with a capital letter or end with a period.

Adapted from Lowther et al. (2005), p. 11. Used with permission.

to say that teachers should develop new rubrics for every assignment. Students can be profitably involved in developing a rubric, but they also can use one that was developed, for example, last year. Indeed, teachers can amend an existing rubric and thus save time in developing a new one, a process that could take a significant amount of class time.

Sadler and Andrade (2004) also suggest that rubrics be used as instructional scaffolds with students. When co-created with students, and when they use language appropriate to students, rubrics can be employed to promote self-regulation. Specifically, Sadler and Andrade assert that instructional rubrics can be used for (a) planning and goal setting, (b) revising, and (c) editing.

A common writing rubric may employ the 6+1 Trait Writing Model (Northwest Regional Educational Laboratory, 2001/2005). This model employs seven traits that are common across all examples of good writing. The seven characteristics are ideas, organization, voice, word choice, sentence fluency, conventions on mechanics, and presentation. Originally, just the first six were included; however, presentation has been added because of the advances in word processing and multimedia.

Using Technology with Rubrics. A number of Web sites can help teachers produce effective rubrics. Probably one of the most well-known and well-used sites is RubiStar (**http://rubistar.4teachers.org**). See Figure 8.6. RubiStar provides templates for common projects and assignments. The rubrics can be stored (for free) or you can print them. Two other sites, **teach-nology.com** and **2learn.ca,** are also good places to start. Be aware, however, that one of the limitations of online rubric makers is that they do not make explicit how weighting of criteria should occur. Weighting can happen one of three ways. First, you can add a multiplying factor, such as "x2," to the levels of performance. Second, you can add a weighting column to the rubric, specifying a percentage for each criterion. Finally, you can append additional criteria, or sub-criteria, to be more specific, increasing the overall weight for certain requirements. For example, a criterion of "grammar" may be further divided with sub-criteria of capitalization, ending punctuation, and so forth.

As briefly described in Chapter 2, there are a group of evaluation tools for improving writing. Two of the most well-known and respected are Criterion from Educational Testing Service (ETS) and SAGrader. These performance-based writing assessments use reliable criteria to gauge students' writing. The writing scorers employ sophisticated internal rubrics to analyze many of the criteria outlined in the 6+1 Trait Writing Model. While these scorers are not inexpensive, some early research (see e.g., Forbess & Grant, forthcoming) suggests they may provide more consistent feedback to students over time and across revisions. While this is not to suggest that these scorers replace teacher judgement, the scorers may offer more continuous formative feedback to students and inform teacher decision-making about student progress.

Portfolios

If we can characterize checklists and rubrics as examples of performance-based methods that apply to a particular assignment, we can characterize portfolios as performance-based methods that can be applied to a whole set of assignments. A portfolio is a collection of a student's work that can represent multiple snapshots of student achievement or effort, whereas checklists and rubrics are the instruments that aid the students in creating snapshots.

There are three main types of portfolios: working, showcase, and assessment (Danielson & Abrutyn, 1997). Working portfolios include works in progress and are used to show progress over time. These portfolios evolve as the student's work evolves.

Figure 8.6 RubiStar, housed at 4teachers.org, is one of the most well-done and well-used rubric makers on the Internet. Teachers can create original rubrics or search for previously generated ones. The rubrics can be saved into RubiStar's system by logging in, or rubrics can be printed out or downloaded.

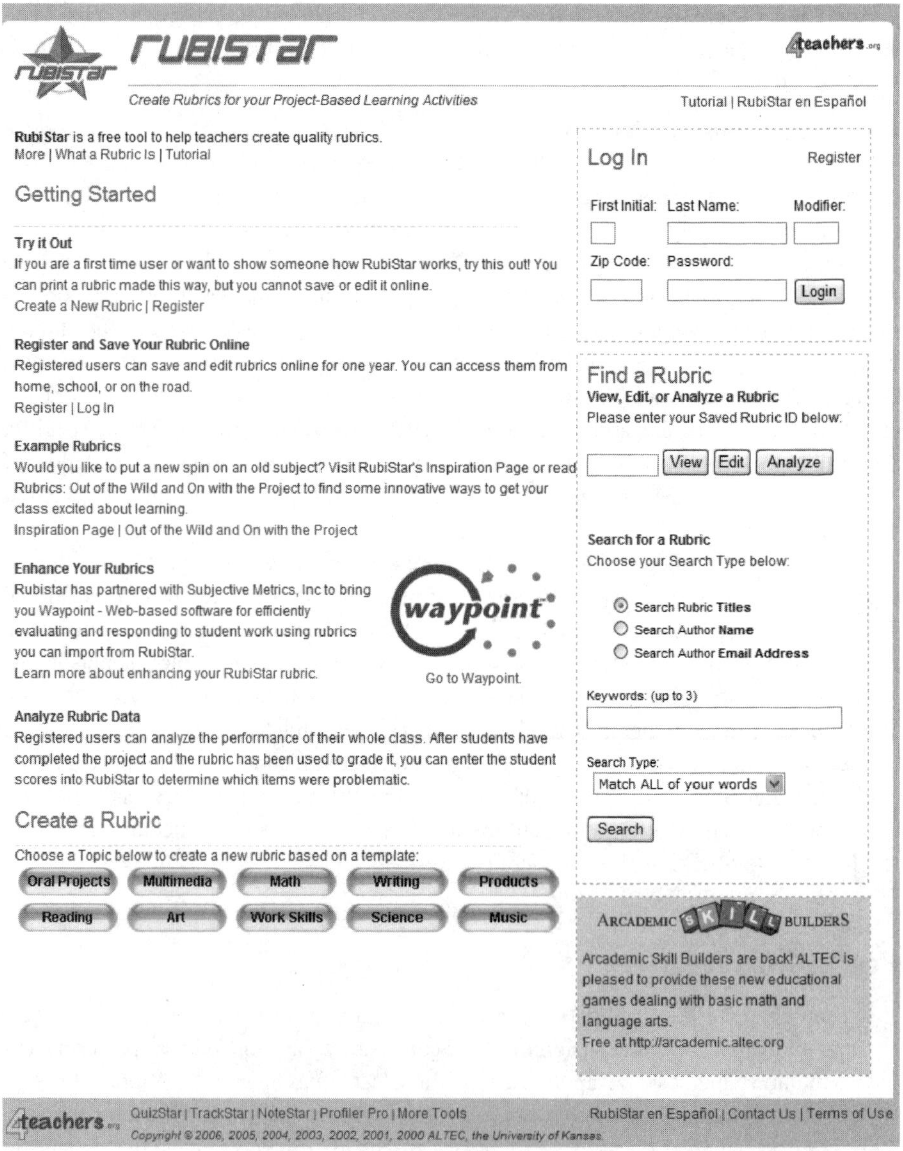

Screenshot copyright 1995–2006 ALTEC, the University of Kansas. Funded by the U.S. Department of Education, Regional Technology in Education Consortium, 1995–2005 to ALTEC (Advanced Learning Technologies in Education Consortia) at the University of Kansas, Center for Research on Learning.

On the other hand, showcase portfolios reflect a student's best work. These are indicative of professional portfolios for job searches, but they may also be used with admission to special academic programs, such as gifted-and-talented classes or governor's schools. Finally, assessment portfolios represent standardized portfolios across a class, grade level, or school. Specific assessments dictated by the curriculum, such as a persuasive writing sample, are required in all students' portfolios. These make portfolios more objective and make it easier to compare across students.

Certainly a rubric should be used to evaluate the portfolio, just as a rubric or checklist should be used to evaluate any assignment. However, the portfolio is perhaps the best example of the super-grade for performance-based assessments. This means that a portfolio does not have to include only projects that were "successful" in terms of grades. A portfolio could include a failed assignment that by a student's own admission provided a needed learning experience, for example, effective time management, the value of clear communication in a collaborative assignment, or the importance of paying attention to details.

Electronic Portfolios. Electronic portfolios, called e-portfolios and e-folios, are one mechanism to bridge the production of digital products with performance-based assessment (Wade, Abravi, & Slater, 2005). Even three-dimensional products, such as collages and visual performances, can be captured for inclusion. Electronic portfolios offer an opportunity for students to help in the creation of the portfolio (Siegel, 2002), using technology skills that may not be emphasized elsewhere. Whether electronic portfolios are online or offline, students, parents, and administrators can have access to the student work either through the Internet or through copies of the portfolio on external storage media, such as CD-ROM.

Electronic portfolios can be created as part of a sophisticated computer system or simply as part of hyperlinked text in a classroom. A number of electronic portfolio systems are available, such as iWebfolio (**http://www.iwebfolio.com/**) and Chalk and Wire (**http://chalkandwire.com/**). There is also an open-source software solution, Open Source Portfolio (**http://www.osportfolio.org**) that would be suitable for a school or district. To implement these types of systems takes significant time and resources, so determining the costs and returns on investments are decisions no single teacher should assume. An alternative to these solutions that is feasible for every teacher is to create a "home grown" electronic portfolio. This can easily be created using a word processor and inserting hyperlinks to the portfolio contents. For a "how-to" on everyday electronic portfolios, see the Classroom Example at the end of this chapter.

○ When Assessment Occurs

We have taken the position that assessment occurs throughout the learning process and includes both teachers and students. Historically, however, assessment in schools has been limited to "the final grade," which is called summative assessment. In other words, a final grade purports to sum up a student's efforts. Clearly, "THE final grade" refers to the super-grade for a course. But throughout a course, other summative assessments are used to arrive at the final or super-grade, such as mid-term examinations, major papers, weekly quizzes, and final examinations. Also, historically, students have been given an assignment, provided some instruction on how to fulfill the assignment, and, perhaps, given some time in class to complete the assignment before it was due. The process for completing the assignment was linear, and students were often left to their own devices to complete the assignment. This approach to assessment might be characterized by the teacher saying, "I teach, you learn, I grade."

Make no bones about it, providing summative assessments is a professional requirement for teachers. We are in no way demeaning summative assessments. What we are calling into question is the way teachers arrive at a summative assessment. Given the philosophy previously outlined, we advocate a healthy dose of formative assessment that fully informs any summative assessment. In short, the bulk of evaluation can focus on formative assessment, and teachers can actively engage students in the entire evaluative process, both formative and summative.

How does formative assessment promote student learning during the assessment process? Formative assessment generally involves evaluations leading up to a final evaluation or grade. The purpose is to give students feedback on their work so they can improve that work. Thus, formative assessment provides the teacher an opportunity to function as a coach, the person who helps students learn how to be effective (Laney, 1993). The teacher, as a coach, is on the same team as the students. The teacher is interested in giving the students every benefit of his or her expertise by making the process of evaluation transparent. For instance, the teacher might say, "Lillian, as a reader, I like very much the way you describe the cabin you and your family go to during the summer, but as I read your description, I keep wondering about the neighboring cabins and the town close by. Can you tell me more about the location?" The teacher is not directly saying, "Lillian, you'll be evaluated on the depth of detail you give and on how well you anticipate readers' concerns"; instead, the teacher is showing Lillian what a real reader, not just a teacher seeking to provide a grade, looks for (Elbow, 1993). By modeling real readers, you can instill in your students the desire to revise their writing to satisfy real readers' needs.

Formative assessment, however, can be much more concrete by including standards, evident in checklists and rubrics, that are applied throughout the process. For instance, at the beginning of a project, students should be made aware of the standards that will be used to evaluate the project when it is finally due. Those standards should be reinforced throughout formative evaluation at each stage of the evolving products students prepare in response to the initial assignment. This philosophy requires the teacher to be involved in the process of assessment. The old model of assignment, product, and summative assessment is inappropriate. Rather, we endorse the new model of assignment—draft one, draft two, draft three, and so on—and then summative assessment, giving students time to apply evaluative standards to various drafts.

As previously noted, we believe that it is in the best interests of students when teachers involve students in the entire evaluative process, both formative and summative

(Belanoff, 1993). When students become active participants in the evaluation process, they reflect on and apply evaluative standards to their own work and that of their peers. This approach has several advantages. First, students have an opportunity to articulate evaluative criteria. As a class, for instance, students can negotiate evaluative criteria and consider what is appropriate for a particular assignment. Second, students have an opportunity to apply the criteria so that they can see whether the criteria work and so that they can understand that the application of criteria requires judgment. Then they begin to see that assessment is not merely a matter of the objective application of criteria, but that it requires some subjective judgments. Ultimately, we want students to be able to assess themselves and their peers so that students apply the criteria for a particular assignment to help themselves and their peers learn effectively.

Self-, Peer, and Teacher Assessments

We have focused on performance-based methods of assessment because such methods make apparent the criteria students can use to achieve a quality product at the outset of a project. Thus, one thrust of evaluation is to enable students to internalize criteria and become good self-assessors.

We recognize that students may be reluctant to evaluate their own work or that of others. In fact, we have heard teachers say that even though they believe it is important for students to engage in self-assessment, their students don't have the skills to do it. For instance, when students are asked what they learned from completing a project, they often say, "I learned a lot." Such an evaluation is so general that it is practically worthless. But when students are invited to evaluate their work according to a performance-based assessment with specific evaluation criteria, they can learn how to make more careful and critical evaluations. Sadler and Andrade (2004) identify three misconceptions teachers have about self- and peer assessment:

1. Self-assessment is pointless because students will just give themselves As.
2. Peer assessment is pointless because students will just stroke their friends and bash their enemies.
3. Both self- and peer assessment are pointless because students won't revise anyway. (p. 51)

We agree with Sadler and Andrade that teachers should engender a culture of improvement and revision to mitigate some of the issues teachers have with implementing self- and peer assessments.

We also acknowledge that involving students in the evaluation process can be controversial. Should students grade other students? Are they really "expert" enough to make judgments on other students' work? In some ways, these questions are a legacy of the old model of teacher-only evaluation, because they assume that students cannot be effective evaluators because they are not teachers. This assumption, however, does not take into consideration the teacher's responsibility to help students become effective evaluators. We believe that the teacher does have the responsibility to show students how to assess their own work and that of their peers, so we advocate balancing self-, peer, and teacher assessments. How can this be done?

As already noted, rubrics specify exactly what is required for an assignment to be effective. Thus, one way to balance assessments, both formative and summative, is to have each party use the rubric to evaluate a student's product. Figure 8.7 shows how this might be done.

One virtue of comparing self-, peer, and teacher evaluations is that differences among the evaluations can be discussed, and the students can begin to see that assessments must be substantiated by well-grounded reasoning. It is not sufficient to appeal to authority or personal preference. Students need to see that well-intentioned people can have different opinions, but that those opinions must be backed up by good reasons. Assessment becomes an exercise in critical thinking; students discover that it entails both the application of objective standards and subjective professional judgment. This supports Sadler and Andrade's (2004) argument for using rubrics as instructional scaffolds.

Facilitating Formative Assessment

One of the tenets of constructivist pedagogy highlighted in Chapter 1 was the emphasis on *process* and product. As noted, formative assessment helps students improve their final product, increases learning, and uses a model for self-assessments. Finding ways to

Figure 8.7   A Rubric for Self-, Peer, and Teacher Assessment of a Picture Book.

	Self	Peer	Teacher
Illustrations (50%)			
Neatness (10%)	_____%	_____%	_____%
Fit with text (20%)	_____%	_____%	_____%
Color (5%)	_____%	_____%	_____%
Creativity (15%)	_____%	_____%	_____%
Total % for Illustrations	_____%	_____%	_____%
Text (50%)			
Creativity (20%)	_____%	_____%	_____%
Story makes sense (15%)	_____%	_____%	_____%
No errors (15%)	_____%	_____%	_____%
Total % for Text	_____%	_____%	_____%
Total % for Illustrations	_____%	_____%	_____%
Total % for Picture Book	_____%	_____%	_____%

document students' decision-making and learning processes can, however, be easier said than done (c.f., Grant & Branch, 2005). To this end, we provide three strategies to help chronicle the formative assessment process and aid a teacher in managing literacy projects: (a) KWL, (b) reflection, and (c) progress charts.

One monitoring method, KWL (What I Know, What I Want to Know, and What I Learned; Ogle, 1986) can promote self-regulation with learning. Specifically developed for comprehension, the KWL strategy is flexible enough to be expanded to help students monitor their learning during an extended project. For example, students can use this strategy as a method to record what they have accomplished in a class period, where they should begin next, and what else they need to learn to accomplish the task. Fisher, Brozo, Frey, and Ivey (2007) note that the strategy has been elaborated to include summarization (KWL-Plus), sources of knowledge for "how we know" (KWHL) and questioning (KWLQ). The KWL strategy could easily be implemented within a student's personal blog or as part of a continuing word-processing document.

A teacher can engage students in both verbal and written reflection about their work on a daily basis. Using reflection journals is one method for recording the learning that has occurred over time and for demonstrating the growth of a student. This may be as simple as asking each student to share with a partner what he or she learned from a specific lesson. Or, you might end each day with students reflecting on it and writing down the most important thing they learned that day. Also, you can encourage students to learn how to reflect on their work by sending home a worksheet (with their completed work) on which parents write down what their children have learned. This fosters discussions between parents and child as well as communication between school and home. Specifically, double-entry journals (Hughes, Kooy, & Kanevskym, 1997) provide an opportunity for students to reflect on notes they have collected. For the journal, a page is divided in half. On one side, students take notes from readings, online research, lectures, or other class activites; on the other side, students reflect on the meanings of the notes. Students are able to use personal opinions, make connections with previous concepts, and ask questions. These reflections can inform teacher judgement for summative assessments, as well as pinpoint flaws in students' thinking or misconceptions. As suggested above, reflections can be housed within a blog, a personal Web page, or simply inside a word-processing document. The double-entry journal also could be executed with some of the writing aids, such as NoodleTools, that we introduced in Chapter 2. With a blog or a word processing document, the teacher (and other students) can add comments and extend the reflection.

Because of the open-ended nature of constructivist classrooms, it can be difficult to put well-defined parameters around how much time should be committed to any one part of a project, and it can be perplexing to have a solid grasp on every student's progress. Whole-class progress charts can help teachers monitor individual student progress quickly. As described previously with checklists, carefully thinking through the tasks associated with a project and assigning specific deadlines to accomplish individual tasks substantially increases the chances of project completion. The tasks and deadlines are then transferred to the chart. Progress charts can be large poster-sized charts purchased from educational supply stores, small letter-paper-sized charts created in a word processor, or electronic charts inside a teacher's PDA. With paper-based charts, students can check off their progress with a pen or using a sticker. Progress charts allow teachers to visually note where students are in a project's process and to specifically identify whether self-, peer, and teacher reviews have occurred.

COMPUTER CLASSROOM LESSONS

Introducing Electronic Portfolios

Grade Level: Adaptable for 3–8

Objective: Generate motivation for developing an electronic portfolio. Select work to include in electronic portfolio. Write reflection statement for work included in electronic portfolio.

Time: 1–2 days

Problem to Be Solved: Using their own work, students will organize their electronic portfolio and include their first artifact with accompanying reflective statement.

Materials: Computer with Internet access
Four types of candy (e.g., Butterfinger, Snickers, suckers, M&M's)
If available, an artist's portfolio or your own portfolio
An example of a student's electronic portfolio, either a former student's or one you accessed on the Internet
Electronic writing products (word-processed writing, Web pages, electronic presentations, and so forth) to select from

Steps:

1. Allow each student to select and eat one piece of his or her favorite candy that you provide.
2. Ask students who selected Butterfingers why it was their choice. Generate this list on the chalkboard or computer screen. Continue this process for the other three types of candy. Emphasize to students the differences in why students chose their individual pieces of candy.
3. Introduce to students the concept of a portfolio, making connections to the candy activity, and choosing their favorite piece of work to include in their portfolio. Also discuss with students the similarities of an artist's portfolio or your own portfolio, and the electronic portfolios that they will develop.

4. Share an example of a student electronic portfolio, emphasizing the necessity of selecting and writing about their best, favorite work from their saved work samples.

5. Have each student select from his or her saved works his or her first artifact to include in the portfolio. The works to choose from may include any word-processed writing pieces, Web pages, electronic presentations, and so forth that the students have produced. If the students have added illustrations to any of the works after they were created in the computer, then you may need to scan the final piece on a scanner to make it electronic.

6. In dyads or ask small groups, students to discuss why they selected the piece.

7. Next, each student writes a reflection statement that includes the following to accompany the artifact selected: (a) what I selected, (b) why I selected it, and (c) what I learned. Students should word process these reflective statements. Students should now have one selected writing piece and its accompanying reflective statement, which are both electronic.

8. In a new word-processing document, have students create an organizer page for their electronic portfolio. At the top of the page, students should list (a) their name, (b) grade, (c) teacher, and (d) school year. If digital pictures of the students are available, then feel free to include these or have students choose a piece of clip art. Further down the page, students should create a heading that reads, "Electronic Writing Portfolio." Beneath the heading students can create a small subheading that reads, "Artifact 1" or "Writing Sample 1." Under this subheading, students can list the title of the writing piece they are including, and on a separate line, they can type "Reflective Statement" or "Why I Chose This Piece." An example is below. Be sure to save this organizer page. A tip here is to have each student include his or her last name and first initial in the file name.

Lisa Beaufort
4th Grade
Mrs. Bishop's Class
Green River Elementary
2006-2007

Electronic Writing Portfolio

"My Best Friend" Descriptive Writing
Why I Chose This Piece

Scientific Inventors
Why I Chose This Piece

---

9. Highlight the title of the piece of writing the student is including in his or her portfolio and hyperlink this title to the file. Similarly, highlight the reflective statement title and hyperlink this text to the file. Now you should be able to click on each hyperlink and that file will open. As students continue to select writing pieces to include in their electronic portfolios, update this organizer page by adding hyperlinks to the titles of the pieces and reflective statements. Again, students may hyperlink to electronic presentations they have created, Web pages, as well as audio recording files, and scripts. Any electronic file has the potential to be hyperlinked.

Assessment: Using a rubric, holistically assess the quality of the students' artifacts, the rationale statements, and the portfolio.

○ Techno-Teacher Tips

Developing Rubrics

One concern that teachers have about developing rubrics is, ironically, the amount of classroom time it takes to create one. A time-saving tip: Even when you want students to have input in the process, share an existing rubric and ask them to help you modify the rubric. You can create the rubric yourself, borrow one from a colleague, or use one from the previous year as a model. This enables students to have a voice in the assessment process within a short period of time.

Assessing Technology Products

The students will have varying degrees of success producing spreadsheet and database products. We recommend grading these as parts of a whole, either as data collection or as effort and participation or both. Few teachers are competent in all areas of computer technology, and such limitations should be acknowledged in the students as well.

Data-Driven Decision-Making

Many schools are using a variety of computer-based instruction and assessments to improve literacy skills, such as Accelerated Reader, PLATO, and READ180. These comprehensive programs individually track student learning, and teachers are able to produce reports of student progress and deficiencies. Earlier in this chapter is a discussion of using electronic portfolios to document student progress in writing. Similarly, you can use the individual progress reports from the computer-based learning systems that your school is implementing as a portfolio as well. This type of portfolio may be considered a working portfolio (Danielson & Abrutyn, 1997) that tracks student learning over time and is more holistic. By combining the different computer-based assessments that are available, you may have a better depiction of where the student is in your curriculum and more evidence of specific deficiencies.

Careful with the Online Quizzes

A number of sites are available for creating free online quizzes for your students. These sites will allow you to enter questions and answers, creating a Web page and Internet address for your students to visit. These are great tools to be used with testing about writing mechanics and reading comprehension. Be careful, though. If your students are pretty savvy Internet users, which are typical of upper-elementary and middle-school students, your students can sometimes go in and find the answers to the quiz. This is because the quiz tool has to embed the answers to your quiz inside the Web page that it has created for you. So, if your students know how to look at the Web page code (HTML) from their browser, which anyone can do, then it is possible for them to locate the answers as well. If you suspect this is likely the case for your students, or if you suspect it is occurring, then use the online quizzes as a formative assessment and not a summative assessment.

☉ Frequently Asked Questions

1. **Does a portfolio have to be available on the Internet for it to be an electronic portfolio?**

   In a simple answer, no. For students and teachers to benefit from electronic portfolios, they do not have to be available on the Internet. As discussed earlier in this chapter, electronic portfolios benefit students and teachers by documenting learning over time and providing an easier mechanism for students to include multimedia and other types of digital artifacts. If electronic portfolios are online behind a password-protected site or inside an electronic portfolio system, then there are added benefits, such as better communication with parents about student achievement.

2. **Do students always have to choose which writing pieces to include in their portfolios?**

   Definitely not. If your school has an established writing curriculum where portfolios are passed from one grade to another, then your grade or school may have collectively decided specific pieces or types of writing that should be required in each student's writing portfolio. Earlier in the chapter, these types of portfolios were described as assessment portfolios (Danielson & Abrutyn, 1997). For example, your grade may determine that, at the end of the school year, each student should have two samples of descriptive writing and one instance of expository writing in addition to three other writing samples. This writing portfolio is then passed along to the next grade level. Your grade also may be more specific and necessitate a specific topic for the required writing pieces, so that every student in the grade level will have examples under the same topics. If your school has not formalized a writing portfolio system this explicitly, then you can determine specific writing pieces that you would like to include in your students' portfolios. You also can determine which writing assignments students are allowed to choose.

3. **Can smaller writing assignments, such as journal entries, be part of a portfolio assessment even though they have not been through the entire writing process?**

    Yes. You may have an in-class writing assignment where students are unable to complete the entire writing process. Other assignments, such as reflective journal entries, are also appropriate for inclusion in writing portfolios. Some assignments can have a due date that might read, "This writing assignment should be in your portfolio by such-and-such date." The benefit? The teacher isn't swamped all at once with grading assignments.

4. **How does effort play into assessment when technology tools are used to aid in completing the assignment?**

    One of the advantages to using technology (and that is highlighted throughout this book) is that technology tools augment students' abilities and help construct more professional products. Teachers need to be sure that assessments emphasize the objectives and goals delineated in the curriculum, such as writing and grammar. These elements should be weighted heaviest within your assessment rubric. Effort or other elements that are indicative of effort, if included at all, should only constitute a small portion of the grade. Exceeding project requirements, creativity, depth of research, variety of source documents, professionalism, and revisions should be specific criteria within your grading rubric. As always, the assessment rubric should be shared with students when the project is assigned, should be aligned with the requirements in the project, and should be explained as part of the project overview.

5. **I am concerned about giving students a group grade for projects they complete. Do you have any suggestions?**

    We recommend that you provide two grades for each project. The first grade is for the final product, determined according to the rubric developed for the project. Each person in the group receives the same grade for the product. The second grade is an individual grade based on a rubric that assesses the contribution, attitudes, and effort made by each student. Each person in the group completes a one-page rubric that evaluates himself or herself and each member in the group according to criteria, such as completed their part/role on time, got along well with everyone, and helped other team members.

◯ References

Anderson, R. S. (1998). Why talk about different ways to grade?: The shift from traditional assessment to alternative assessment. In R. S. Anderson & B. W. Speck (Eds.), changing the way we grade students' performance: Classroom assessment and the new learning paradigms. (New Directions for Teaching Learning, No. 74). San Francisco: Jossey-Bass.

Anderson, R. S., & Speck, B. W. (Eds.). (1998). *Changing the way we grade student performance: Classroom assessment and the new learning paradigm.* (New Directions for Teaching and Learning, No. 74). San Francisco, CA: Jossey-Bass.

Angelo, R. T., & Cross, K. P. (1993). *Classroom assessment techniques* (2nd ed.). San Francisco, CA: Jossey-Bass.

Applebee, A. N. (1984). *Contexts for learning to write: Studies of secondary school instruction.* Norwood, NJ: Ablex.

Banta, T. W., Lund, J. P., Black, K. E., & Oblander, F. W. (1996). *Assessment in practice.* San Francisco, CA: Jossey-Bass.

Belanoff, P. (1993). What is a grade? In W. Bishop (Ed.), *The subject is writing: Essays by teachers and students* (pp. 179–88). Portsmouth, NH: Boynton/Cook.

Danielson, C., & Abbrutyn, L. (1997). *An introduction to using portfolios in the classroom.* Alexandria, VA: Association for Supervision and Curriculum Development.

Dick, W., & Carey, L. (2005). *The systematic design of instruction.* Boston, MA: Allyn and Bacon.

Dulek, R., & Shelby, A. (1981). Varying evaluative criteria: A factor in differential grading. *Journal of Business Communication, 18*(2), 41–50.

Edwards, D. (1982). Project marking: Some problems and issues. *Teaching at a Distance, 21*, 28–35.

Elbow, P. (1993). Ranking, evaluating, and liking. *College Composition and Communication, 55*(2), 187–206.

Forbess, J., & Grant, M. M. (forthcoming). *The effects of online essay scoring on the improvement of writing of high school sophomores.* Unpublished manuscript, the University of Memphis, Memphis, TN.

Grant, M. M., & Branch, R. M. (2005). Project-based learning in a middle school: Tracing abilities through the artifacts of learning. *Journal of Research on Technology in Education, 38*(1), 65–98.

Greenberg, K. L. (1988). Assessing writing: Theory and practice. In J. H. McMillan (Ed.), *Assessing students' learning* (pp. 47–59). (New Directions for Teaching and Learning, No. 34). San Francisco, CA: Jossey-Bass.

Harp, B. (Ed.). (1993). *Assessment and evaluation in whole language programs.* Norwood, MA: Christopher-Gordon.

Henning-Stout, M. (1994). *Responsive assessment.* San Francisco, CA: Jossey-Bass.

Hirumi, A. (2002). Student-centered, technology-rich learning environments (SCenTRLE): Operationalizing constructivist approaches to teaching and learning. *Journal of Technology and Teacher Education, 10*(4), 497–537.

Honey, M., Culp, K. M., & Spielvogel, R. (1999, 2005). *Critical issue: Using Technology to improve student achievement.* Retrieved August 29, 2006, from http://www.ncrel.org/sdrs/areas/issues/methods/technlgy/te800.htm

Hughes, H. W., Kooy, M., & Kanevsky, L. (1997). Dialogic reflection and journaling. *The Clearing House, 70*(4), 187–190.

Laney, R. (1993). Letting go. In K. Spear (Ed.), *Peer response groups in action: Writing together in secondary schools* (pp. 151–61). Portsmouth, NH: Heinemann.

Lowther, D. L., Grant, M. M., Marvin, E. D., Inan, F. A., Cheon, J., & Clark, F. (2004). *Teacher's technology handbook: A resource to support effective technology integration.* Memphis, TN: Appalachian Technology in Education Consortium at the University of Memphis.

Lowther, Grant, Marvin, Inan, Cheon, & Clark. (2005). *Teacher's technology handbook: A resource to support effective technology integration.* Appalachian Technology in Education Consortium and the University of Memphis, Memphis, TN. Available at: http://teacher handbook.memphis.edu

North West Regional Educational Laboratory. (2001, 2005). 6 + 1 Trait Writing–About. Retrieved September 9, 2006, from http://www.nwrel.org/assessment/about.pho?odelay=1&d=1

Ogle, D. M. (1986). K-W-L: A teaching model that develops active reading of expository text. *Reading Teacher, 39*(6), 564–570.

Peterson, R. (1995). *The writing teacher's companion: Planning, teaching, and evaluating.* Boston: Houghton Mifflin.

Saddler, B., & Andrade, H. (2004). The writing rubric. *Educational Leadership, 62*(2), 48–52.

Siegle, D. (2002). Creating a living portfolio: Documenting student growth with electronic portfolios. *Gifted Child Today, 25*(3), 60–63.

Speck, B. W. (1998a). *Grading student writing: An annotated bibliography.* Westport, CT: Greenwood Press.

Speck, B. W. (1998b). The teacher's role in the pluralistic classroom. *Perspectives, 28*(1), 19–44.

Speck, B. W. (1998c). Unveiling some of the mystery of professional judgment in classroom assessment. In R. S. Anderson & B. W. Speck (Eds.), *Changing the way we grade student performance: Classroom assessment and the new learning paradigm* (pp. 17–32). (New Directions for Teaching and Learning, No. 74). San Francisco, CA: Jossey-Bass.

Tierney, R. J., Carter, M. A., & Desai, L. E. (1991). *Portfolio assessment in the reading-writing classroom.* Norwood, MA: Christopher-Gordon.

Wade, A., Abrami, P. C., & Sclater, J. (2005). An electronic portfolio to support learning. *Canadian Journal of Learning and Technology 31*(3). Retrieved August 29, 2006, from http://www.cjlt.ca/content/vol31.3/wade.html

White, E. M.(1985). *Teaching and assessing writing.* San Francisco, CA: Jossey-Bass.

White, E. M., Lutz, W. D., & Kamusikiri, S. (Eds.). (1996). *Assessment of writing: Politics, policies, practices.* New York: Modern Language Association of America.

Wilkinson, D. C. (1979). Evidence that others do not agree with your grading of letters. *The ABCA Bulletin, 42*(3), 29–30.

Zak, F., & Weaver, C. C. (Eds.). (1998). *The theory and practice of grading writing: Problems and possibilities.* Albany: State University of New York Press.

Index